T0330399

Environmental Accounting in Action

Environmental Accounting in Action

Case Studies from Southern Africa

Glenn-Marie Lange

Research Associate Professor and Co-Director, Institute for Economic Analysis, New York University, USA

Rashid Hassan

Professor of Environmental Economics and Management and Director, Centre for Environment and Economic Policy in Africa, University of Pretoria, South Africa

Kirk Hamilton

Team Leader, Policy and Economics Unit, Environment Department, World Bank, USA

With a contribution from

Moortaza Jiwanji

Fellow, Overseas Development Institute, UK

Edward Elgar
Cheltenham, UK • Northampton, MA, USA

Published by
Edward Elgar Publishing Limited
Glensanda House
Montpellier Parade
Cheltenham
Glos GL50 1UA
UK

Edward Elgar Publishing, Inc.
136 West Street
Suite 202
Northampton
Massachusetts 01060
USA

A catalogue record for this book
is available from the British Library

Library of Congress Cataloging in Publication Data

Lange, Glenn-Marie.
　　Environmental accounting in action: case studies from southern Africa/Glenn-Marie
　　Lange, Rashid Hassan, Kirk Hamilton; with a contribution from Moortaza Jiwanji.
　　　　p.cm.
　　Includes index.
　　1. Natural resources – Africa, Southern – Accounting – Case studies. 2. National
income – Africa, Southern – Accounting – Case studies. 3. Environmental auditing –
Africa, Southern – Accounting – Case studies. I. Hassan, Rashid M. II. Hamilton,
Kirk, 1951– III. Jiwanji, Moortaza. IV. Title.
HF5686.N3 L36 2003
333.7′14 ′0968 – dc21　　　　　　　　　　　　　　　　　　　　　　　　　　2002072182

ISBN 1 84376 076 2

Typeset by Cambrian Typesetters, Frimley, Surrey
Printed and bound in Great Britain by MPG Books Ltd, Bodmin, Cornwall

Contents

v

Figures

Tables

Boxes

xi

Preface

In 1993, the Untied Nations Statistical Division published a handbook, *Integrated Environmental and Economic Accounting*, and there has been much progress on environmental accounting since then. Many industrialized countries have compiled environmental accounts, but the experience has been more limited in developing countries. The purpose of this book is to show how environmental accounts have actually been implemented and can influence policy in developing countries, based on case studies from southern Africa. The case studies focus on Namibia, Botswana and South Africa, the core countries in a unique regional programme to develop environmental accounts that has been under way since 1995.

The regional programme grew out of a recognition in southern Africa that resource constraints pose an increasing challenge to economic development, that economic principles are increasingly important for sustainable resource management, and that decision-making in the past has often not been grounded in economic assessment of the availability and quality of natural resources. A framework for information and integrated environmental-economic policy analysis was needed to support sustainable natural resource management, and environmental accounts provide such a framework.

In response to the recognized need for environmental accounts, discussions were held with stakeholders in southern Africa in 1993–94, and a three-phase, long-term strategy was designed for building environmental accounts throughout the region. In the first phase of the project, 1995 to 1997, environmental accounts were introduced at a demonstration site, Namibia, in order to test the feasibility of constructing these accounts and the usefulness of the accounts for policy makers. The combination of accounts compilation and policy analysis was to characterize all future work on environmental accounting in the region. This pioneering effort was accompanied by outreach to other countries in the region.

Under the direction of eight government and non-governmental organizations in Botswana, Namibia, South Africa and Swaziland, the second phase began in 1998 and ran for more than three years until 2001. Environmental accounts were constructed for two additional countries in the region (Botswana and South Africa); an accounting framework was developed for regional, transboundary resource management issues; technical training and outreach in the region was greatly expanded, and the groundwork was laid to establish a regional institution capable of supporting this work in the longer term. This last objective was achieved in 1999 with the establishment of the Centre for Environment and Economic Policy in Africa (CEEPA) at the University of Pretoria, under the directorship of Professor Rashid Hassan.

The regional approach to environmental accounting has had several distinct advantages. First, it facilitated the development of a common methodology for data compilation and analysis that ensures comparability across countries. This can be clearly seen in Chapters 2 and 5, dealing with minerals and water in all three countries. The regional approach also facilitated the application of the accounting approach to economic evaluation of transboundary resources such as water. Finally, there have been clear economies of scale in regional cooperation for training and capacity building.

The third phase of this initiative would expand environmental accounting to several other countries in east and southern Africa; further develop environmental accounting as a tool for transboundary resource management in key areas such as water, wildlife and tourism; and advance policy initiatives based on environmental accounts. Some of the results are presented in this book, but much work remains to be done in the area of policy analysis and indicators, particularly monetary valuation.

This book attempts to bring together much of the work that has been done on environmental accounting in southern Africa. Reflecting the spirit of the regional initiative, the chapters integrate both construction of the accounts and policy analysis. Water is a particularly important issue for southern Africa and was a major focus of the accounting work. Only a small portion of the work could be reported here; a more comprehensive reporting of the water accounts, including monetary valuation, will be published in a future volume.

The work presented in this book is the result of a vast collaboration among many people, those within the three countries where the work has been carried out, as well as our many advisors and supporters throughout the world. We would like to thank our collaborators, especially the late Professor Glenn T. Magagula. Professor Magagula was one of the founding members of the regional steering committee that initiated the southern Africa environmental accounting project. Professor Magagula passed away while he was serving as a member of the steering committee. He held the position of the Vice-Chancellor of the University of Swaziland at that time after having worked as the Deputy Director of the African Development Bank for five years. He devoted his life to supporting capacity building in African professionals in the fields of agricultural and natural resource economics. His wisdom and guidance have been sorely missed.

We also want to express our gratitude for several international donors who provided much of the financial support for this work, notably the Swedish

International Development Cooperation Agency, the United States Agency for International Development and the World Bank.

Glenn-Marie Lange
Rashid Hassan
Kirk Hamilton

1. Basic concepts and methods of natural resource and environmental accounting

Glenn-Marie Lange, Rashid Hassan and Kirk Hamilton

1.1 INTRODUCTION

All economies are heavily dependent on the environment as a source of materials and energy, as a sink for waste products and as the physical habitat for human communities. This capacity of the environment constitutes our 'natural' capital. Over the past few decades, most countries have come to embrace the notion of sustainable development, expressed in popular form by the Brundtland Commission Report, *Our Common Future*, as 'development that meets the needs of the present without compromising the ability of future generations to meet their own needs' (WCED, 1987).

There has since been a search for concepts to operationalize this notion: a clear definition of sustainable development and tools to help achieve it. One approach to operationalize sustainable development has been in the area of national accounting: incorporating the role of the environment in the economy more fully into the System of National Accounts (SNA) through a system of satellite accounts for the environment.

The SNA is particularly important because it constitutes the primary source of information about the economy and is widely used for analysis and decision-making in all countries. However the SNA has had a number of well-known shortcomings regarding the treatment of the environment. With regard to minerals, for example, until recently the SNA recorded only the income from mining but not the corresponding depletion of this natural capital. Similarly, a country could appear to enjoy high economic growth as it depleted its forests or fisheries, followed by economic collapse when these resources were exhausted because the depletion of natural capital was not accounted for. The 1993 revision of the SNA (UN et al., 1993) addresses some of these problems, notably by expanding the asset boundary to include a broader range of natural assets such as minerals, natural forests and capture fisheries. Even with the expanded coverage of the environment by the 1993 SNA, significant gaps remain; for example, the valuation of non-marketed environmental services and environmental damage. Satellite accounts called the System of Environmental and Economic Accounts (SEEA), were developed to address these gaps (UN, 1993, 2001).

The issue of sustainable management of natural capital is especially acute in many developing countries where natural resources are a principal source of income. All too often an abundance of natural wealth – oil, forests and fisheries – has failed to substantially improve the lives of many citizens. In fact resource-rich countries seem to run a high risk of below-average economic growth and development.

At first glance resource-rich economies would appear to have an advantage over less well-endowed economies because resources could provide funds for rapid development and poverty reduction. However the economic performance of resource-rich compared with resource-poor economies over the past three decades has been surprisingly weak.

Auty and Mikesell (1998) found that as a group, resource-rich developing countries performed worse economically than resource-poor developing countries over the previous 30 years,[1] a phenomenon known as the 'resource curse'. Their results are summarized in Table 1.1: per capita GDP growth in resource-rich countries was well under 2 per cent over the period 1960 to

Table 1.1　Resource endowments and economic growth in developing countries

	Number of countries	Annual per capital GDP growth 1960–90 (%)
Resource-rich		
Large economies	10	1.6
Small economies, of which	55	1.1
Non-mineral exporter	31	1.1
Ore exporter	16	0.8
Oil exporter	8	1.7
Resource-poor		
Large economies	7	3.5
Small economies	13	2.5
All countries	85	1.6

Source:　Based on (Auty and Mikesell, 1998, Table 6.1, p. 86).

1990, while the growth of resource-poor developing countries averaged 2.5 per cent or higher. Among the resource-rich countries, the ore exporters have done the worst, averaging annual GDP growth of only 0.8 per cent.

The reasons for the poor performance of resource-rich countries are complex. Part of the problem may result from the 'Dutch disease' where a surge in foreign exchange earnings from mineral exports leads to currency appreciation, which makes the domestically manufactured tradable goods uncompetitive in world markets, generally discouraging economic diversification and growth. This problem is exacerbated when the resource sector causing the economic boom does not have strong economic linkages with other sectors of the economy.

Another aspect of the problem results from political pressure to use revenues from the exploitation of natural resources to fund current consumption without putting aside anything to compensate for the loss of natural capital. This is particularly the case in developing countries, where many basic needs remain unmet and rent-seeking behaviour may be especially difficult to resist. None of these problems are insurmountable and the chapters in this book provide examples of prudent resource management as well as poor resource management. However, the use of resources for sustainable economic growth requires careful macroeconomic management. The case studies of the management of specific resources and the use of revenues generated by natural resources identify policies that have contributed to sustainable development and those that have not.

The principal concern of sustainability and of environmental accounting is the impact of our ill-informed social choices on intergenerational equity. Intergenerational equity requires that opportunities of future generations, measured by their total national wealth including natural capital, should not decline over time (Hartwick, 1977; Solow, 1974, 1986, 1992). Environmental accounts provide a way to measure total wealth and to monitor changes in this indicator of sustainability.

Environmental accounts also improve our ability to weigh the trade-offs among competing uses of ecosystems, and the changing capacity of ecosystems to supply critical goods and services for present and future well-being. As we alter some ecosystems to increase the supply of commercial products (for example the conversion of forest into agricultural land to raise cattle), we reduce the capacity of the ecosystem to provide other goods and services. The loss of goods and services that have market prices, such as commercial timber, can be readily measured but many other ecosystem services, such as flood control and carbon sequestration, are not easily measured and are often omitted from economic assessment. The net effect of an ecosystem change may be a gain in social welfare when only the impacts on market goods and services are measured but may be a loss when all environmental goods and services are accounted for. Environmental accounts expand the measure of goods and services to include many non-market benefits, in principle, measuring total economic value.

In 1995 a regional project to construct environmental accounts in southern Africa was initiated, based around three core countries, Botswana, Namibia and South Africa. This book reports the experiences of these countries with environmental accounting, providing case studies that show how the environmental accounts have actually been implemented and how they can be used to influence policy decisions in southern Africa.

The next section of this chapter provides an overview of the three countries whose environmental accounts are presented here with a focus on the degree of dependence of these economies on natural resources. Sections 1.3 and 1.4 provide the conceptual overview for the case studies. Rent (section 1.3) is a key concept in environmental accounting and sustainable resource management: the value of natural capital is measured as the discounted value of the rent it can generate in the future. How a resource is exploited affects the amount of rent it generates; in some instances, resource exploitation may be highly inefficient and generate no rent at all. Who appropriates rent and how it is used both influence whether resources contribute to sustainable development or not. Government policy is an important factor influencing all these decisions. Section 1.3 defines resource rent and explains the role it plays in proper resource management.

The general structure and methods of constructing environmental accounts are discussed in section 1.4. Issues in the construction of environmental accounts specific to each resource will be discussed in the relevant chapter. Section 1.5 highlights a key indicator derived from environmental accounts: 'genuine savings' illustrates the use of environmental accounting to measure progress towards sustainable development. The final chapter briefly outlines the plan of the book.

1.2   ECONOMIC DEPENDENCE ON NATURAL RESOURCES IN SOUTHERN AFRICA

Botswana, Namibia and South Africa are neighbouring countries with strikingly different economic and political histories. South Africa, the largest economy, was colonized in the 16th century and in the 20th century introduced an apartheid system to institutionalize racially discriminatory practices. Under this system two very different and separate economies developed: a traditional (sometimes called communal) sector, in which the majority of the people were restricted to a disproportionately small land area and practiced mostly subsistence agriculture, and a commercial economy based on manufacturing, export-oriented mining and agriculture controlled by a minority. Namibia was colonized by Germany in the 19th century and administered by South Africa after the First World War, introducing many of the same apartheid practices and also developing a dualistic economy.

Namibia achieved independence in 1990 and South Africa dismantled apartheid in 1994. Both countries now face the enormous task of integrating the traditional and the commercial economies. Rapid economic growth is a primary objective of virtually all countries but this goal has added significance in Namibia and South Africa because of the urgency of reducing the great social and economic inequalities.

By contrast Botswana, with the highest per capita income in 1999, was never formally colonized, although it was a British protectorate until 1966. At independence it had virtually no infrastructure and the economy was based on extensive livestock grazing. The discovery of diamonds several years later was to change all that (see Chapter 2), and Botswana's exemplary government has transformed Botswana from one of the poorest countries to one of the fastest growing economies in the world. Botswana also suffers from income inequality but this is not as severe as in Namibia and South Africa.

Botswana and Namibia are rather similar in size and population compared South Africa, which is larger by an order of magnitude. Their sparse population reflects very low average rainfall and relatively poor agricultural conditions; most of the land is used for extensive livestock grazing. While South Africa's average rainfall is also low, it is considerably higher than in Botswana or Namibia. The climate is more varied and its agricultural potential is also higher (see Chapter 5 for further discussion).

Primary sector activity dominates the 1999 GDP of Botswana (36 per cent) and Namibia (20 per cent) but is much smaller in South Africa (9 per cent) (Table 1.2). However if the processing of primary products is added, South Africa joins the other two countries as an economy highly dependent on natural resources: primary production plus processing accounts for 38 per cent, 28 per cent and 26 per cent of GDP in Botswana, Namibia and South Africa respectively. With its more highly developed economy, South Africa carries out much more processing of materials – mainly agriculture, wood and minerals – than the other two. Botswana processes very little of its primary products; in Namibia, processing of livestock and fish is a major component of GDP.

All three economies are very open, with exports accounting for roughly a quarter (South Africa) to a half (Namibia and Botswana) of GDP. Exports of primary products or processed primary products dominate, accounting for 76 per cent, 79 per cent and 46 per cent of total exports in Botswana, Namibia and South Africa respectively. Minerals are clearly the most important sector of the Botswana economy. Agriculture, fish and minerals are all important in

*Table 1.2   Structure of the economies of Botswana, Namibia and South
              Africa in 1999*

	Botswana	Namibia	South Africa
Area of country (thousands of km^2)	582	842	1221
Population (millions)	1.61	1.80	42.1
Land per capita (km^2 per capita)	0.36	0.47	0.03
GDP (in millions of currency units)	Pula 25 208	N$ 21 124	R 723 247
GDP (millions of US$)	5458	3469	118 757
GDP (US$ per capita)	3390	1927	2821
Structure of GDP (% of total)			
Primary sectors	35.9	20.1	9.4
Agriculture, forestry, fisheries	2.6	10.4	3.5
Mining	33.3	9.7	5.9
Non-primary	64.1	79.9	90.6
Food processing	2.0	8.0	8.5
Wood products	*	*	3.2
Mineral and metal processing	*	*	5.1
Manufacturing	4.9	10.2	27.1
Other manufacturing	2.9	2.2	1.1
Services and other	59.2	67.6	45.7
Exports as % of GDP	56.0%	46.8%	25.9%
Structure of exports (% of total)			
Agricultural and processed			
food products	1.9	16.0	8.9
Fish and fish products	*	23.0	*
Forest and wood products	*	*	3.3
Minerals	73.7	40.1	34.3
Other (non-primary)	24.4	20.9	53.7

Notes: *Less than 0.1 per cent
Foreign exchange rates used: Pula = 0.2165 US$. Rand and Namibia $ = 0.1642 US$

Source: Botswana: Bank of Botswana (2001), Central Statistics Office (1999). Namibia: Central
Bureau of Statistics (2000). South Africa: SSA (2001) and SARB (March 2001).

Namibia. Agriculture, forest products and minerals are the primary sector
drivers in South Africa. High economic dependence on primary products
makes efficient management of natural capital critical both for current
economic performance as well as for sustainability.

1.3   RESOURCE RENT AND SUSTAINABLE
         MANAGEMENT OF RESOURCES

The term 'rent' is used for a range of different phenomena. Resource rent is a
central concept for management as well as for valuation of natural resources.
In this section we explain what is meant by resource rent and distinguish it

from other notions of rent.[2] Hotelling rent, a concept critical for determining optimal extraction paths of non-renewable resources, is also discussed. The role of rent in resource management is discussed in this section; its role in valuation is discussed later in this chapter in the section on methodology.

Economic rent refers to the price paid for a resource whose supply is fixed and inelastic to price at the moment. The supply of the resource may or may not be increased in the future in response to price changes but at any given moment the supply is fixed.[3] Oil is a useful example: the proven economic reserves at any time are fixed and generate a certain rent. Over time, the supply may be increased by exploration and the development of new technology; however, at any given moment the supply is fixed. An economic rent can accrue to any scarce factor of production, including for example an exceptionally talented sports figure. When economic rent accrues to natural resources, the term 'resource rent' is often used.

Resource scarcity rent is measured by the unit price of *in situ* reserves and represents the present value of future benefits from an additional unit of resource stock. For many resources, however, markets for *in situ* resources are absent or very limited. For such resources, rent is realized only after extraction and sale of a resource. Resource rent is thus incorporated in the market price of the extracted resource along with the costs of other inputs employed for extraction. It is commonly measured as the difference between the market price and the long-run marginal costs of production (including a normal return to fixed capital).

Ricardian rent refers to different payments made to different units of what appears to be a homogeneous resource. These rents arise when the units of the resource actually differ in some way that effects their value in production. For example, one hectare of farmland may command a higher payment than another if it has higher fertility or closer proximity to markets.

Resource rent and Ricardian rent may occur together, and it is important in measuring rent to distinguish between the two. For example, the difference in the spot-market price for low-sulphur crude oil and high-sulphur crude oil results from a Ricardian rent because the value in production (the production of refined petroleum products) of low-sulphur crude is higher than the value of high-sulphur crude. The resource rent, due to scarcity, will depend on the relative scarcity of the two forms of petroleum.

Monopoly rent refers to increased prices obtained due to artificial restrictions placed on the provision of a product, rather than constraints arising from any natural cause, for example monopoly rights for providing telecommunications services.

The Hotelling rent (Hotelling, 1925) addresses the situation of the owner of a non-renewable resource who must decide at what rate to extract the resource. The owner could extract and sell the entire stock at the current price (assuming that this supply would not affect market price) or could wait and extract the resource over a period of time. Hotelling rent measures the dynamic scarcity value of resource assets, based on the opportunity cost of waiting rather than liquidating the resource now, and establishes the rules for optimal resource exploitation over time.

Extraction of a non-renewable resource reduces the stock available for future generations; to maintain social welfare, they must be compensated for this depletion of natural capital. Two questions arise with respect to this. First, what then is the share of resource rents realized from liquidation of natural assets today that must be saved for future generations? Second, how is that current income converted into capital assets and transferred to the future? The rest of this section deals with various aspects of capturing and managing resource rents.

Management of Resource Rents

Building national wealth from natural capital involves transforming one form of wealth, natural capital, into other forms of wealth.[4] This is, of course, essential in the case of non-renewable resources like minerals, which will eventually be depleted, but it is also important in the management of renewable resources, which will not be depleted if managed sustainably. There are three steps in the transformation of natural capital into other forms of wealth:

1. natural resources must be managed to maximize the generation of resource rent;
2. resource rent must be recovered by an agent capable of reinvesting it;
3. resource rent must be used for productive investments.

The role of government policy is critical in each of these steps. Broadly speaking, there are two approaches to the management of natural resources. Natural resources can be commercially exploited to maximize economic rent, which is then appropriated by the government for use on behalf of society. Alternatively, resources may be managed to achieve a combination of economic and social or political objectives in which the assessment of the purely economic benefits and costs of a given resource management strategy may play a more limited role in decision-making. Countries often adopt the first approach – commercial exploitation – for some resources and the second approach – use for both economic and non-economic objectives – for other resources. Minerals are typically suitable for commercial exploitation because of large economies of scale. Other resources, and even minerals under certain circumstances, may have a tradition of artisanal exploitation that may not be economically efficient.

There are a number of arguments that can be made for rent recovery by government:

1. For non-renewable resources, economic sustainability requires reinvestment of rent. In the case of resource exploitation by foreign companies, it is highly likely that large amounts of the rent will be repatriated rather than reinvested in the country providing the resource. In the case of domestic companies, they may limit their domestic investment to private opportunities, and are likely to underinvest in capital that is critical for most developing countries: human capital and infrastructure.
2. For renewable resources, low taxation of rent creates incentives for inefficient levels of exploitation above both maximum economic yield and sometimes above maximum sustainable yield. Rent may be dissipated on excess capacity.
3. Low rent capture also tempts private companies exploiting natural resources, renewable and non-renewable, to over-extract and harvest as fast as possible in anticipation of future revisions of government policy to improve rent capture. These rates of extraction are likely not to be optimal ones.
4. An argument can be made that rent recovery promotes intragenerational equity: the revenues can then be used to support development projects such as education or health that benefit many citizens, not just the small minority involved in resource exploitation.
5. Under the appropriate conditions, taxes on rent are less distortionary than other taxes such as sales or profit taxes (Common, 1995; Dasgupta and Heal, 1979). To the extent that taxes on resource rent can replace these other taxes, economic distortions can be reduced.
6. Unrecovered rents artificially increase private sector profits, which reduces the incentive for efficient economic production in the extracting industry or in downstream resource processing industries (Day, 1998).

These justifications will be examined further in the subsequent chapters of this book. Whatever choice is made about the economic efficiency of resource exploitation, the rent that is generated must then be transformed into other forms of wealth. Resources such as commercial forest plantations and aquaculture fish stocks are usually privately owned. Under private ownership, all the rent accrues to the private sector and it is the responsibility of the private sector to reinvest the rent. However, in many instances the state is the legal owner of resources – this is most often the case for minerals, marine fisheries and natural forests. When a resource belongs to the state, government has the right to charge for the use of these resources as any private business would, and it also bears the responsibility for reinvesting the rent in other assets.

Because of the predominance of public ownership of natural capital, we will focus here on policy issues related to building national wealth under public ownership.

Governments must recover resource rent and must reinvest it productively. The following chapters will present an analysis of the extent to which resource rent is captured by taxes. As we will see, rent recovery has been greater for some resources than for others and some countries have been more successful than others. Once the rent is recovered, it must be reinvested productively. None of the countries of southern Africa have dedicated funds for the reinvestment of resource rent such as the Alberta Heritage Fund or the Alaska Permanent Fund, which manage part of the rent obtained from oil and natural gas in Canada and the United States (Warrack and Keddie, 2000). However, even without a formal rule for reinvestment of resource rent, some countries have used rent to build national wealth. Methods to assess per capita wealth and more specifically, whether the depletion of natural capital is being offset by the creation of other capital will be discussed in this chapter; trends in total wealth will be presented in Chapter 6, synthesizing the work presented in separate chapters for each resource.

1.4   STRUCTURE OF ENVIRONMENTAL ACCOUNTS

Environmental and resource accounts have evolved since the 1970s through the efforts of individual countries and practitioners, each developing their own frameworks and methodologies to represent their environmental priorities. Since the late 1980s, concerted efforts have been under way through the United Nations Statistics Division, the European Union, the OECD, the World Bank, country statistical offices and other organizations to standardize the framework and methodologies. The United Nations published an interim handbook on environmental accounting in 1993 (UN, 1993), which was revised in 2001. The environmental and resource accounts of southern Africa have been based on the UN's System of Integrated Economic and Environmental Accounting (SEEA) so an overview of the framework and methodologies are provided here.

As a system of satellite accounts the SEEA has a similar structure to the SNA, recording stocks and flows of environmental goods and services. It provides a set of aggregate indicators to monitor environmental economic performance at both the sectoral and macroeconomic levels, as well as a detailed set of statistics to guide resource managers toward policy decisions that, hopefully, will improve environmental economic performance in the future. Environment and natural resource accounts have four components:

1. Natural resource asset accounts, stocks of natural resources constructed to revise the balance sheets of the System of National Accounts (SNA) and improve resource management.
2. Pollutant and material (energy and resources) flow accounts, which provide information at the industry level about the use of energy and materials as inputs to production and final demand, and the generation of pollutants and solid waste. These accounts are linked to the supply and use tables of the SNA, which are used to construct input–output tables and social accounting matrices.
3. Environmental protection and resource management expenditure accounts, which identify expenditures in the conventional SNA incurred by industry, government and households to protect the environment or manage resources.
4. Environmentally adjusted macroeconomic aggregates, which include indicators of sustainability such as environmentally adjusted net domestic product (eaNDP).

It can be seen from this brief description that the SEEA differs from other databases about the environment in two fundamental ways. First, the SEEA directly links environmental data to the economic accounts through shared structure, definitions and classifications. The advantage of this database is that it provides a tool to integrate environmental economic analysis and to overcome the tendency to divide issues along disciplinary lines, in which analyses of economic issues and environmental issues are carried out independently of one another.

Second, the SEEA covers all the important environmental economic interactions, a feature that makes it ideal for addressing environmental issues with strong cross-sectoral linkages, such as sustainable forestry or the emission of greenhouse gases. As a system of satellite accounts to the SNA, the SEEA is linked to the full range of economic activities; with a fairly comprehensive classification for environmental resources, the SEEA includes information about all critical environmental stocks and flows relevant to an environmental issue.

This book is primarily concerned with measuring the natural resource assets (minerals, forestry, fisheries) and so only the asset component of the environmental accounts is discussed here. This section provides a general discussion of asset accounts applicable to all resources. Special considerations unique to a particular resource such as constructing asset accounts for age classes of growing biological resources like forests are discussed in the relevant chapter. The chapter on fisheries addresses resource management expenditures but data are not sufficient for construction of full accounts. Macroeconomic aggregates based on asset accounts are discussed in other sections of this chapter.

The chapter on water addresses only the flow accounts because information about water stocks is not readily available at this time. The flow of economic benefits from minerals and fisheries is already included in the national accounts and does not require special treatment. However, with forestry we also consider some aspects of the flow accounts as well as the asset accounts – goods and services produced by forests that are at least partly omitted from the national accounts. Some of these economic benefits are conceptually a part of the national income accounts but have not yet been included because of measurement problems. This includes goods and services such as fuel wood, traditional medicines and foods. Other economic benefits of forests include services of the ecosystems such as the value of pollination services provided to agriculture and the value of carbon sequestration. These issues are taken up in the chapter on forestry.

Physical and Monetary Asset Accounts

Natural resource asset accounts follow the general structure of the accounts for fixed assets in the SNA, with data for opening stocks, closing stocks and changes during the year. The changes that occur during the period are divided into those that are due to economic activity (for example extraction of minerals or harvesting of forests), and those that are due to natural processes (for example growth, births and deaths) or other factors. There is some controversy over how to treat new discoveries of minerals: as an economic change (the result of exploration activities) or as part of other volume changes. The monetary accounts for resources have an additional component, like manufactured capital, for revaluation (Table 1.3).

Table 1.3   Structure of environmental asset accounts

	Physical accounts	Monetary accounts
Opening stocks	X	X
Changes in stocks	X	X
Extraction or Harvest	X	X
Net Natural Growth (renewable resources only)	X	X
Other Volume Changes	X	X
Revaluation (monetary accounts only)		X
Closing stocks	X	X

Measurement of the physical stocks can present problems in terms of what to measure as well as how to measure. In some earlier versions of subsoil (mineral) asset accounts, only economically proven stocks were included in the asset accounts. Some countries have modified this to include a portion of probable and possible stocks, based on the probability of these stocks becoming economically feasible to mine. Certain resources like marine capture fisheries are not observed directly and require biological models to estimate stocks and changes in stocks. It is not always possible to determine net natural growth, so that the changes in stocks include only extraction and other volume changes. The particular challenges associated with constructing physical accounts for each resource are described in the relevant chapters.

Two methods have been used to value natural assets: net present value (NPV) and net price. In much of the early work on environmental accounting (for example Repetto et al., 1989, Bartelmus et al., 1992, Van Tongeren et al., 1991, UN, 1993) the net price method was used to value assets rather than NPV. The net price method simply applies the net price, price minus extraction costs, in a given year to the entire remaining stock. Based on an interpretation of Hotelling's Rule it is equivalent to the NPV method under the restrictive assumption that the real net price increases every year at the same rate as the discount rate (Hartwick and Hageman, 1993). Although this assumption is unrealistic, the net price method was widely used because it appeared to avoid the need to project future net price or extraction paths. However, the method did not really avoid the need to make these projections, it simply made it unnecessary to make them explicit.

The NPV method, that is the discounted sum of its future net income stream or rent, is the theoretically correct method for asset valuation and it has been recommended by the revised SEEA. Rent is calculated as the value of production minus the marginal exploitation costs, which include intermediate consumption, compensation of employees, consumption of fixed capital and the opportunity cost of capital invested in the business. In actual implementation average cost is used rather than marginal cost because data about marginal costs are not generally available. This practice may introduce an upward bias into the measure of rent because average cost is usually lower than marginal cost.

The resource rent is calculated from:

$$R_t = TR_t - IC_t - CE_t - CFC_t - NP_t \tag{1.1}$$

$$NP_t = i_t K_t \tag{1.2}$$

Where,

R = the resource rent
TR = total revenue from the mining sector
IC = intermediate consumption
CE = compensation of employees
CFC = consumption of fixed capital
NP = 'normal' profit, a return on fixed capital
K = fixed capital stock invested in an industry
i = the rate of return considered the opportunity cost of capital

It is best to calculate net rent from establishment data but when such information is not available, aggregate data from the national accounts are used. Whatever the source of data, it is necessary to estimate two components of cost included in the operating surplus or mixed income part of value-added. The first is the cost of capital or so-called 'normal profit,' which is usually viewed as either the cost of borrowing capital or the opportunity cost of equity capital. The second component is the earnings of the self-employed. This is essentially a payment for labour, which is not included in compensation of employees because as the owners of business, the self-employed do not pay themselves an explicit wage. Where resource exploitation is undertaken by the self-employed, for example fishing in Norway, this can be a significant component of costs.

The NPV formula for calculating the value of mineral assets V at period τ is:

$$V\tau = \sum_{t=\tau}^{T} \frac{p_t Q_t}{(1 + r)^t} \tag{1.3}$$

$$p_t = \frac{R_t}{Q_t} \tag{1.4}$$

$$T_t = \frac{S_t}{Q_t} \tag{1.5}$$

Where,

V = value of the asset
p = unit rent price of the resource
Q = quantity of resource extracted
r = the discount rate
R = total resource rent
T = the remaining lifespan of the resource
S = the stock of mineral reserves at the close of the accounting period

In the case of a renewable resource, which is being harvested at a constant, sustainable rate, the formula reduces to:

$$V_t = \frac{p_t Q_t}{r} \qquad (1.6)$$

More important in the case of valuing renewable assets is the fact that biological resources such as trees and wildlife are capable of growth and natural regeneration. As biological resources complete a growth cycle over a length of time before reaching maturity, the standing stock of such resource assets at any point in time consists of a mixture of different age-groups. In this case, applying one price to all standing stocks may generate biased estimates of the values of renewable assets values. Accordingly the used net price or discounted sum of rents (NPV) methods should be modified to allow for a distinction between age-groups in terms of maturity (quality) and hence value.

The NPV method of valuation requires assumptions about future prices and costs of extraction, the rate of extraction, and the discount rate. It is often assumed that net price and level of extraction remain constant, although when information is known about planned extraction paths or expected future prices, this information can be incorporated. A wide range of discount rates have been used by different countries.

Regardless of the method there are several qualifications to this approach to valuation that must be noted. This estimate of rent is based on the *private costs* of extraction. The *social costs* of extraction, and hence the social value of rent, may diverge from the private value of rent for several reasons. First, in many developing countries wages may be artificially higher than the shadow wage rate in highly profitable resource sectors such as mining, especially for unskilled labour. This would have the effect of increasing private costs above social costs and reducing the private value of rent relative to the social value of rent. Where labour costs are rather small, such as capital-intensive mining operations, this effect is probably quite small and can be ignored.

The second source of divergence between the private and social values of rent occurs when government covers part of the costs of exploitation. In some instances government may provide some of the fixed capital necessary for resource exploitation such as roads, water and electricity supply or other infrastructure. In the national accounts these capital costs are reported as part of public sector investment and not associated with mining operations. Hence the true capital costs (return to fixed capital and depreciation) of resource exploitation may be underestimated. The omission of government investment reduces the private costs of mining and increases the private value of rent relative to the social value.

In other instances there may be extensive resource management costs borne by government. For example, management of marine capture fisheries requires extensive research to assess the state of a fishery each year and to establish the total allowable catch – the amount of fish that can be caught on a sustainable basis. In addition the government must undertake extensive monitoring, control and surveillance activities to enforce its policies and to prevent illegal fishing. These costs are included in a separate component of environmental accounts – the environmental protection and resource management expenditure accounts. There is no recommendation yet that resource management costs be included with private costs for the calculation of rent but it is clear that resource management is an essential component of social, if not private, extraction costs.

For some resource extraction activities where rent is very large relative to extraction costs, the inclusion of full costs including government investment and resource management costs would probably not make much difference. However, for marginal undertakings the inclusion of all costs could push the extraction costs high enough to result in near zero or negative rents.

Another source of divergence between the private and social costs occurs when there is substantial environmental damage from resource extraction, such as air and water pollution, mine tailings and the disruption of natural habitat. All resource exploitation has the potential to damage ecosystems resulting in loss of environmental function. Including such costs would reduce the value of rent and of the asset.

Finally, most asset valuation has focused on the dominant commercial use of a resource. Some assets may have multiple uses, providing environmental services both of a commercial nature and a public goods nature. For example forests, in addition to providing timber, may have a direct commercial use for the recreation industry, as well as providing grazing land, wild foods and medicine to local communities. In addition, forests provide other important but indirect uses, for example carbon sequestration or watershed protection. In principle all these values should also be included in the value of the forest.

Constant Value Asset Accounts

As with many economic variables, in order to assess trends over time, values must be converted to constant value measures. There are two approaches to estimating the constant value of mineral assets. The Australian Bureau of Statistics treats the annual unit rent as the price of the asset. Constant price asset accounts are obtained by using the price for the benchmark year in the calculation of the monetary accounts (Johnson, pers. comm.). There are practical problems with this method for resources with highly volatile prices: there may still be years when the price is zero, even if price averaging is used. If such a year were chosen as the benchmark year, the constant value of natural capital would be zero for the entire time series. In addition, the revaluation component drops out of the calculation. The constant price method is based on a cost of production approach and provides little more information than the physical accounts. An alternative approach, under consideration by Statistics Canada (Gravel, pers. comm.) is to apply the GDP deflator to annual rent to calculate the constant or 'real' value of the asset. This is an income-based approach that adjusts for the changing relative value of the income a resource generates over time. It is similar to deflating wages or other incomes. While the GDP deflator approach seems conceptually the better method, since there has been no experience with it yet, the constant unit rent method is used for the accounts presented in this book except for the case of forestry where historical records on actual prices and costs were used.

The Social Discount Rate

In calculating the value of natural capital, a discount rate must be used, reflecting the fact that income received in the future is not as valuable as income received today. Discounting is reflected in the way people behave: consumers' behaviour reflects 'impatience' regarding future consumption, that is, they must be paid to save (positive rate of time preference) and producers invest only where the productivity of capital is positive (opportunity cost of capital). In valuing public assets, the social discount rate is typically used rather than a private discount rate.

Growth theory tells us that the formula for the social discount rate r is as follows:

$$r = i + u \cdot \frac{\Delta c}{c},$$

where i is the pure rate of time preference (also termed the rate of impatience), u the elasticity of the marginal utility of consumption, and $\Delta c/c$ the percentage growth rate in per capita consumption. The rate of impatience represents the rate at which people trade off future welfare against current welfare. The term in the growth rate of per capita consumption represents, roughly speaking, how well off people will be in the future relative to the present, while the elasticity term u adjusts for differing effects on utility at the margin associated with different levels of consumption.

This formula provides a starting point for countries wishing to establish their social discount rate. For the UK, for example, Pearce and Ulph (1999) estimate the pure rate of time preference to be about 1.4 per cent per year and the elasticity of the marginal utility of consumption to be about 0.8, leading to an estimated social discount rate as low as 2.6 per cent.

The social discount rate is the rate applied by an agency like the government which is concerned with social well-being, often over many generations, while the discount rate is the rate that an individual might apply to decisions affecting his or her own economic well-being, often over a much shorter time period, usually not more than a lifetime (even models of overlapping generations are not able to completely overcome these differences).

The social discount rate may be lower than the private discount rate for several reasons (see Hanley and Spash, 1993 for a concise summary):

1. Market failure: there may be positive externalities which private savings decisions, made on the basis of a higher discount rate, do not take into account.
2. Individuals act in two very different roles: as consumers concerned with private benefits and as citizens concerned with the well-being of society. The discount rate expressed for costs and benefits as consumers is typically higher than the discount rate expressed as citizens. Government should act as a disinterested party promoting the well-being of society and use the lower discount rate.
3. Finally, some economists have argued that it is not ethical to discount the well-being of future generations because they have no say in the decisions made today that will affect them. This argument is particularly strong for environmental issues such as preventing climate change for which near-term costs are relatively high, but benefits accrue far in the future; the costs are lightly discounted while the benefits are heavily discounted.

The social opportunity cost of capital is also lower than the private opportunity cost of capital, largely due to taxation and, in some instances, differences in risk. There is considerable controversy over these arguments and a number of alternative approaches to calculating an appropriate social discount rate have emerged. Most countries have adopted a rate – or a range of rates – based on criteria considered appropriate to their circumstances. We will not comment on them here but note that these rates are often higher in developing countries than in developed countries. The subsequent chapters will discuss the discount rates adopted for asset valuation in each country.

Depletion and Depreciation

One of the major motivations for the compilation of environmental accounts has been to include the cost of the depletion and degradation of natural capital in the national accounts in order to provide a more accurate measure of net domestic product. This is particularly important for resource-rich countries, which may appear to perform well according to conventional economic indicators but in fact are living off their (natural) capital in a manner that cannot be sustained indefinitely. In early work, the cost of depletion was measured as the value (net price) of extraction of non-renewable resources, and for renewable resources, the value of the volume of harvest above sustainable yield.

It has since been recognized that this concept, derived from ecological concepts of sustainability, is not consistent with the economic concept of depreciation used for manufactured assets in the SNA. (For further discussion, see Davis and Moore, 2000; Vincent, 1999.) The revised SEEA proposes a measure of depletion cost more consistent with economic depreciation: the change in the asset value from one period to the next. The El Serafy method (1989) is consistent with the concept of economic depreciation under certain assumptions (Hartwick and Hageman, 1989). However, several alternative ways to measure this cost have been proposed and no consensus has yet been reached (United Nations, 2000).

In the national accounts, depletion is defined to include only those asset losses due to economic activities, such as over-harvesting, but not losses resulting from other causes, such as natural disasters. This raises an additional problem for measurement of depletion because the year-to-year fluctuations of some resources, like fish stocks, are not always well understood, making it impossible to determine how much of a change may be due to economic activities. As a result of the uncertainty over measurement of depreciation of natural capital, most countries do not measure it. An example of depreciation calculation of natural assets using the change in asset value method is provided in the chapter on forestry.

1.5   INDICATORS OF SUSTAINABILITY: GENUINE SAVINGS

One of the key roles played by resource and environmental accounting is to provide the basis for measuring progress towards sustainable development. It is certainly arguable that government commitments to achieving sustainability, in the absence of concrete indicators, are only so many words.

The original definition of sustainable development provided by the Brundtland Commission is serviceable enough, but it is useful to make this definition more precise in the context of economic theory. Fortunately Pezzey (1992) has provided an exhaustive analysis of different definitions, summarizing some 40 appearing even at that early point in the literature. The definition used by Pezzey and by most economists today is apparently quite simple: a development path is sustainable if welfare per person does not decline anywhere along it.

This simple definition is actually quite broad. As long as the social welfare function is sufficiently general, embracing all the different aspects of economy, society and environment that people value, then this definition permits a rich analysis of the prospects for sustainability facing an economy.

Pearce and Atkinson (1993) postulate that non-declining social welfare can be equated to non-declining total wealth. That is, (weak) sustainability requires that:

$$K_t = K_t^P + K_t^N + K_t^H$$

and

$$K_{t+1} \geq K_t$$

where

K = total wealth
K^P = produced capital
K^N = natural capital
K^H = human capital.

For total capital to provide an accurate measure of trends in sustainability, it is essential that all forms of capital are included and are properly measured. An alternative to direct measurement of total capital is to measure changes in total wealth with a properly adjusted measure of savings. As long as savings are non-negative, a country's wealth is non-declining. Chapter 6 presents a key result from the theoretical literature which makes the linkage between savings, wealth, welfare and sustainability explicit.

Pearce and Atkinson provided the first empirical estimates of a net saving measure adjusted for environmental depletion and degradation. The World Bank (1999), in its *World Development Indicators*, now publishes estimates of genuine saving for roughly 150 countries each year. These estimates span major minerals and mineral fuels, net forest depletion (that is, where harvest exceeds natural growth), damages from CO_2 emissions and expenditures on education which aim at increasing human capital.

Figure 1.1 presents World Bank estimates for genuine saving for the countries of eastern and southern Africa in 1997. As can be seen, negative savings rates are more than a theoretical possibility with Ethiopia, Malawi, Mozambique and Namibia exhibiting declines in total wealth per capita. It is important to note that depletion of fisheries, subsoil water and diamonds and degradation of cropland, are omitted from these figures, so the estimates are if anything optimistic. However, the lack of data on diamonds in the World Bank

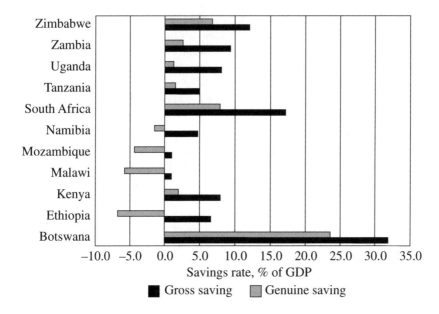

Source: Derived from World Bank (1999).

Figure 1.1   Gross vs. genuine saving rates for eastern and southern Africa, 1997

data set overstates the positive savings for Botswana. This gap is filled in Chapter 2.

Figure 1.1 helps to motivate much of the material on resource and environmental accounting presented in this book. More refined and complete accounting for total national wealth can provide decision-makers with more useful indicators of sustainability. This in turn should motivate better development policies for the countries in the region.

1.6   PLAN OF THE BOOK

Over the next four chapters, accounts for each of the major resources are presented: minerals, forestry, fisheries and water. For minerals and water, accounts were constructed for all three countries and these accounts reveal interesting contrasts in policy. Only South Africa has constructed accounts for forestry; preliminary forest accounts had been constructed for Namibia, but there were simply not enough data for Namibia and Botswana to construct full forest accounts. Forest resources are not as economically important in

Botswana and Namibia as in South Africa. Fisheries accounts were constructed only for Namibia. Fish are not economically important for Botswana, a landlocked country with no marine fisheries and limited inland fisheries. South Africa's fishing industry is similar in size to Namibia's, but given the much larger economy of South Africa, fishing is economically insignificant, accounting for less than 1 per cent of GDP.

Each of the four chapters is intended to provide a useful assessment of resource management, as well as sufficient information to help guide other countries in the construction of environmental accounts. The chapters begin with a description of the economic and policy context for exploitation of the resource in each country. This is followed by a detailed discussion of the resource-specific methodologies, data sources and assumptions made in constructing the accounts. A comprehensive set of physical and monetary accounts is presented and analysed in the main text and appendices, which readers can use for their own calculations. Some of the basic policy applications are included, for example the analysis of the generation and distribution of resource rent. The book concludes with a chapter that synthesizes the work and discusses total national wealth.

NOTES

1. While this may also be true in industrialized countries, the dependence of these economies on non-renewable resources is often much lower than in the developing countries under consideration, hence the management of this wealth is less critical.
2. Alchian, A. 1987.
3. *Quasi-rent* occurs when the insensitivity of supply to price change is temporary. With free entry under perfect competition, *quasi rents* will eventually be eroded.
4. Natural capital can also be transformed into another form of natural capital. For example, mineral wealth can be used to develop forests or improve land.

REFERENCES

Alchian, A. (1987), 'Rent', in J. Eatwell, M. Milgate and P. Newman (eds), *The New Palgrave*, London, Macmillan Press.

Auty, R.M. and R. Mikesell (1998), *Sustainable Development in Mineral Economies*, Oxford, Clarendon Press.

Bank of Botswana (2001), *Annual Report 2000*, Gaborone, Botswana.

Bartelmus, P., E. Lutz and S. Schweinfest (1992), 'Integrated environmental and economic accounting: a case study for Papua-New Guinea', World Bank Environmental Working Paper No. 54.

Central Bureau of Statistics (2000), *National Accounts 1993–1999*, National Planning Commission, Windhoek, Namibia.

Central Statistics Office (1999), *Statistical Bulletin*, Government Printer, Gaborone, Botswana.

Central Statistics Office (2000), *Environment Statistics*, Government Printer, Gaborone, Botswana.

Common, M. (1995), *Sustainability and Policy*, Cambridge, Cambridge University Press.

Daly, H. (1996), *Beyond Growth: The Economics of Sustainable Development*, Boston, Beacon Press.

Dasgupta, P. and G. Heal (1979), *Economic Theory and Exhaustible Resources*, Cambridge, Cambridge University Press.

Davis, G. and D. Moore (2000), 'Valuing mineral stocks and depletion in green national income accounts', *Environmental and Development Economics*, 5 (1 and 2): 109–28.

Day, B. (1998), 'Who's Collecting the rent? Taxation and super-profits in the forest sector', Environment Department Working Paper (draft), Washington DC, World Bank.

El Serafy, S. (1989), 'The proper calculation of income from depletable natural resources', in Y. Ahmad, S. El Serafy and E. Lutz (eds), *Environmental Accounting for Sustainable Development*, Washington, DC, World Bank.

Hanley, N. and C. Spash (1993), *Cost-Benefit Analysis and the Environment*, Cheltenham, Edward Elgar Publishing.

Hartwick, J. (1977), 'Intergenerational equity and the investing of rents from exhaustible resources', *American Economic Review*, 67(5): 972 – 4.

Hartwick, J. (1990), 'Natural resources, national accounting, and economic depreciation', *Journal of Public Economics*, 43: 291–304.

Hartwick, J. and A. Hageman (1993), 'Economic depreciation of mineral stocks and the contribution of El Serafy', in Y. Ahmad, S. El Serafy and E. Lutz (eds), *Environmental Accounting for Sustainable Development*, Washington, DC, World Bank.

Hotelling, H. (1925), 'A general mathematical theory of depreciation', *Journal of the American Statistical Association*, 20: 149–52, 340–53.

Lawn, P. (1998), 'In defence of the strong sustainability approach to national income accounting', *Environmental Taxation and Accounting*, 3 (1): 29–47.

Pearce, D. and G. Atkinson (1993), 'Capital theory and the measurement of sustainable development: an indicator of "weak" sustainability', *Ecological Economics*, 8: 103–8.

Pearce, D. and D. Ulph (1999), 'A social discount rate for the United Kingdom', in D. Pearce, *Economics and Environment: Essays on Ecological Economics and Sustainable Development*, Cheltenham, Edward Elgar.

Pearce, D., K. Hamilton and G. Atkinson (1996), 'Measuring sustainable development: Progress on indicators', *Environment and Development Economics*, 1: 85–101.

Pezzey, J. (1992), Sustainable development concepts: an economic analysis. World Bank Environment Paper No. 2, Washington, DC,World Bank.

Pezzey, J. and M. Toman (forthcoming), 'Progress and problems in the economics of sustainability', in T. Tietenberg and H. Folmer (eds), *International Yearbook of Environmental and Resource Economics 2002/2003*, Cheltenham, Edward Elgar.

Repetto, R., W. Magrath, M. Wells, C. Beer and F. Rossini (1989), *Wasting Assets: Natural Resources in the National Accounts*, World Resources Institute, Washington.

Ricardo, D. (1821), *The Principles of Political Economy and Taxation*, 3rd edition, London, Johan Murray.

SARB *see* South Africa Reserve Bank.

Solow, R. (1974), 'Intergenerational equity and exhaustible resources', *Review of Economic Studies*, 41: 29–45.

Solow, R. (1986), 'On the intergenerational allocation of natural resources', *Scandinavian Journal of Economics*, 88 (1): 141–9.

Solow, R. (1992), 'An almost practical step towards sustainability', Paper prepared for Resources for the Future, Washington, DC.

SSA *see* Statistics South Africa.

South Africa Reserve Bank (2001), *Quarterly Bulletin March 2001*, Pretoria, South Africa.

Statistics South Africa (2001), *The 1998 Social Accounting Matrix*, Pretoria, South Africa.

United Nations (1993), *Integrated Environmental and Economic Accounting*, Studies in Methods, Handbook of National Accounting, Series F, No. 61, New York.

United Nations (2001), *Integrated Environmental and Economic Accounting 2000*, Draft available through the UN website: www.un.org.

United Nations, Commission of the European Communities, International Monetary Fund, Organisation for Economic Cooperation and Development and World Bank (1993), *System of National Accounts*, United Nations, New York.

Van Tongeren, J., S. Schweinfest and E. Lutz (1991), 'Integrated environmental and economic accounting: a case study of Mexico', World Bank Environment Working Paper No. 50. Washington, DC, World Bank.

Vincent, J. (1999), 'Net accumulation of timber resources', *Review of Income and Wealth*, 45 (2).

Warrack, A. and R. Keddie (2000), 'Albert Heritage Fund vs. Alaska Permanent Fund: a comparative analysis', Draft paper obtained from the website of the Alaska Permanent Fund Corporation website: www.apfc.org.

WCED (1987), *Our Common Future*, Oxford, Oxford University Press.

World Bank (1999), *World Development Indicators*, Washington, DC, World Bank.

2. Mineral accounts: managing an exhaustible resource

Glenn-Marie Lange and Rashid Hassan

2.1 INTRODUCTION

Minerals are a principal source of income for many developing countries, including many in southern Africa. At first glance mineral-rich economies have an advantage over those less well endowed because minerals provide funds for rapid development and poverty reduction. However, as discussed in Chapter 1, resource abundance does not necessarily lead to economic prosperity for a variety of reasons grouped together under the 'resource curse'. It is hoped that this chapter will shed some light on policies that can be taken to avoid the 'resource curse'.

Mining has played a vital role in the economic development of South Africa, Botswana and Namibia by financing growth in all sectors of the economy. Mining in all countries is dominated by large-scale commercial operations, although some small-scale artisanal mining does take place.

Commercial mining in southern Africa had its origin in South Africa in the 19th century with the opening up of the Kimberley diamond mines in the 1860s followed by the Witwatersrand gold mines in the 1880s. With the discovery of gold and diamonds, the South African economy underwent rapid growth and dramatic structural change from a predominantly agricultural economy and rural population to a more urban economy centred around mining and supporting industries. The share of agriculture in employment dropped from 75 per cent to 33 per cent between 1865 and 1921. Exports grew rapidly during the same period with a steadily declining share of agricultural products matched by an increase in mineral exports. The profits from diamonds and gold also became the main source of revenue for the government and the source of finance for private investment in the rapidly expanding industries (Natrasse, 1981).

Coal mining initially developed to meet domestic energy demands, but later became an important export. South Africa also became one of the world's top producers of asbestos, aluminium, chromium, iron, lead, nickel, manganese, platinum, silicon, titanium, vanadium and zirconium. The bulk of the mining industry is now controlled by five mining investment houses, marked by complex interlocking ownership. Government involvement in mining has been minimal except in oil and natural gas. These are considered strategic resources because of the international sanctions during the apartheid period. Since the end of the apartheid system in 1994, most restrictions on capital have been removed and the mining industry has been restructuring to make it more competitive in world markets. South Africa's mining industry is presently dominated by coal, gold and platinum; although diamonds are mined, they no longer play a very large role in the industry. In 1999 South Africa produced more than 55 different minerals from about 723 mines and quarries including 60 coal mines and 49 gold mines (USGS, 1999).

Namibia's mining industry also developed relatively early, based mostly on diamonds discovered at the turn of the century (Hartmann, 1986). Like South Africa's diamond mines, the initial reserves were relatively high-quality gem and near gem-quality diamonds, extracted from relatively inexpensive onshore mining sites. As in South Africa, mining was a major contributor to the development of the Namibian economy. Other metals (mainly copper, zinc and lead) were exploited in the post-Second World War period, and uranium mining began in the early 1970s. In more recent years a gold mine has opened up, a new zinc mine is planned and an offshore natural gas field has been discovered. These new developments will help offset the decline of diamond and uranium mining. Namibia has largely exhausted its early diamond reserves and has now moved to offshore diamond mining; although there appear to be extensive diamond reserves they are much more expensive to mine. The global outlook for uranium has not been good for some time; although the reserves have not yet been exhausted, there is not a strong market for uranium. Namibia's mining industry today is dominated by diamonds, uranium and gold; zinc and new copper mines are likely to become important in the future.

Until independence, mining was controlled by foreign companies. Diamond mining was largely under the control of a single company, Consolidated Diamond Mines (CDM), which was based in South Africa and owned by De Beers. After independence a new company was formed, Namdeb, as an equal partnership between CDM and the government of Namibia. Namdeb still accounts for 90 per cent or more of diamond mining but government has opened up the coastal region, Sperrgebiet (Forbidden Territory), for others and there are now five other companies with rights to mine diamonds. Namibia's single uranium mine is owned by Rossing, a company based in Britain, and many other mining operations are owned by South African companies.

Botswana is a relative newcomer to mining: its diamonds were discovered only after independence in the late 1960s and not developed until the 1970s.

Discovered by De Beers, the South African mining company, diamonds are mined by Debswana, a company owned jointly by the government of Botswana and De Beers, with Botswana holding a 50 per cent share of the company. Three diamond mines are currently in operation. One of the poorest countries in the world in the 1960s, with an economy based largely on live-stock, Botswana has become the largest global producer of gem-quality diamonds. This mineral wealth has been used to transform the economy and has greatly improved the lives of its people.

Copper/nickel (which occur together with a small amount of cobalt), coal and soda ash are also mined in Botswana but are not economically significant. Coal reserves are extensive but of very low quality and are used only by the domestic electric power company (a parastatal) and a few other government institutions. Copper/nickel mining was profitable in the early 1980s but has been marginal in the 1990s. Government also has a share in these mining operations, but unlike diamond mining, these operations are majority controlled by private companies (USGS, 1998). Soda ash is a newer development but it also is not highly profitable.

Botswana, Namibia and South Africa have a broad range of minerals and each one of them is a major world producer for at least one mineral (Table 2.1). South Africa accounted for 18 per cent of the world's gold production in 1999, and 6 per cent of world coal. It has become a major coal exporter, accounting for 11 per cent of coal exports in 1999. Botswana's coal production is negligible. Namibia produced 9 per cent of the world's uranium, making it the fourth-largest producer. Its production of gold, while important domestically, accounts for less than 1 per cent of the world total. Botswana's gold production, largely a by-product of other mining, is even smaller than Namibia's.

Diamonds are mined in all three countries although the industry's economic importance varies. Botswana accounts for 27 per cent of the lucrative diamond gemstone production, 9 per cent of the industrial diamonds, and 22 per cent of the estimated value of world production. By the late 1990s Botswana became the world's largest producer of gem-quality diamonds, surpassing Australia and Russia. Namibia and South Africa contribute 3 per cent and 7 per cent respectively to gemstone production. South Africa contributes more to the industrial diamond market, reflecting the depletion of its most valuable diamonds over the last century. However, the total value general by South Africa's diamonds is not insignificant on the world market: 13 per cent. Like gold, Namibia's diamond industry is important domestically but accounts for a negligible share of the value of world diamond production.

In terms of both economic importance and property rights, the mining industry differs markedly among the three countries. Mining is most important in Botswana: as a share of GDP, mining peaked at 51 per cent in 1988 and has

Table 2.1 World production of major minerals and shares produced by Botswana, Namibia and South Africa, 1999

	Diamonds		Total value (US$ million)	Gold (tons)	Coal 10^{15} BTUs	Uranium (000s of tons U)
	Gemstone (000s of carats)	Industrial (000s of carats)				
Botswana	27%	9%	22%	*	*	0%
Namibia	3%	*	*	*	0%	9%
South Africa	7%	10%	13%	18%	6%	3%
World Production	59 200	58 200	7353	2540	85	31.1

Notes: *less than 1%.
The value of diamond production is estimated. The figure for uranium production is equivalent to 36.6 thousand tons of $U_3 O_8$.

Sources: Adapted from: Diamond and gold: USGS (1999), value of diamonds: World Diamond Council (2001), Coal: Energy Information Agency (2000), Uranium: World Nuclear Association (2001).

since declined to about one-third of GDP, as Botswana has sought to diversify its economy and to lessen its vulnerability to changing market conditions for diamonds (Figure 2.1a). Diamonds account for 95 per cent or more of the value-added generated by mining in Botswana. By contrast, mining currently contributes only about 10 per cent and 6 per cent to the GDPs of Namibia and South Africa respectively. Mining is a much older industry in these countries and in earlier years played a much larger role in their economies. As recently as 1980, mining accounted for 40 per cent of Namibia's GDP and was still over 20 per cent until 1990. South Africa's mining industry peaked much earlier: by 1970 it contributed only 13 per cent of GDP. In contrast to Botswana and Namibia, however, South Africa has an extensive downstream mineral processing industry, contributing a significant share of value-added and employment.

Despite varying contributions to GDP, minerals remain the single largest export for all three countries (Figure 2.1b). Minerals accounted for over 73 per cent of exports in each country in 1980 but have since declined to 72 per cent, 40 per cent and 57 per cent in Botswana, Namibia and South Africa respectively.

As a capital-intensive industry, mining does not generate a great deal of employment in Botswana or Namibia. While production of diamonds, Botswana's principal mineral, has increased fourfold from 1980 to 1999, its share of employment has declined from 9 per cent to less than 4 per cent of formal sector employment (Figure 2.1c). Namibia does not regularly compile employment statistics, but the available data indicate that mining's share of employment is very low and declining as mineral production has declined. In 1997 mining accounted for roughly 2 per cent of formal sector employment (Ministry of Labour, 2001). In South Africa on the other hand, a significant share of its labour force is still employed in mining: 9 per cent in 1997 compared with 13 per cent in 1980. While this is not an issue that can be addressed here, it is interesting to note that the labour-intensity of production is much higher in South Africa than Botswana. Differences in labour-intensity reflect the dominance of different mining subsectors in the two countries. Gold and coal mining, which contribute more than 70 per cent of the mining income and account for more than 68 per cent of total employment in South Africa, are more labour-intensive than diamond mining, which dominates the Botswana economy. In 1998 the labour-intensity of gold mining in South Africa was 10.7 full-time jobs per million rand of output, which was more than three times that of diamonds: 3.4 full-time jobs per million rand of output (DME, 2000).

Mineral property rights differ among the three countries. Under Botswana and Namibian law, all sub-soil assets, including minerals, are the property of the state. The state grants rights to private companies for the extraction of the

minerals and levies taxes for this right. The governments of both Botswana
and Namibia are more directly involved in diamond mining as partners with
De Beers, the major international diamond mining company. In South Africa
sub-soil assets belong to the owner of the land and not to the state, although
this policy is currently being changed. Government is less directly involved in
mining activities in South Africa.

The difference in ownership has important implications for policies to

2.1a   GDP

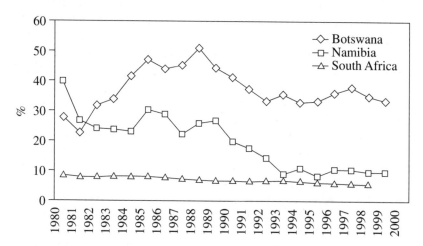

2.1b   Exports

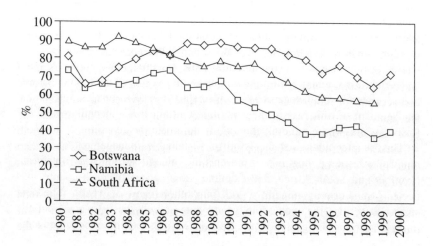

2.1c   Employment

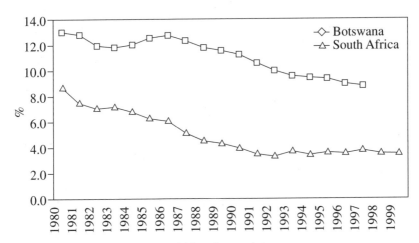

Note: Namibia does not compile annual labour force statistics

Source: Based on Lange (2001b, 2001c) and Hassan and Blignaut (2001).

Figure 2.1   *Contribution of mining to GDP, exports and formal employment, 1980 to 1999/2000 in Botswana, Namibia and South Africa*

promote sustainable development. Under private ownership, all resource rent from mining accrues to the private sector and reinvestment to compensate for the depletion of minerals is entirely in private hands. Under public ownership, government charges mining companies for the exploitation of these resources, but it also bears the responsibility for reinvesting some portion of the revenues in other assets to compensate for mineral depletion. This situation raises two related policy issues for government: is the resource rent being recovered under public ownership, and is the rent used for investment to offset the depletion of mineral wealth regardless of ownership? For all countries, sustainable management of mineral resources is important but it is especially important for Botswana, where minerals thoroughly dominate the economy.

This chapter addresses the issue of sustainable management of a non-renewable resource: minerals. It presents the mineral accounts for Botswana, Namibia and South Africa, and examines how successful each country has been in transforming mineral wealth into other forms of wealth. The next section describes the methodology and data sources used to construct the mineral accounts for each country. Section 2.3 presents the mineral accounts in physical and monetary terms and compares trends in mineral wealth among the three countries over time. Section 2.4 discusses the policy implications: the rent generated by mining, the recovery of rent by government, and the use of that rent – whether rent is used to effectively transform mineral wealth into other forms of wealth. Of the three countries only Botswana has developed an explicit policy linking use of mineral revenues with development objectives. The success and limitations of this policy are assessed. Concluding remarks are provided in the final section.

2.2   METHODOLOGY AND DATA SOURCES

Relative to other resources, minerals are probably the most commonly constructed set of accounts. Table 2.2 shows the countries where there are official environmental accounting programmes, and the most important minerals in their asset accounts. There have been one-off consultancy reports and academic studies as well but these are too numerous to include here. Both industrialized and developing countries compile mineral accounts and, not surprisingly, mineral accounts are compiled in countries where minerals play an important economic role. Accounts for petroleum and natural gas predominate.

Mineral accounts for Botswana, Namibia and South Africa have been constructed based on the SEEA (UN, 2001) and the general methodology described in Chapter 1. The discussion here is based on reports compiled for each country; more detailed information can be obtained from the following sources: Botswana: Lange (2001c); Namibia: Lange (2001b); and South Africa: Blignaut and Hassan (2001), Hassan and Blignaut (2001).

Although each country mines a wide range of minerals, just a few minerals account for virtually all of the economic contribution. In Botswana diamonds, copper/nickel and coal account for more than 99 per cent of mining GDP and the mineral accounts include these three minerals (Table 2.3). At present diamonds, uranium and gold account for more than 95 per cent of Namibia's mining GDP and accounts have been compiled only for these minerals. Copper and zinc mines are under development and mineral accounts in the future should also include them. In South Africa, mineral accounts have only been constructed for coal and gold, which account for more than 70 per cent of mining income and export earnings in 1998. The other important mineral is platinum (contributing 21 per cent of export income in 1998), for which physical and monetary accounts are currently under construction. These three minerals contributed more than 82 per cent of mining exports income in 1998 (DME, 2000). Data problems have so far prevented the construction of detailed accounts for other minerals either because information is classified

Table 2.2   Countries that have constructed mineral accounts

Country	Minerals included in the sub-soil asset accounts
Australia	bauxite, diamonds, lead, coal, zinc, petroleum, natural gas, uranium
Canada	petroleum, natural gas, coal, metals (copper, zinc, nickel, lead, gold, silver, molybdenum, iron, uranium), potash
Chile	copper, gold, coal, calcium carbonate
Denmark	petroleum, natural gas
France	petroleum, natural gas
Indonesia	petroleum, natural gas
Mexico	petroleum
Namibia	diamonds, uranium, gold
Netherlands	petroleum, natural gas
Norway	petroleum, natural gas
Philippines	gold, silver, cobalt, copper, lead, chromite, molybdenum, zinc, nickel, iron, manganese
UK	petroleum, natural gas
US	petroleum, natural gas, coal, metals (iron ore, copper, lead, zinc, gold, silver, molybdenum), other minerals (phosphate rock, sulfur, boron, diatomite, gypsum, potash)

Source: Based on Lange (2001a)

Table 2.3   Minerals in the asset accounts of Botswana, Namibia and South Africa

Country	Minerals	% of mining GDP from these minerals
Botswana	diamonds, copper/nickel, coal	99+
Namibia	diamonds, uranium, gold	95+
South Africa	coal, gold	70

(platinum and diamonds) or because no detailed statistics are currently available (especially on reserves) and hence published information aggregates all other minerals.

Physical Accounts: Methodological Issues and Data Sources

Construction of physical accounts is a relatively straightforward application of the general methodology described in Chapter 1. Accounts consist of opening stocks, changes in stocks and closing stocks. Changes consist of extraction, new discoveries and redefinition of assets. Redefinition refers to the categories of probability of economically feasible extraction and, in this respect, the mineral accounts differ from the general model of accounts provided in Chapter 1.

The mining industry has developed a system referred to as the McKelvey Box, to classify mineral reserves according to combined criteria of geological certainty (proved, probable, possible or undiscovered reserves) and economic feasibility of extraction (economic or sub-economic reserves). For example, exploration may establish a proven reserve of 100 000 tons of ore at a given site, of which half may be profitable to mine given the current market price for ore and the cost of extraction (economic reserves) and half might be too expensive to extract (sub-economic reserves). Reserves that are both proven and economic are referred to as economically proven reserves.

There has been some controversy over whether mineral accounts should include only economically proven reserves or whether both proven and probable reserves should be valued. In the past, most countries included only proven reserves because of the difficulties in valuing probable reserves. The costs of extraction, and hence the per unit rent for probable reserves, may differ significantly from extraction costs for proven reserves.

Increasingly, countries are including other categories of reserves, weighted by their probability of economic extraction because omission of these reserves gives a misleading picture of the mineral assets. For example, the proven petroleum reserves of UK have shown no depletion for the last 20 years, despite massive extraction (Harris, 2000). Even when probable reserves were added to proven reserves no depletion was seen. Only when all three categories of reserves – possible, probable and proven – were included could the depletion of reserves due to extraction be seen. This is because depletion of proven reserves was constantly being offset by further development of probable and possible reserves which added to proven reserves. 'Proving' reserves – undertaking the exploration and development necessary to move reserves from probable or possible into proven – is expensive and companies do not undertake this expense until it is profitable for them to do so, that is when the current level of proven reserves has declined sufficiently.

In principle the mineral accounts for Botswana, Namibia and South Africa would include at least some of all categories of reserves. In practice, the category of reserves included depends on the information available for each mineral discussed below.

Botswana

The Department of Mines published figures annually for extraction, production and reserves for copper/nickel until 1987. Reserves included both proven and probable, though the distinction was dropped after 1982 and appeared to combine the two categories. After 1987 the Department of Mines discontinued its series on reserves, so for 1988 to the present, reserves are calculated as closing stock in 1987 (1.1 million tons) minus extraction in each subsequent year. Any changes in reserves since that time have not been included in the mineral accounts. In 1992 the Department of Mines further reduced published information, reporting only the quantity of copper/nickel in the final product, a copper/nickel matte. This is insufficient for calculating changes in reserves because there are substantial production losses during mining and initial processing, which had been reported in the past. The mineral accounts for copper/nickel calculate the losses based on the last published loss rates. Discussions are underway with the Department of Mines to improve the data in future.

Eleven coalfields have been identified in Botswana but reserves have been measured for only two of these fields: Morupule and Mmamabule. Measured coal reserves at the two coal fields are vast relative to annual extraction and will last thousands of years at current rates of extraction. Botswana's reserves are of very low quality and are used only domestically, mainly for power production. The other coalfields are considered to have no value and are omitted from the accounts. Data about coal reserves and extraction were obtained from (CSO, 2000).

Information about extraction of diamonds is publicly available from the Annual Reports of the Department of Mines but until recently, information about the reserves of diamonds was a closely guarded secret, making it impossible to publish the full accounts for diamonds. However, in its 1999 Annual Report De Beers, the major partner of Debswana, adopted a new policy of openness and transparency and published the estimated reserves for each of its mines throughout the world, which have been used for the mineral accounts.

In Botswana, De Beers reported reserves for the three mines in operation: Orapa, Jwaneng and Letlhakane. Reserves were classified as probable, indicated and inferred, which roughly correspond to proven, probable and possible. The geological characteristics of Botswana's diamond mines make the probability of economically feasible mining very high, even for the inferred reserves, so Botswana's diamond accounts include all three categories.

Diamond reserves have not been reported for earlier years, so reserves prior to 1999 were calculated by adding back annual extraction. Consequently the accounts for the period 1980 to 1999 do not show new discoveries and other volume changes. This should not distort the accounts because the major discoveries were already identified by the late 1970s although it took a number of years to bring these discoveries into production.

Namibia
Annual figures for extraction are published by the Ministry of Mines and Energy. No figures on reserves are collected or published so a survey was undertaken of the four companies that mine Namibia's three major minerals. Uranium has been mined by one company at a single location since the mine was first opened in the early 1970s. Gold mining is also limited to one company in a single location. Two companies mine virtually all the diamonds although Namdeb, the partnership between the government of Namibia and De Beers mining company, is by far the largest company. The survey requested data for economically proven reserves, changes in reserves and new discoveries, as well as information about annual investment since the opening of the mine in order to compile the monetary accounts. Because of confidentiality requirements, information about reserves for individual minerals cannot be published.

South Africa
Data for gold and coal have been obtained mainly from statistics published by the Department of Minerals and Energy (DME annual, 2000) as well as from surveys of informal sources. Data for coal were readily available but gold was more problematic. The *Handbook of the South African Mining Industry* reported the level of gold reserves fixed at 20 000 tons from 1983 until 1990 (Chamber of Mines, various years). Later editions of the handbook published different figures of gold reserves ranging between 40 000 tons (1994) and 35 000 tons (1998). Surveys of other unofficial sources (independent estimates through personal communications with the Chamber of Mines, Institute for Geological Sciences and the Minerals Bureau) confirmed the reliability of the published 1998 estimate of gold reserves of 35 000 tons. No information was available on new additions and other volume changes.

Volumes sold, and not production figures, were published for the years 1966 to 1975 and hence volumes sold were used as estimates of production for that period. After 1976 only production data were available leading to indirectly deriving volumes sold from the value of sales and average gold prices. Reserves for earlier years were calculated by adding annual production to the gold reserves figure for 1998.

Monetary Accounts: Methodological Issues and Data Sources

As described in Chapter 1, the value of minerals like any other asset, is the net present value of the stream of income they are expected to generate in the future, or future resource rents. Rent is calculated as the revenue minus the costs of extraction, including full capital costs (depreciation of fixed investment plus a 'normal' return on fixed capital).

The rent for minerals in Botswana and South Africa was calculated with data obtained from the national accounts. The primary source of financial information in South Africa has been mining censuses conducted by Statistics South Africa. These censuses commenced in 1966 and are done approximately every three years with the latest available census being for 1993. In Botswana only three companies are involved in the mining of gold, copper/nickel and coal. These companies provide detailed economic information to the Central Statistics Office each year.

Namibia only developed its own national accounts after independence in 1990, so there is no repository of statistical surveys and historical time series are rather limited. In Namibia part of the information necessary to calculate rent is obtained from unpublished national accounts data: production value and some extraction costs. However the costs of capital cannot be easily calculated for each mineral because there is no historical time series of fixed capital by mining company. (There is a times series of fixed capital for all mining in Hartmann, 1986 but this did not adequately distinguish different minerals.) A company survey was carried out to develop the time series, which is now updated with information on annual investment obtained from surveys by Namibia's Central Bureau of Statistics.

In calculating the value of resource rent, an assumption must be made about the return to fixed capital or normal profit. Different assumptions were used in each of the countries, largely reflecting conditions within each country. Where there is extensive public borrowing to finance investment, these interest rates can be used. However, this has only been the case in South Africa; the economies of Botswana and Namibia are too small and the number of companies involved is too few for much public borrowing. The nominal interest rate on bonds issued by mining companies in South Africa ranged from 7 per cent to 16 per cent over the period 1966 to 1993. A 10 per cent rate of return was used for the calculations reported here for all countries. In all three countries sensitivity analysis was carried out using different rates of return.

In calculating the asset value another assumption must be made about the discount rate to apply to future earnings. All three countries use the same social discount rate of 10 per cent, which is the medium rate used by these governments for project evaluation. In the original work for South Africa, a 3 per cent discount rate was used; for this report a 10 per cent discount rate was used for greater comparability with the results from the other two countries.

In Chapter 1, several reasons for a potential divergence between private and social cost in calculating rent were discussed. To varying degrees this divergence occurs in all three countries and will be discussed in the following section.

Mineral prices can fluctuate a great deal from one year to the next, so the real value of mineral assets is not always best represented by the per unit rent in any single year. In order to reduce volatility and better represent the longer-term value of mineral assets, a number of countries use a multiple-year moving average per unit rent in calculating asset values. Australia and Canada, for example, use a multiple-year, lagged moving average. To better reflect the longer-term value of mineral assets, a five-year lagged moving average of the unit rent is used for the mineral accounts in Botswana and Namibia.

In estimating the value of the resource, no information about future market prices or production levels is available, so the conventional approach was used: assume constant levels of extraction and unit rent. With regard to diamonds, the most valuable mineral for Botswana and Namibia, this assumption may raise some questions. In the past the price of diamonds has been artificially maintained through a marketing cartel. The diamond market may change in the future because of several factors. World diamond producers have become more independent and difficult to control, with some producers looking to get a 'free ride' and benefit from the high prices established by the Central Selling Organization (CSO), but not selling through the CSO. This threatens the ability of CSO to maintain its monopoly control over prices. In part for this reason DeBeers, the main producer, is changing its marketing strategy from one of controlling supply (acting in essence as a 'buyer of last resort') to emphasis on sales promotion. Another factor is the potential effect of a public campaign against diamonds, viewed as supporting wars in Africa, which could reduce demand. Botswana does not expect its diamond revenues to be much affected in the future. Its level of production is expected to stay high because it is the lowest-cost producer in the world and its costs are not expected to increase significantly in the future. Namibia, as a relatively high-cost producer, is more vulnerable. The only factor that would affect the value of Botswana's diamonds would be a severe decline in the market price of diamonds. However, while De Beers has abandoned its strategy of controlling supply, it still controls over 60 per cent of world production and expects that its marketing and advertising efforts will maintain the high price of diamonds. It is too early to tell whether the campaign against so-called 'conflict' diamonds will affect the overall diamond market and the price of diamonds.

2.3 MINERAL ACCOUNTS AND RESOURCE RENT FROM MINING

Physical Accounts for Minerals

The extraction of minerals is shown in Table 2.4 and an index of physical mineral reserves is shown in Figure 2.2. Detailed physical and monetary accounts are given in Appendix A, except for Namibia whose reserves cannot be publicly reported. Although both Botswana and Namibia produce diamonds, Botswana's production is far greater than Namibia's: between 10 and 20 times as great by the end of the 1990s. South Africa's coal production similarly dwarfs Botswana's and its gold production is more than 100 times Namibia's.

Despite high production over the past 20 years, less than 25 per cent of Botswana's known diamond reserves have been extracted. The extraction of copper/nickel has been offset in the past by new discoveries and reclassification of reserves but by 1998, about 30 per cent of copper/nickel reserves had been extracted. Less than 1 per cent of the known coal reserves have been extracted. South Africa still had more than 90 per cent of its coal reserves in 1980 and almost 80 per cent of its gold reserves. No information on new reserves discovered over the period is yet available.

Resource Rent and the Monetary Accounts for Minerals

The mining sector has generated substantial amounts of resource rent (Table 2.5). In Botswana and Namibia most of this rent has been generated by diamonds. In some years the rent generated by diamonds surpassed total rent from mining due to negative rents from other mining activities in those years. More detailed information for Botswana shows the trends for each mineral (Table 2.6). Rent per carat of diamonds has shown a fairly steady increase over time. The rent generated by copper/nickel has been extremely volatile, significant in some years but low and even negative in others. Coal has generated very little rent in all years. Indeed coal is only purchased by government agencies required to use coal, at the price government is willing to pay for it and not a competitive market price. It is quite likely that without a government-determined price, it would not be profitable to mine coal and rent would be zero or even negative.

Table 2.6 also shows the sensitivity of rent estimates to the rate of return to fixed capital in Botswana. For diamonds in the mid-1980s, the difference between using a 20 per cent rate of return to fixed capital in rent calculations and a 10 per cent rate of return were significant: the higher rate reduced rent by as much as 20 per cent to 30 per cent, relative to the lower rate of return.

Table 2.4 *Extraction of minerals in Botswana, Namibia and South Africa, 1980–99 (diamonds in millions of carats, coal in millions of tons, other minerals in tons)*

	Botswana			Namibia			South Africa	
	Diamonds	Copper/nickel	Coal	Diamonds	Gold	Uranium	Gold	Coal
1980	5.1	44.5	0.4	1.3	0	5.5	675.1	115.0
1981	5.0	41.9	0.4	1.0	0	5.3	662.2	133.0
1982	7.8	41.8	0.4	0.8	0	5.1	662.7	172.9
1983	10.7	48.4	0.4	0.8	0	5.2	677.9	170.8
1984	12.9	51.0	0.4	0.7	0	4.9	681.9	197.2
1985	12.6	53.6	0.4	0.6	0	4.4	672.9	213.7
1986	13.1	53.1	0.5	1.0	0	4.6	640.0	219.6
1987	13.2	53.5	0.6	0.8	0	4.8	604.3	214.4
1988	15.2	53.3	0.6	0.9	0	4.9	619.9	225.4
1989	15.3	51.0	0.7	0.8	0	4.2	607.7	223.2
1990	17.4	48.5	0.8	0.6	0	4.3	605.1	213.9
1991	16.5	48.3	0.8	0.8	0	3.3	601.0	222.1
1992	15.9	47.9	0.9	0.9	0	2.3	613.0	212.3
1993	14.7	50.9	0.9	0.6	2.0	2.3	619.3	229.4
1994	15.6	51.0	0.9	0.7	2.3	2.6	580.2	242.9
1995	16.8	47.0	0.9	0.6	2.0	2.9	523.8	258.7
1996	17.7	55.4	0.8	0.7	2.1	3.5	498.3	266.0
1997	20.1	48.8	0.8	0.8	2.5	4.1	490.1	281.4
1998	19.8	54.9	0.9	1.5	NA	3.3	464.2	289.5
1999	20.7	47.6	0.9	NA	NA	NA	NA	NA

Note: NA: not available

Source: Appendix A tables.

2.2a   Botswana

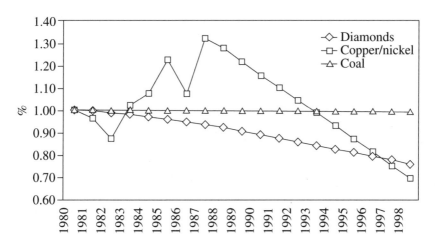

2.2b   South Africa

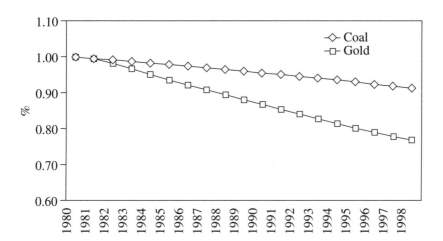

Source: Derived from data in Appendix A Tables A1 and A2.

*Figure 2.2   Index of mineral reserves in Botswana and South Africa,
             1980–98 (1980 = 1.00)*

Table 2.5   Resource rent from mining in Botswana, Namibia and South Africa, 1980–97

	Botswana		Namibia		South Africa		
	Total	Diamonds	Total	Diamonds	Total	Coal	Gold
1980	118	117	355	281	7459	6962	497
1981	57	75	179	93	4675	3773	901
1982	186	224	189	57	5317	3532	1785
1983	276	311	157	86	5599	4186	1413
1984	555	539	190	66	5676	4150	1527
1985	893	890	482	159	10 809	6929	3879
1986	950	992	538	199	10 676	6932	3744
1987	1380	1291	395	201	5956	4642	1314
1988	2546	2189	579	414	8647	5401	3246
1989	2403	2134	769	466	9094	4296	4798
1990	2458	2404	380	241	3673	641	3032
1991	2406	2388	364	370	5089	250	4839
1992	2282	2320	355	343	5058	433	4625
1993	3030	3025	151	150	3415	884	2532
1994	3129	2973	462	400	3078	1589	1489
1995	3779	3545	279	237	795	512	283
1996	5263	4841	759	595	1036	1580	–544
1997	6409	6042	761	590	NA	NA	NA

Notes: NA: not available
Rent calculated using a 10% rate of return to fixed capital.

Source: Based on Lange (2001b, 2001c) and Hassan and Blignaut (2001).

Table 2.6   Resource rent per unit of mineral for different rates of return to fixed capital in Botswana, 1980–96

	Rent calculated assuming 10% return on capital			Rent calculated assuming 20% return on capital		
	Diamonds (pula per carat)	Copper/nickel (pula per ton)	Coal (pula per ton)	Diamonds (pula per carat)	Copper/nickel (pula per ton)	Coal (pula per ton)
1980/81	26.8	179.7	1.9	20.6	-160.8	1.2
1981/82	22.9	-31.9	2.2	15.9	-389.0	1.4
1982/83	24.4	-255.8	1.9	17.5	-634.2	1.0
1983/84	25.3	-354.0	2.0	18.8	-734.1	1.0
1984/85	27.6	-357.3	1.7	21.3	-742.0	0.6
1985/86	37.1	-349.7	1.2	31.3	-733.6	0.1
1986/87	49.2	-415.7	0.6	44.1	-801.0	-0.6
1987/88	62.9	100.7	0.6	58.1	-281.0	-0.7
1988/89	85.9	1584.3	0.4	80.9	1182.8	-1.0
1989/90	105.5	2558.6	1.7	99.8	2105.2	0.0
1990/91	119.1	2704.8	5.6	112.8	2182.4	3.6
1991/92	132.9	2866.8	10.2	125.7	2266.9	7.5
1992/93	142.5	2367.7	10.6	134.2	1674.5	7.2
1993/94	154.8	1039.6	11.2	145.1	248.7	7.3
1994/95	165.0	621.2	9.3	154.1	-265.7	4.9
1995/96	179.5	1452.5	5.6	167.5	448.0	0.7
1996/97	205.3	2968.2	1.6	192.6	1879.7	-3.5
1997/98	236.3	4628.6	1.9	223.5	3440.0	-3.4

Note: 5-year moving average unit rent.

Source: Based on data in Lange (2001c).

43

This difference has dropped considerably since then. Presently a 20 per cent rate of return reduces rent by only 5 per cent relative to the 10 per cent rate of return. These differences can be explained in terms of the development of the diamond mining industry. In the early 1980s, Botswana was still developing its diamond mines and diamond prices were quite low, so Botswana's mines were not operating at full capacity. Hence capital costs per unit of production were quite high. Since the mid-1980s production has expanded to capacity and the market price of diamonds has increased, so that capital costs per unit have declined and the rate of return to fixed capital has less of an impact on rent calculations.

Per unit rent for both copper/nickel and coal is not only highly volatile but also fairly sensitive to the rate of return used. In some years for both copper/nickel and coal, a higher rate of return results in negative rents. Rent estimates for Namibia's mining industry are quite sensitive to the rate of return to fixed capital (Table 2.7). At a 15 per cent rate of return, total rents earned over the entire period would have been 70 per cent lower than rents earned using a 10 per cent rate of return, with negative rents in some years. At a rate of return to fixed capital of 20 per cent, negative rents would be earned in eight out of the 19 years. Namibia is a mature mineral economy with large capital investments, but declining and increasingly costly production (Auty and Mikesell, 1998). Relative to Botswana, Namibia's capital costs are much higher. During the past 20 years, one major mine (Tsumeb Copper) and numerous smaller ones have closed down in Namibia. Namibia's onshore diamond industry was largely exhausted, requiring development of completely new sites offshore and demand for uranium has been extremely volatile.

Short-term losses in mining due to fluctuations in world mineral prices can be expected and are no cause for concern if the industry makes a positive net economic contribution over the long term. However, evaluation of long-term performance should include the full social costs. Three reasons for a divergence of private and social costs were mentioned in section 2.2: artificially high wages, provision of investment by government and environmental damage.

In all three countries, mining wages have been higher than average wages, particularly for unskilled workers, which would lead to an underestimation of the rent. In Botswana and Namibia, where mining employs very little labour, this distortion is minor. It may be more important in South Africa where labour forms a relatively greater share of mining costs. In Botswana, government has provided a great deal of infrastructure for copper/nickel and coal and thus, for these minerals, the true rent may be overestimated.

Finally, mining has caused some environmental damage in all three countries. Botswana's copper/nickel operations generate considerable amounts of pollution. The air and water around the copper/nickel mine are monitored and concentrations in the past have been within the standards set by government,

Table 2.7   *Resource rent for different rates of return to fixed capital in Namibia, 1980–98 (millions of Namibian dollars)*

	Rates of return to fixed capital		
	10%	15%	20%
1980	355	341	297
1981	179	97	48
1982	189	71	15
1983	157	37	−24
1984	190	67	6
1985	482	355	289
1986	538	358	278
1987	395	162	76
1988	579	408	312
1989	769	513	402
1990	380	57	−70
1991	364	33	−99
1992	355	10	−129
1993	151	−256	−401
1994	462	116	−33
1995	279	−70	−228
1996	759	85	−141
1997	761	329	139

Source: Based on data from Lange (2001b).

although there have been concerns about more recent levels of pollution (CSO, 2000). The big mining operations in Namibia are far from urban centres and have not generated much pollution, although dust from diamond mining has recently caused conflict with grape growers, an important export crop for Namibia. Under Namibian law, mining companies are required to set aside funds for mining site rehabilitation in the future. Of greater concern for both Botswana and Namibia is the potential damage to fragile and unique natural habitats both from mining operations themselves and from the infrastructure – roads and railways – necessary for the exploitation of their minerals. Namibia's offshore diamond mining may have damaged its rock lobster population. In addition, mining is a very water-intensive industry (see Chapter 5) and the depletion of water resources is a concern.

In South Africa there are serious concerns about environmental damage to air and water from mining operations. Contamination of ground and surface water with salt and heavy metals and run-off from stockpiles are the major problems in some areas. South African coal has a high ash content and high levels of pyrite (iron sulphide), which leads to the formation of sulphuric acid when exposed to air and water, causing water and atmospheric pollution (Fuggle and Rabie, 1999). Gold is also associated with pyrite as well as arsenic compounds that when oxidized lead to the formation of sulphur dioxide, sulphuric acid and arsenic trioxide. While coal mining occurs mainly in areas historically reserved for agriculture such as the Highveld, some coal mines are near major river systems such as the Vaal, Olifants, Usutu, Pongola and Tugela rivers, causing major impacts on water quality. The environmental impacts of coal mining in South Africa are most evident in Northern Natal, Springs-Witbank and Ermelo Coal Fields, where mining has gone on the longest.

Air pollution is caused by numerous factors in the mining industry including dust and toxic chemical release. Oxides of sulphur are released through high-temperature exhaust fumes, discharged by both underground and coal discard dump fires. The Witbank area in South Africa, in particular, is marred by significantly poor air quality due to these coal-burning fires, which are further compounded by industrial emissions. Another common residual effect of gold extraction is the establishment of slime dams and the associated dust pollution.

Surface mining, especially opencast mining, is associated with the greatest impacts on land resources. There are extensive deposits of displaced materials in tailing dams for gold or in spoils for coal. Soil contamination, surface subsidence and sinkholes resulting from the dewatering of dolomitic compartments, unstable land and underground fires are major land impacts of gold and coal mining. Although the direct effects of mining activities on land are relatively localized and restricted to mine sites, their off-site impacts are also significant.

Historically the Mines and Works Act did not contain any provision for the rehabilitation of mining surfaces. Current regulations require that prospecting permit applications must be accompanied by rehabilitation plans, which must be approved prior to the commencement of any mining activity. The regulations also require that topsoil removed for opencast mining must be stored for rehabilitation and as far as possible the surface must be restored to its former state once mining has ceased. Water and air pollution control is also provided for in recent legislation (Fuggle and Rabie, 1999).

The evidence suggests that there are serious environmental impacts of mining in South Africa which should be included in valuation of the asset. However, at this time it is not yet possible to quantify the damage.

Table 2.8 reports the monetary value of minerals in current and constant prices and converts these figures to constant 1993 US dollars for comparison. It should be noted that the volatile nature of resource prices makes constant price calculations extremely sensitive to the base year chosen, even when the

Table 2.8 Total mineral wealth in Botswana, Namibia and South Africa, 1980–97

	Botswana (millions of pula and US$)			Namibia (millions of Namibia and US$)			South Africa (millions of rands and US$)		
	Current prices	Constant 1993 prices	Constant 1993 US$	Current prices	Constant 1993 prices	Constant 1993 US$	Current prices	Constant 1993 prices	Constant 1993 US$
1980	1441	8323							
1981	1146	8078	3340	778	3792	1161	46 684	24 120	7383
1982	1905	12 448	5146	624	3341	1023	53 113	28 523	8731
1983	2726	17 076	7059	1534	3346	1024	55 902	28 500	8725
1984	3555	20 431	8446	1451	2989	915	56 662	31 470	9634
1985	4686	20 046	8287	923	2894	886	107 919	33 163	10 152
1986	6440	20 799	8598	2695	3281	1004	106 622	33 352	10 210
1987	8364	20 996	8680	3036	3175	972	59 495	32 277	9881
1988	13 765	24 053	9943	3567	3135	960	86 360	33 713	10 320
1989	17 164	24 067	9949	883	2632	806	90 857	33 297	10 193
1990	21 698	27 207	11 247	3475	2422	741	36 719	32 230	9866
1991	23 057	25 921	10 716	3212	2702	827	50 883	33 077	10 126
1992	23 636	25 073	10 365	2878	2514	769	50 569	32 160	9845
1993	23 236	23 236	9606	2136	2136	654	34 127	34 127	10 447
1994	25 859	24 451	10 108	1888	2227	682	30 743	35 075	10 737
1995	30 489	26 267	10 859	1709	2191	670	7941	36 015	11 025
1996	37 056	27 566	11 396	2397	2402	735	15 786	36 464	11 162
1997	48 072	30 892	12 771	3061	2546	779	NA	NA	NA

Notes: NA: not available
Values calculated assuming a 10% return on fixed capital. Constant asset value calculated using 1993/94 unit rents.

Source: Mineral accounts based on Lange (2001b 2001c); Hassan and Blignaut (2001). Exchange rates Bank of Botswana (2001) Bank of Namibia (2000)

unit rent is averaged over five years. Botswana's total mineral wealth is much greater than Namibia's, US$12 771 million compared with US$779 million in 1997, which is consistent with Botswana's extensive and much more valuable diamond reserves. South Africa's mineral wealth in 1996 was US$11 162 million, significantly higher than Namibia's and similar to Botswana's.

The total mineral wealth of Botswana and South Africa has been rising over time, Botswana's roughly threefold from US$3.4 billion to US$12.8 and South Africa's at a much slower rate, only 63 per cent over the period from US$6.8 billion to US$11.2 billion. Since a constant unit rent is used to calculate wealth and most mineral reserves have been declining in physical terms (see Figure 2.2 and Appendix A tables), this may seem surprising. The rising value of the stock results from a shift toward receiving more rent sooner, brought about by an increase in extraction rates (Table 2.4). Discounting future income (the method used to calculate the value of mineral assets) reduces the value of assets that will only be exploited far in the future: a 10 per cent discount rate reduces rent accruing ten years in the future by 60 per cent, while rent accruing 50 years in the future is worth less than 1 per cent of its nominal value. Rents that are received sooner through more rapid extraction are discounted less, which increases the present value of the mineral.

The extraction of Botswana's most valuable mineral, diamonds, has increased considerably: in 1980 only 5.1 million carats were extracted but in the late 1990s roughly 20 million carats were extracted annually. In the early 1980s the rate of diamond extraction relative to reserves was quite low. This is not surprising since Botswana was still at a relatively early stage of mineral development, having just begun large-scale diamond mining in the late 1970s. The extraction of other minerals has not changed so dramatically but they are of negligible importance (Table 2.9).

Although South Africa has been mining for a long time and extraction of gold has declined by about 25 per cent between 1980 and 1996, extraction of coal increased dramatically over the same period, more than doubling. The rapid increase in coal extraction was largely induced by international sanctions against South Africa, making it extremely difficult to purchase petroleum products. South Africa responded by producing liquid fuels from domestically available coal. The increased value of coal due to higher extraction more than offset the declining value of gold.

Namibia represents a different story (Auty and Mikesell, 1998). Namibia's mineral wealth has fallen by about 40 per cent from US$1295 billion in 1980 to US$779 billion in 1997. It has continued to mine diamonds but they are of lesser quality and much more expensive to produce. Extraction levels have fallen for diamonds and uranium. Gold extraction began in 1993 but is still a very small component of Namibia's mineral wealth.

Diamonds have clearly accounted for virtually all of Botswana's mineral

Table 2.9 Value of mineral assets by type of mineral in Botswana and South Africa, 1980–97

	Botswana (millions of pula in current prices)				South Africa (millions of rands in current prices)		
	Diamonds	Copper/nickel	Coal	Total minerals	Gold	Coal	Total minerals
1980	1367	67	7	1441	69 508	4966	74 474
1981	1137	–	8	1146	37 670	9015	46 684
1982	1897	–	8	1905	35 260	17 853	53 113
1983	2719	–	8	2726	41 773	14 129	55 902
1984	3548	–	7	3555	41 396	15 266	56 662
1985	4681	–	5	4686	69 125	38 794	107 919
1986	6437	–	3	6440	69 185	37 438	106 622
1987	8314	46	3	8364	46 354	13 141	59 495
1988	13 045	718	2	13 765	53 903	32 457	86 360
1989	16 045	1108	12	17 164	42 876	47 981	90 857
1990	20 539	1114	45	21 698	6395	30 324	36 719
1991	21 820	1157	80	23 057	2493	48 390	50 883
1992	22 608	932	96	23 636	4319	46 249	50 569
1993	22 722	414	99	23 236	8811	25 316	34 127
1994	25 534	241	84	25 859	15 857	14 886	30 743
1995	29 916	523	50	30 489	5114	2827	7941
1996	35 926	1117	12	37 056	15 786	–	15 786
1997	46 481	1576	15	48 072	NA	NA	NA

Notes: NA: not available
'–' indicates negative rent in a given year and consequently a zero value for the asset in that year.

Source: Based on Lange (2001b and 2001c); Hassan and Blignaut (2001).

wealth (93 per cent or more in current prices) (Table 2.9). The share of copper/nickel has fluctuated with the world price and coal has never accounted for even 1 per cent of mineral wealth. In South Africa, values for both gold and coal have been extremely volatile; of the two, gold has been more valuable in most years. Figures for Namibia cannot be publicly reported.

2.4   POLICY IMPLICATIONS FOR RESOURCE MANAGEMENT

As discussed in Chapter 1 and again in section 2.2 of this chapter, sustainable management of mineral resources requires that resource rent be reinvested in other activities which will generate income after the mineral is exhausted. When the government is the owner of sub-soil assets, as is the case in Botswana and Namibia, and will be the case soon in South Africa, the government bears this responsibility for assuring the transformation of mineral wealth into other forms of wealth. This requires establishing taxes to recover resource rent, and a commitment to reinvest the rent.

On the first count, recovery of resource rent, Botswana has been rather successful in recovering rent, averaging 76 per cent (Table 2.10). Botswana's rent has been rising at a fairly steady rate over the past 20 years, which makes tax policy easier. Namibia and South Africa have both had much more volatile rent. The Namibian mining industry has paid on average at least 50 per cent of the rent in taxes, whereas South Africa's industry has generally paid less. In the 1970s hardly any taxes were paid at all. However, this is consistent with its past property rights regime in which the private landowner also owned the minerals underneath the land and, consequently, the rent belonged to the landowner.

While there are general theoretical guidelines for reinvesting mineral rents which were discussed in Chapter 1, there are no specific rules for determining the amount of rent that must be reinvested, with the exception of the 'user cost' rule developed by El Serafy. El Serafy's rule specifies the minimum amount of rent that must be reinvested in order to maintain total wealth intact. This is a sensible appeal, based on a minimum amount of reinvestment that should take place, to governments that have been squandering their mineral resources such as Nigeria or Saudi Arabia. However, if minerals are to be harnessed to support economic development in relatively poor developing countries, such a rule is not sufficient because it does not take into account population growth and the need to increase national income in order to improve material standards of living. Both these factors require increasing levels of capital stock, not just non-decreasing levels.

Recognizing this deficiency, the government of Botswana has developed a

Table 2.10 Taxes on resource rent in Botswana, Namibia and South Africa, 1966–97

	Botswana			Namibia			South Africa		
	Rent	Taxes	% of rent accruing to government	Rent	Taxes	% of rent accruing to government	Rent	Taxes	% of rent accruing to government
1966							237	110	46
1970							246	97	39
1975							1207	13	1
1978							1724	41	2
1980	118	101	85	355	183	52	7459		
1981	57	77	134	179	151	85	4675	2542	54
1982	186	100	54	189	55	29	5317		
1983	276	194	70	157	48	31	5599		
1984	555	376	68	190	110	58	5676	2392	42
1985	893	581	65	482	134	28	10 809		
1986	950	845	89	538	242	45	10 676		
1987	1380	1034	75	395	317	80	5956	3398	57
1988	2546	1508	59	579	315	54	8647		
1989	2403	1596	66	769	322	42	9094		
1990	2458	2005	82	380	199	52	3673	1591	43
1991	2406	1888	78	364	140	39	5089		
1992	2282	1866	82	355	211	59	5058		
1993	3030	2279	75	151	302	200	3415	1052	31
1994	3129	2349	75	462	309	67	3078		
1995	3779	2591	69	279	188	67	795		
1996	5263	3640	69	759	231	30	1036	1344	130
1997	6409	4681	73	761	249	33			

Note: No entry means datat not available.

Source: Based on Lange (2001b, 2001c) and Hassan and Blignaut (2001).

51

measure, the Sustainable Budget Index (SBI), to monitor whether the mineral revenues it collects are being used in a manner that promotes sustainable development, that is, whether mineral wealth is being transformed into other assets.

In Botswana fiscal policy is firmly based in a tradition of prudence and medium-term planning, developed at a time when subsistence under harsh and drought-prone conditions taught the value of effective use of limited resources and saving at times when surpluses occurred. This tradition has been carried over to subsequent years since the early 1970s, when the successful development of large, low-cost diamond mines dramatically increased public revenues. Recognizing that the revenues from diamonds represented mainly asset sales rather than value-added in production, the government of Botswana saw the need for reinvestment of these revenues in order to sustain development (see for example Ministry of Finance and Development Planning, 1991, p. 27).

Without a formal investment rule the emphasis was on reserving all mineral revenues for investment expenditure. From the mid-1990s, a formal rule was introduced which is now routinely included in the various assessments of economic performance produced by the government (Ministry of Finance and Development Planning, 1997). This measure which, following Salkin (1994), has been labelled by commentators the Sustainable Budget Index (SBI), is simply the ratio of non-investment spending to recurrent (non-mineral) revenues.

$$SBI = \frac{Spending_{non\text{-}investment}}{Revenue_{recurrent}} \qquad (2.1)$$

An SBI value of 1.0 or less has been interpreted to mean that current government consumption is sustainable because it is financed entirely out of revenues other than from minerals and that all the revenue from minerals is used for public investment. An SBI value greater than 1.0 means that consumption relies in part on the mineral revenues, which is fiscally unsustainable.

To calculate the SBI, the government expands the definition of public sector investment so that it includes not only the capital and development budget, but also a portion of the recurrent budget interpreted as investment in human capital. Government has used a rule of thumb that 30 per cent of the recurrent budget is investment in human capital, rather than identifying specific expenditures which should be reclassified. The 30 per cent approximates the combined share of health and education in the recurrent budget over the past 20 years. Thus non-investment spending in the SBI is equal to 70 per cent of the recurrent budget.

Such a rule has the obvious advantage that it is clear and easy to understand. Moreover it is very similar to the budgetary rules of thumb that have been adopted by governments elsewhere, although it is not without problems. Wright (1995, 1997) identified several weaknesses. An obvious problem is the assumption that all capital and development spending is productive investment or as productive as the mineral wealth it replaces. It is not necessary and may be harmful to insist on fiscal sustainability in every year as the SBI proposes. It may be more useful to consider fiscal sustainability averaged over time (though it can be more difficult to hold politicians to such a concept). Capital projects typically occur over multiple years while mineral revenues can fluctuate a great deal from year to year due to causes beyond the control of the government. It would be counterproductive to curtail capital projects, or postpone new ones deemed necessary because of short-term fluctuations in mineral revenues. Also, without an intertemporal dimension to the SBI, there are ways in which mineral revenues not invested immediately can subsequently be used to fund recurrent spending.

Botswana's capital and development budget, narrowly defined as public sector investment, constitutes a large share of both government budget and GDP, averaging 38 per cent of the total government budget and 13 per cent of GDP over the past 25 years (Lange and Wright, 2001). Over most of the past two decades the SBI has been below 1.0 and all mineral revenues have been reinvested in public capital. It remained well under 1.0 until the 1990s (Figure 2.3), first passed 1.0 in 1994/95 and has been over 1.0 since 2000.

Human capital is an especially important component of public investment and the SBI. Figure 2.3 highlights the component of the SBI that includes recurrent expenditures for education and health. Without adding such expenditures, the SBI would have averaged 1.07 from 1976 to 2001, which is over the sustainability rule.

The assumption of the SBI that 100 per cent of mineral revenues must be reinvested is quite a conservative rule; even more restrictive is the assumption that it must all be used for public sector capital. The SBI and its strong bias toward reinvestment of all mineral revenues has served Botswana well in the past but may be less useful for the future. There is evidence that not all of public sector investment has been productive (Lange and Wright, 2001), and that a better allocation of mineral revenues might improve the sustainability of the economy. In section 2.2 it was pointed out that the policy rule for reinvestment of Botswana's mineral revenues was not based on an objective with a well-defined target such as a given percentage increase in per capita GDP against which the action could be measured. Consequently there are no criteria for allocation of mineral revenues.

Government can use mineral revenues in a combination of four ways:

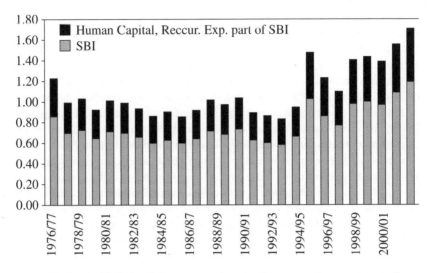

Note: The Sustainable Budget Index measures the ratio of government's recurrent expenditures to its recurrent (non-mineral) revenues.

Source: Lange and Wright (2001).

Figure 2.3   Sustainable Budget Index for Botswana, 1976–2001

1.   invest in foreign financial assets;
2.   invest in infrastructure and human capital;
3.   fund public consumption;
4.   fund private consumption by returning some of the revenues to citizens.

Until recently government has used revenues only for the first two purposes, both investment. In recent years, however, an increasing part of the revenues have been used for the third purpose, funding public consumption. A closer examination shows that less of the revenues have been used for investment than the SBI would reveal (Lange and Wright, 2001). Some spending does not add to productive capacity (defence, agriculture and most of social services). Though not quantifiable, there is an increasing tendency toward 'monuments' which are not productive. Some of the investments may even be harmful, leading to the depletion of other natural capital. For example overinvestment in water supply infrastructure for which the user is not charged, encourages depletion of fossil groundwater, an asset which has not yet been valued but is clearly very important in arid Botswana.

One alternative would be to reduce the capital and development budget and to put more revenues into foreign financial assets. Another alternative would be to remit part of it to citizens to fund private consumption or investment. For example, the Alaska Permanent Fund manages oil revenues, investing part in financial assets and remitting a portion of the amount beyond what is necessary to maintain the value of the fund every year to the citizens of the state (Warrack and Keddie, 2000). A country may try to use its resource endowment as a means to rapid development, but could also use the resources to improve the circumstances of the current generation by allowing greater consumption. Reflecting this, in Botswana the emphasis on saving resources for investment in the future has been questioned at a time when so many currently live in conditions of poverty.

2.5 CONCLUSIONS

In Chapter 1, we identified several criteria that must be met in order to build a sustainable economy based on non-renewable natural resources:

1. policies that maximize resource rent generated by mining;
2. recovery of resource rent by an agency able and willing to reinvest rent;
3. reinvestment of rent in productive activities that are capable of generating income and employment once resources are exhausted.

Due to the capital-intensive nature of production, minerals are often most efficiently exploited, maximizing rent generation, by large-scale commercial operations. The policies of all three countries have promoted such commercial exploitation for most of their mining and in most instances maximize resource rent. There are some exceptions, however, such as copper/nickel and coal mining in Botswana, which generate little or no rent or receive indirect subsidies. Coal is indirectly subsidized by setting the selling price above international market prices. Copper/nickel mining has received indirect subsidies in terms of infrastructure and water pricing. Government has also provided finance to copper/nickel mining at times. These mines are kept open for the employment they provide and, in the case of coal, for energy security. Although Botswana's policy toward coal and copper/nickel do not contribute to maximizing rent from mining, these two minerals are relatively unimportant in Botswana's mining industry and, consequently, do not distort rent maximization significantly.

Namibia's mining operations generally operate efficiently and maximize resource rents. South Africa has traditionally used relatively labour-intensive technologies for mining, and mining is an important source of high-wage, unionized employment. In recent years, mining companies have attempted to increase labour productivity and reduce the use of labour, but this has met with stiff opposition. It is not clear at this time the extent to which the emphasis on labour-intensive production has affected the generation of resource rent.

The second criterion, recovery of resource rent, depends very much on the property rights regime: the resource rent should accrue to the owner of the resource. In Botswana and Namibia, minerals belong to the state, while in South Africa, minerals belong to the landowner, hence, one would expect government to recover most of the rent in Botswana and Namibia, but in South Africa, the private sector would receive the rent. The pattern of rent recovery is generally consistent with the system of property rights in each country. The government of Botswana has had a long-standing partnership with the private diamond mining company and has been highly successful in recovering rent. The Namibian government has been moderately successful, whereas most of the rent in South Africa has accrued to the private sector. Whether sustainable development requires that government should recover the rent depends critically on the likelihood that rent will be productively reinvested by the party to whom rent accrues, our third criteria.

Only Botswana has developed a formal rule for assessing reinvestment of rent in productive activities, the Sustainable Budget Index. Given the importance of minerals to the Botswana economy it is perhaps not surprising that Botswana should do this. However, most resource-rich economies do not have such a far-sighted rule. Minerals were as important to the economies of Namibia and South Africa in the past, but these countries failed to develop such rules. Botswana stands out as a model for mineral economies in the management of mineral revenues. Over the past 20 years, Botswana has reinvested virtually all of its mineral revenues in produced and human capital. Only in the last few years has the rate of reinvestment started to slip below 100 per cent. There are, in fact, questions over whether Botswana has overinvested in non-productive projects. In the future, Botswana will benefit from setting objectives for use of mineral revenues not just in terms of overall reinvestment, but in assessing the quality of investments as well.

While the data are not available to trace the disposition of mineral rents in South Africa, it would seem that much was reinvested domestically. This is partly due to fortunate circumstances – the large size of South Africa and the resulting range of opportunities for profitable reinvestment by the private sector – and partly due to the restrictions on capital movements during the later apartheid period. The mining sector, mostly owned by South Africans, had to find domestic investments for their profits. It is less certain that mineral rents were reinvested in productive domestic activities in Namibia. Namibia is a very small economy with limited investment opportunities. In addition, most mining has been controlled by foreign companies and not as much rent was recovered by government as in Botswana. Of course, in South Africa prior to the end of apartheid in 1994 and in Namibia prior to independence in 1990, rent that was recovered by government was used in part to support the apartheid system, including a heavy defence component, which could not be considered productive use of rents. More information is needed to better assess the role that minerals have played in the long-term development of the Namibian and South African economies.

REFERENCES

Auty, R.M. and R. Mikesell (1998), *Sustainable Development in Mineral Economies*, Oxford, Clarendon Press.

Bank of Botswana (2001), *Annual Report*, Gaborone, Botswana.

Bank of Namibia (2000), *Annual Report*, Windhoek, Namibia.

BCL Mines (1998), Unpublished data about copper/nickel extraction and reserves.

Blignaut, J. and R. Hassan (2001), 'A natural resource accounting analysis of the contribution of mineral resources to sustainable development in South Africa', *South African Journal of Economic and Management Sciences*, SS No. 3 (April).

Bureau of Economic Analysis, US Department of Commerce (1994), 'Accounting for mineral resources: issues and BEA's initial estimates', in *Survey of Current Business*, 74 (4): 50–72.

Central Statistics Office (various years), *Statistical Bulletin*, Gaborone, Botswana.

Central Statistics Office (various years) *External Trade Statistics*, Gaborone, Botswana, Central Statistics Office.

Central Statistics Office (various years), *Labour Statistics*, Gaborone, Botswana.

Central Statistics Office (1996), Unpublished data about value-added, capital stock and taxes, Gaborone, Botswana.

Central Statistics Office (1997), *Population Projections, 1991–2021*, Gaborone, Botswana.

Central Statistics Office (1998), 'National accounts statistics – capital stock', in Stats Brief No. 98/7 (June), Gaborone, Botswana.

Central Statistics Office (2000), *Environmental Statistics*, Gaborone, Botswana.

Chalk, N. (1998), 'Fiscal sustainability with non-renewable resources', Working Paper of the International Monetary Fund, WP/98/26, Washington, DC, IMF.

Chamber of Mines (annual), *Handbook of the South African Mining Industry*, Pretoria, South Africa.

CSO *see* Central Statistics Office.

Department of Geological Surveys (1998), Unpublished data about coal reserves, Gaborone, Botswana.

Department of Mines (various years), *Annual Report*, Gaborone, Botswana, Ministry of Mines, Energy and Water Resources.

Department of Mines (1998), Unpublished data about mineral extraction and reserves, Gaborone, Botswana.

Department of Mines and Energy (annual), *Mineral Statistics*, Pretoria, South Africa.

Department of Mines and Energy (2000), *South Africa's Mineral Industry 1998/99*, Pretoria, South Africa.

DME *see* Department of Mines and Energy.

Energy Information Agency (2000), *International Energy Annual 1999*, United States Department of Energy, EIA, Washington, DC.

Fuggle, R.F. and M.A. Rabie (1999), *Environmental Management in South Africa*, Cape Town, Juta and Co.

Harris, R. (2000), 'Sub-soil asset accounts for the United Kingdom', paper presented at the International Workshop on Environmental and Economic Accounting, 18–22 September, Manila, the Philippines.

Hartmann, P. (1986), 'The role of diamond mining in the economy of South West Africa 1950–1985', unpublished MSc Thesis, Department of Economics, University of Stellenbosch, South Africa.

Hartwick, J.M. (1977), 'Intergenerational equity and the investing of rents from exhaustible resources', *American Economic Review*, 67 (5): 972–4.

Hartwick, J. and A. Hageman (1993), 'Economic depreciation of mineral stocks and the contribution of El Serafy', in Y. Ahmad, S. El Serafy and E. Lutz (eds), *Environmental Accounting for Sustainable Development*, Washington, DC, World Bank.

Hassan, R. and J. Blignaut (2001), 'Resource rent from mining: revisiting the SSA census of mining', (Memo), Centre for Environmental Economics and Policy in Africa (CEEPA), University of Pretoria, South Africa.

Lange, G. (2001a), 'Policy applications of environmental accounts', draft discussion paper for Environment Department, Washington DC, World Bank.

Lange, G. (2001b), 'Mineral accounts for Namibia', unpublished paper for the Directorate of Environmental Affairs, Ministry of Environment and Tourism, Windhoek, Namibia.

Lange, G. (2001c) 'The contribution of minerals to sustainable economic development in Botswana', Final report to the Botswana Natural Resource Accounting Programme, Gaborone, Botswana.

Lange, G. and D.J. Motinga (1997), 'The contribution of resource rents from minerals and fisheries to sustainable economic development in Namibia', DEA Research Discussion Paper #19. Directorate of Environmental Affairs, Ministry of Environment and Tourism, Windhoek, Namibia.

Lange, G. and M. Wright (2001), 'The contribution of minerals to sustainable economic development: the example of Botswana', paper presented at the Conference of the United States Society for Ecological Economics Duluth, Minnesota; 11–13 July.

Ministry of Finance (1994), *Economic Review 1994*, Windhoek, Namibia.

Ministry of Finance and Development Planning (various years), *Annual Economic Report*, Gaborone, Botswana.

Ministry of Finance and Development Planning (1997), *Mid-Term Review of NDP7*, Gaborone, Botswana.

Ministry of Labour (2001), *The Namibia Labour Force Survey 1997*, Windhoek, Namibia.

Natrasse, J. (1981), *The South African Economy: Its Growth and Change*, Cape Town, Oxford University Press.

Russell, C. (1991), 'Coal mining – custodian or culprit?', *Mining Survey*, Number 1, pp. 7–14.

Sengupta, M. (1993), *Environmental Impacts of Mining: Monitoring, Restoration, and Control*, London, Lewis Publishers.

Statistics Canada (1997), *Eco-connections: Linking the Environment and the Economy*, Ministry of Industry, Ottawa, Canada.

Statistics South Africa (annual), *Census of Mining*, Pretoria, South Africa.

United Nations (1993), *Integrated Environmental and Economic Accounting*, Studies in Methods, Handbook of National Accounting, Series F, No. 61, United Nations, New York.

United Nations (2001), *Integrated Environmental and Economic Accounting 2000*, draft available at website: www.un.org.

United States Geological Survey (annual), *Minerals Information: Commodity Statistics and Information*, available at website: www.usgs.gov/minrals/pubs/commodity.

USGS *see* United States Geological Survey.

Warrack, A. and R. Keddie (2000), 'Albert Heritage Fund vs. Alaska Permanent Fund: a comparative analysis', draft paper obtained from the website of the Alaska Permanent Fund Corporation website: www.apfc.org.

World Diamond Council (2001), 'Diamond production estimates 1999', available at website: www.worlddiamondcouncil.com/etimate.shtml.

World Nuclear Association (2001), 'World uranium mining', in *Information and Issue Briefs*, June, available at website: www/world-nuclear.org/info/inf23.htm.

Wright, M. (1995), 'Reservation principle in sustainable budgeting: the case of Botswana', in *Research Bulletin of the Bank of Botswana*, 13 (1): 1–21.

Wright, M. (1997), 'The use of mineral revenues in Botswana: super caution vs. pragmatism', in *Research Bulletin of the Bank of Botswana*, 15 (1): 35–47.

Environmental accounting in action

APPENDIX A: DETAILED MINERAL ACCOUNTS

Table A.1   Physical asset accounts for minerals in Botswana, 1980–99

a.   Diamonds (millions of carats)

	Opening stocks	Extraction	New discoveries	Other volume changes	Closing stocks
1980	1053	5.1	NA	NA	1048
1981	1048	5.0	NA	NA	1043
1982	1043	7.8	NA	NA	1035
1983	1035	10.7	NA	NA	1024
1984	1024	12.9	NA	NA	1012
1985	1012	12.6	NA	NA	999
1986	999	13.1	NA	NA	986
1987	986	13.2	NA	NA	973
1988	973	15.2	NA	NA	957
1989	957	15.3	NA	NA	942
1990	942	17.4	NA	NA	925
1991	925	16.5	NA	NA	908
1992	908	15.9	NA	NA	892
1993	892	14.7	NA	NA	878
1994	878	15.6	NA	NA	862
1995	862	16.8	NA	NA	845
1996	845	17.7	NA	NA	828
1997	828	20.1	NA	NA	807
1998	807	19.8	NA	NA	788
1999	788	20.7	NA	NA	767

Note: NA: not available.

b. Copper/nickel (in tons)

	Opening stocks	Extraction		New discoveries	Other volume changes	Closing stocks
		Total extraction	Final production (metal content matte)			
1980	872 618	44 478	30 995	NA	14 253	842 394
1981	842 394	41 879	36 097	NA	−38 946	761 569
1982	761 569	41 830	36 131	NA	171 859	891 599
1983	891 599	48 363	38 477	NA	94 581	937 817
1984	937 817	51 007	40 075	NA	182 601	1 069 411
1985	1 069 411	53 574	41 257	NA	−78 020	937 817
1986	937 817	53 056	40 310	NA	267 897	1 152 658
1987	1 152 658	53 480	35 461	NA	15 821	1 114 998
1988	1 114 998	53 274	46 967	NA	NA	1 061 725
1989	1 061 725	51 038	41 468	NA	NA	1 010 687
1990	1 010 687	48 518	39 634	NA	NA	962 169
1991	962 169	48 318	39 870	NA	NA	913 851
1992	913 851	47 929	39 286	NA	NA	865 922
1993	865 922	50 939	41 753	NA	NA	814 984
1994	814 984	51 022	41 821	NA	NA	763 962
1995	763 962	47 030	38 549	NA	NA	716 932
1996	716 932	55 381	45 394	NA	NA	661 552
1997	661 552	48 772	39 977	NA	NA	612 780
1998	612 780	54 870	44 975	NA	NA	557 910

Note: NA: not available.

Environmental accounting in action

c. Coal (in thousands of tons)

	Opening stocks	Extraction	New discoveries	Other volume change	Closing stocks
1980	7 188 645	371	0	0	7 188 273
1981	7 188 273	381	0	0	7 187 893
1982	7 187 893	415	0	0	7 187 478
1983	7 187 478	395	0	0	7 187 083
1984	7 187 083	393	0	0	7 186 690
1985	7 186 690	437	0	0	7 186 253
1986	7 186 253	499	0	0	7 185 754
1987	7 185 754	579	0	0	7 185 174
1988	7 185 174	613	0	0	7 184 561
1989	7 184 561	663	0	0	7 183 898
1990	7 183 898	794	0	0	7 183 104
1991	7 183 104	784	0	0	7 182 320
1992	7 182 320	901	0	0	7 181 419
1993	7 181 419	890	0	0	7 180 529
1994	7 180 529	900	0	0	7 179 629
1995	7 179 629	898	0	0	7 178 730
1996	7 178 730	763	0	0	7 177 967
1997	7 177 967	777	0	0	7 177 190
1998	7 177 190	928	0	0	7 176 262

Source: Diamonds: extraction obtained from Department of Mines Annual Reports. 1999 closing stocks: De Beers 1999 Annual Report. See Lange (2001c) for method of estimating other years stocks.
Copper/nickel: Department of Mines Annual Reports and estimation methods described in Lange (2001c).
Coal: CSO, 2000.

Table A.2   Physical asset accounts for minerals in South Africa, 1980–99

a.   Gold (million kg)

	Opening stocks	Extraction	Other volume changes	Closing stocks
1980	46.0	0.7	0.0	45.3
1981	45.3	0.7	0.0	44.7
1982	44.7	0.7	0.5	44.5
1983	44.5	0.7	0.0	43.8
1984	43.8	0.7	0.0	43.1
1985	43.1	0.7	0.0	42.5
1986	42.5	0.6	0.0	41.8
1987	41.8	0.6	0.0	41.2
1988	41.2	0.6	0.0	40.6
1989	40.6	0.6	0.0	40.0
1990	40.0	0.6	0.0	39.4
1991	39.4	0.6	0.0	38.8
1992	38.8	0.6	0.0	38.2
1993	38.2	0.6	0.0	37.6
1994	37.6	0.6	0.0	37.0
1995	37.0	0.5	0.0	36.4
1996	36.4	0.5	0.0	36.0
1997	36.0	0.5	0.0	35.4

b.   Coal (million tons)

	Opening stocks	Extraction	Other volume changes	Closing stocks
1980	39 269	115	–0	39 154
1981	39 154	133	100	39 121
1982	39 121	173	0	38 948
1983	38 948	171	–0	38 777
1984	38 777	197	0	38 580
1985	38 580	214	0	38 366
1986	38 366	220	–	38 147
1987	38 147	214	0	37 932
1988	37 932	225	–0	37 707
1989	37 707	223	–0	37 484
1990	37 484	214	0	37 270
1991	37 270	222	–0	37 048
1992	37 048	212	0	36 835
1993	36 835	229	0	36 606
1994	36 606	243	–0	36 363
1995	36 363	259	–0	36 104
1996	36 104	266	0	35 838
1997	35 838	281	0	35 557

Source: Hassan and Blignaut (2001).

*Table A.3   Monetary asset accounts for minerals in Botswana, 1980–97
(million pulas)*

a.   Diamonds

	Opening stocks	Extraction	New discoveries	Other volume changes	Revaluation	Closing stocks
1980	1350	137	–	–	154	1367
1981	1367	114	–	–	–116	1137
1982	1137	190	–	–	949	1897
1983	1897	272	–	–	1093	2719
1984	2719	355	–	–	1185	3548
1985	3548	468	–	–	1601	4681
1986	4681	644	–	–	2401	6437
1987	6437	832	–	–	2709	8314
1988	8314	1308	–	–	6039	13 045
1989	13 045	1609	–	–	4608	16 045
1990	16 045	2067	–	–	6561	20 539
1991	20 539	2194	–	–	3474	21 820
1992	21 820	2272	–	–	3060	22 608
1993	22 608	2280	–	–	2394	22 722
1994	22 722	2566	–	–	5378	25 534
1995	25 534	3017	–	–	7398	29 916
1996	29 916	3635	–	–	9645	35 926
1997	35 926	4752	–	–	15 306	46 481

Environmental accounting in action

b.   Copper/nickel

	Opening stocks	Extraction	New discoveries	Other volume changes	Revaluation	Closing stocks
1980	117	8	NA	3	−44	67
1981	67	−1	NA	1	−69	0
1982	0	−11	NA	−44	33	0
1983	0	−17	NA	−33	16	0
1984	0	−18	NA	−65	47	0
1985	0	−19	NA	27	−46	0
1986	0	−22	NA	−111	89	0
1987	0	5	NA	2	50	46
1988	46	84	NA	NA	756	718
1989	718	131	NA	NA	521	1108
1990	1108	131	NA	NA	137	1114
1991	1114	139	NA	NA	181	1157
1992	1157	113	NA	NA	−111	932
1993	932	53	NA	NA	−465	414
1994	414	32	NA	NA	−142	241
1995	241	68	NA	NA	351	523
1996	523	164	NA	NA	758	1117
1997	1117	226	NA	NA	684	1576

Note: NA: not available.

c. Coal

	Opening stocks	Extraction	New discoveries	Other volume changes	Revaluation	Closing stocks
1980	6	1	0	0	1	7
1981	7	1	0	0	2	8
1982	8	1	0	0	0	8
1983	8	1	0	0	1	8
1984	8	1	0	0	−1	7
1985	7	1	0	0	−1	5
1986	5	0	0	0	−2	3
1987	3	0	0	0	1	3
1988	3	0	0	0	−1	2
1989	2	1	0	0	10	12
1990	12	4	0	0	38	45
1991	45	8	0	0	43	80
1992	80	10	0	0	25	96
1993	96	10	0	0	14	99
1994	99	8	0	0	−7	84
1995	84	5	0	0	−29	50
1996	50	1	0	0	−37	12
1997	12	1	0	0	4	15

Source: Table A.1 and method described in the text, based on Lange (2001c).

Table A.4   *Monetary asset accounts for minerals in Namibia, 1980–97 (million Namibia $ in current prices)*

	Opening stocks	Extraction	New discoveries	Other volume changes	Revaluation	Closing stocks
1980	2625	283	0	10	0	2352
1981	2352	158	0	66	−483	1778
1982	1778	103	0	−39	−11	1624
1983	1624	105	0	11	3	1534
1984	1534	83	0	−13	14	1451
1985	1451	81	250	−19	322	1923
1986	1923	151	0	−13	936	2695
1987	2695	159	35	107	359	3036
1988	3036	239	14	18	738	3567
1989	3567	276	0	−234	826	3883
1990	3883	248	26	−101	−84	3475
1991	3475	354	0	57	34	3212
1992	3212	396	0	94	−32	2878
1993	2878	268	4	26	−504	2136
1994	2136	307	29	17	14	1888
1995	1888	268	112	225	−248	1709
1996	1709	373	29	322	711	2397
1997	2397	444	32	473	603	3061

Note: Figures combine values for diamonds, uranium and gold because figures for individual minerals cannot be published.

Source: Lange (2001b).

Table A.5 Monetary asset accounts for minerals in South Africa 1980–98 (million rands in current prices)

	Gold					Coal				
	Opening stocks	Extraction	Other volume changes	Revaluation	Closing stocks	Opening stocks	Extraction	Other volume changes	Revaluation	Closing stocks
1980	76 470	6962	3	0	69 508	5463	497	0	0	4966
1981	69 508	3773	5	−28 070	37 670	4966	901	678	4272	9015
1982	37 670	3532	2663	−1541	35 260	9015	1785	0	10 624	17 853
1983	35 260	4186	49	10 650	41 773	17 853	1413	0	−2311	14 129
1984	41 773	4150	−72	3845	41 396	14 129	1527	0	2663	15 266
1985	41 396	6929	−14	34 672	69 125	15 266	3879	0	27 407	38 794
1986	69 125	6932	27	6964	69 185	38 794	3744	0	2388	37 438
1987	69 185	4642	33	−18 221	46 354	37 438	1314	0	−22 983	13 141
1988	46 354	5401	−1	12 951	53 903	13 141	3246	0	22 562	32 457
1989	53 903	4296	−2	−6729	42 876	32 457	4798	0	20 322	47 981
1990	42 876	641	8	−35 848	6395	47 981	3032	0	−14 625	30 324
1991	6395	250	−4	−3648	2493	30 324	4839	0	22 905	48 390
1992	2493	433	0	2259	4319	48 390	4625	0	2484	46 249
1993	4319	884	0	5375	8811	46 249	2532	0	−18 401	25 316
1994	8811	1589	−1	8636	15 857	25 316	1489	0	−8941	14 886
1995	15 857	512	−17	−10 213	5114	14 886	283	0	−11 777	2827
1996	5114	1580	66	12 186	15 786	2827	−544	0	−3371	0

69

3. Forestry accounts: capturing the value of forest and woodland resources

Rashid Hassan

3.1 INTRODUCTION

The social and economic benefits of forests and woodland (F&WL) resources are many. Tangible products such as fuel wood, wild foods and medicinal products are harvested from F&WL for direct consumption by millions of people around the world. Timber is also extracted from F&WL by commercial logging firms for further processing and by households for various domestic uses (fencing and construction). Non-timber products of F&WL such as gum and rattan are also processed and traded. In addition F&WL resources provide several other direct and indirect use benefits and ecological services. Examples include recreational amenities, watershed protection and carbon sequestration benefiting other economic sectors. F&WL also serve as the habitat for highly valuable biological resources and provide many social, religious and cultural benefits to human communities. As the source of these many benefits to people, F&WL resources clearly constitute an important part of total national wealth, and depletion (appreciation) and degradation of quality will decrease (increase) long-term social welfare. Unfortunately neither the flow benefits of F&WL resources nor their asset values are adequately captured in the current system of national accounts (SNA).

Various factors contribute to the inadequacy of the SNA to fully capture F&WL resources' contributions to economic welfare. The fact that the SNA includes values of produced outputs that are traded in the market is the main reason for missing non-market flow benefits of F&WL resources. Although the production and asset boundaries have been expanded in the new SNA and the more recent system of integrated environmental and economic accounting (SEEA) to include non-produced natural assets and their goods and services (UN, 1993), a number of challenges remain in terms of adequately accounting for the value of F&WL resources. Among the main issues is the difficulty associated with capturing the value of non-traded products and measuring non-market values of intangible goods and services of F&WL resources such as biodiversity and carbon sink functions. More technical aspects of proper valuation of the stocks and depreciation of biological resource assets such as growing trees remain a constraint to adequately measuring the true contribution of F&WL resources to economic welfare. Also the diversity in key institutional and management factors governing the supply and use of F&WL goods and services creates additional operational difficulty in capturing asset values of the resource. For example the distinctions between F&WL under private and public ownership or open access and whether a forest is old-growth, managed second growth or a cultivated plantation have important implications for measuring and accounting for the value and depreciation of F&WL resource assets. The factors mentioned also influence many policy dimensions of crucial importance to sustainable management and exploitation of F&WL resources, such as appropriation and deployment of forest resource rents.

This chapter is devoted to addressing aspects of F&WL resource accounting and how deficiencies in the current SNA in this regard can be addressed and corrected. To achieve this goal, the chapter uses examples of case study applications drawing on the results of forest resource accounting efforts in South Africa. The chapter is organized in five sections. The following section addresses the issue of accounting for flow benefits of F&WL resources. Section 3.3 deals with correcting for asset values and depletion of natural capital in the form of F&WL resources. Measures of income and wealth of the current SNA are adjusted for the missing values of F&WL resources in section 3.4. Conclusions and implications for policy and sustainable use of the F&WL resources in South Africa are distilled in section 3.5.

3.2 ACCOUNTING FOR FLOW BENEFITS OF FOREST AND WOODLAND RESOURCES

Due to the way the SNA is structured, ownership of the resource asset and tradability of its products and services are key determinants of how its benefits are accounted for. When the goods and services provided are traded in the market, their values are typically captured by the SNA (timber harvested by commercial logging companies). On the other hand even tangible F&WL products that directly contribute to consumption and economic welfare such as fuel wood and wild foods do not register in the SNA because they are directly harvested by households for own use from open access, F&WL resources and hence escape trade (market exchange). Similarly, indirect use benefits and ecological services (watershed protection, carbon storage, bio-habitat functions) of F&WL do not pass through the market and their values are usually attributed to the wrong economic activities (recipient sectors).

Flow benefits of F&WL resources in South Africa were measured for all the biomes described in Box 3.1. Data for cultivated plantations (CPLNT)

BOX 3.1   FOREST AND WOODLAND RESOURCES IN SOUTH AFRICA

F&WL resources, which span a wide range of biomes originally covered more than half a million km² (about 56 million ha) in South Africa, which amounted to more than 42 per cent of the total area of the country. The most extensive of those resources is the open savanna woodlands originally covering about 42 million ha (32 per cent of South Africa). Woodlands were also the most depleted and transformed through extensive conversion for agricultural expansions and excessive harvesting by rural communities. It is estimated that the current area under woodlands is half of what was originally there (Low and Rebelo, 1996). Less than 10 per cent of this resource are currently conserved (for example contained within protected areas). Closed-canopy forests, on the other hand, extend over a much smaller area that is similarly believed to have been reduced by more than 40 per cent over the years through human activities to stand at 400 000 ha today. However the conservation status of this resource is much better than the savanna woodlands, especially for the relatively smaller and rare types such as coastal and sand forests (Low and Rebelo, 1996; DWA&F, 1997).

Vegetation type	Area		
	Million ha	(% of total)	% conserved
FORESTS	**2.15**	**(3.85)**	–
Cultivated plantations	1.43	(2.56)	–
NATURAL FORESTS	0.72	(1.29)	18.1
Afromontane forest	0.59	(1.06)	17.6
Coastal forest	0.09	(0.16)	9.5
Sand forest	0.04	(0.07)	44.6
THICKET	**4.19**	**(7.51)**	**4.4**
WOODLANDS	**41.76**	**(74.88)**	**9.3**
FYNBOS	**7.67**	**(13.76)**	**11.5**
Grassy fynbos	0.59	(1.06)	16.2
Other fynbos	7.08	(12.70)	11.1
Total F&WL	**55.77**	**(100)**	**9.1**

Source: Cultivated forest data from DWA&F (1997) and the rest adapted from Low and Rebelo (1996).

The thicket biome, a transitional vegetation type between ever-green closed forests and woodlands, appear to be the least conserved. Fynbos (Cape Floral Kingdom) resources were simi-larly depleted as a result of invasion by alien species and increased commercialisation and urbanisation. On the other hand, cultivation of exotic tree species in commercial timber plan-tations expanded rapidly to more than 3.5 times the current area under natural forests. About 10 per cent of all plant species in the world (24 000 plant taxa) are estimated to exist in the woody vegetation of SA, which covers an area equivalent to only 1 per cent of the total earth surface (Low and Rebelo, 1996).

The spatial spread and distribution of these resources show important patterns. Natural forests in general, are confined to narrow strips along the East Coast, mainly in the Eastern and Western Cape provinces, with the exception of sand forests, which are entirely contained in Kwazulu–Natal. These comprise frost-free areas extending from sea level to about 2100 m above sea level (Low and Rebelo, 1996). On the other hand fynbos resources are confined to the Cape provinces. Woodlands are more extensive in the northern semi-arid parts of the country and Kwazulu-Natal. Cultivated forests concentrate in Mpumalanga, Kwazulu-Natal and Eastern Cape provinces.

were taken from published and unpublished official statistics (Hassan, 2001). The flow of goods and services from natural forests, thicket and woodlands (NFWDL) were estimated from data generated by three indepen-dent studies conducted in different geographic regions of the country (Shackleton et al., 2001). A separate study was carried to assess the status and economic value of fynbos vegetation in South Africa (Turpie et al., 2001). NFWDL and fynbos studies adopted survey techniques, where measurements were based mainly on household estimation of direct extrac-tion rates. In many cases these were supplemented with direct measurement of mass and actual counts of loads extracted, standing homestead structures, poles and kraals. As some degree of trade was observed at least locally, price levels were reported for most of the extracted products. In the absence of market price information, the opportunity cost of collection or replacement of structures was used as a proxy to the value of the goods and services extracted.

The total contribution of F&WL resources to production measured as value-added is summarized in Table 3.1 (more detailed flow accounts are

Table 3.1   Flow benefits of F&WL resources in South Africa (R million of value-added in 1998 prices)

Types of values	Cultivated forest	Natural woodlands	Fynbos	Total	% of total
Direct consumptive use values[a]	1856	2613	79	4584	73.1
Direct non-consumptive use values[b]	NAP[d]	NA[e]	29	29	0.5
Indirect use values	−225	1021	799	1595	25.7
Water	−225	NAP	NAP	−225	−3.6
Honey and pollination	NAP	NA	786	786	12.7
Livestock grazing	NAP	1021	13	1034	16.6
Non-use values[c]	NA	NA	43	43	0.7
Total value-added (VAD)	1631	3634	950	6215	100
% of total VAD	26.2	58.5	15.3	100	

Notes:
a. Tangible timber and non-timber products for final consumption or intermediate use.
b. Intangible forest amenities for example recreation.
c. Option and existence values.
d. NAP: not applicable (the sector's contribution to such values is insignificantly small).
e. NA: not available, indicating that the value of such services has not been estimated.

74

given in the appendices). This includes values already accounted for as well as values currently missing from the SNA. Of the total value of R6215 million, 59 per cent came from NFWDL, 26 per cent from CPLNT, and 15 per cent is contributed by fynbos. The goods and services provided by F&WL are classified according to four categories of value: direct consumptive use, direct non-consumptive use, indirect use and non-use values.

Direct Consumptive Use Values

This category consists of those timber and non-timber products extracted by logging firms for commercial use (timber logs, gum) or directly harvested by households mainly for their own use, either for final consumption (fuel wood and wild foods) or for other purposes (fencing, construction, tools, furniture). Consumptive use value is the single largest component of total value-added, accounting for 73 per cent of the total economic contributions of F&WL, most of which is generated by NFWDL (59 per cent). Direct consumptive use activities in CPLNT consist of commercial logging as no other direct use benefits were reported for this forest resource type.

The main categories of direct consumptive use items from NFWDL include timber products for energy purposes (fuel wood), construction (buildings, fencing, kraals) and carving (crafts) wood; non-timber products for food (edible fruits and vegetables), medicinal purposes, thatch, weaving reeds and bush meat. Accessible NFWDL represent the typical open access-case, where products are freely collected by rural and urban populations living close to the resource. Some of the harvested products are sold locally and some even find their way to farther away markets (for example honey, fruits, carvings, thatch products). However, trade in these products is limited and usually happens in small informal markets and hence remains to a large extent unrecorded in the official accounts.

The most important foods harvested from fynbos are sour figs (*Carpobrotus* spp.) and honeybush tea (*Cyclopia* spp.). Buchu (*Agathosma* spp.) is exploited for essential oils used in flavouring, perfumery, medicine and brandy (Cowling and Richardson, 1995). Thatching reed (*Thamnochortus* spp.) is harvested in substantial quantities from the wild, even today. Currently the most important species harvested in the wild are flowers and other products for the ornamental industry. Substantial growth in demand for these products in the past 20 years has led to increased flower cultivation, mostly for the export trade. Today the ratio of veld-derived to cultivated harvests is in the region of 80:20 for the dried flower industry. There has also been a large increase in the cultivation of flowers for the fresh flower industry.

Direct Non-Consumptive Use Values

This refers to the case where benefits of the resource are enjoyed without harvesting or consuming the physical stocks. Recreation is an example of such value, which has been estimated only for fynbos accounting for merely 0.5 per cent of total value-added. There do not appear to be significant non-consumptive uses for CPLNT and recreation values have not been estimated for NFWDL resources; and hence non-consumptive use values are believed to be underestimated.

Indirect Use Values

This category of environmental services, which are used as intermediate inputs into the production of other economic (owned and traded) goods and services contributed a total of 26 per cent of the aggregate value-added. Since the value of such goods and services of nature (water, nutrients, carbon sequestration, watershed protection, deposition of pollutants, and so on) is included in the value of the produced and traded economic goods and services, it is usually captured in the national accounts measures of production and income (for example value-added).

Only four intermediate use services were measured in this study: pollination, livestock grazing, water abstraction and carbon sequestration. While carbon sequestration is an indirect environmental service of tree cover, it was treated in this study as a stock variable and added to changes in forest asset values rather than part of current production. Water abstraction is considered an environmental disamenity of CPLNT for reducing the normal run-off and, consequently, the amount of water available for downstream users. The water abstraction externality is a serious environmental cost imposed by cultivated forests, comprising mostly exotic species that are highly water-absorbing (Box 3.3); it is not considered a problem for other types of forest, which consist of naturally-occurring species.[1] Pollination was estimated only for fynbos (Box 3.2), and livestock grazing[2] occurs only in NFWDL and fynbos vegetation and not in CPLNT. Of the four environmental services, livestock grazing and pollination are the most important, accounting for 17 per cent and 13 per cent respectively of the total value-added of F&WL reported in Table 3.1. The water abstraction externality has a relatively small negative value.

Non-Use Value

This refers to what is known as option or existence value, was estimated only for fynbos vegetation, and is relatively insignificant, accounting for only about 1 per cent of total value-added.

BOX 3.2   VALUE OF POLLINATION SERVICES OF FYNBOS VEGETATION

The Cape honeybee *Apis mellifera capensis* is endemic to the fynbos region, where it is naturally limited in population size by available nesting sites (Rebelo, 1987). Hives are kept throughout most of the fynbos region and are used both for the production of honey and for providing a pollination service to fruit farmers.

Honey Values

It has been estimated that there are a minimum of 58 000 hives in this region, in the fynbos region. Bees are kept on fynbos or other indigenous vegetation for most of the year. It is estimated that approximately 50 per cent of the honey production in the fynbos region is attributable to foraging on fynbos vegetation. Eucalyptus flowers serve to boost honey production substantially, while the diversity of fynbos plants with differing flowering times, ensures that honeybees can forage throughout the year. Honeybees thus 'overwinter' in the natural vegetation where they build up their reserves and strengthen their colonies. On average, hives yield 20 kg of honey per year and honey fetched a wholesale price of R10/kg and a retail price of approximately R25/kg in 1997. Based on the estimated total number of hives for the fynbos region a total wholesale value of honey was derived, part of which is attributed to Eucalyptus plantations based on the proportion of the time spent in fynbos (50 per cent). The contribution of fynbos was accordingly derived to be R65 of VAD per hive per year in terms of honey production.

Pollination Services' Value

Approximately 15 000 hives are used for pollination of fruit orchards. Hives are used for two pollination cycles per year, for which beekeepers are paid R147 per hive per cycle by fruit farmers in 1997. The total income accrued to beekeepers for this service was accordingly calculated. Based on the assumption that bees spend 80 per cent of their time foraging in the fynbos vegetation, it was estimated that an equivalent of R39.56/hive/year in value-added in pollination services is attributable to fynbos. Estimates of the number of hives kept in different vegetation types in the Western Cape are given below based on which estimates of average annual income per ha from beekeeping in each vegetation type was derived.

Estimated density of hives and value-added in Rand/ha of beekeeping in fynbos (1998 prices)

Fynbos type	Total hives	Hives /ha	VAD in honey/ha	VAD in pollination /ha	Total VAD/ha
Mountain fynbos	15 000	0.007	0.46	0.27	0.73
Laterite fynbos	1000	0.036	2.34	1.42	3.76
Limestone fynbos	20 000	0.098	6.37	3.88	10.25
Sand plain fynbos	10 000	0.064	4.16	2.53	6.69
Stranveld	12 000	0.061	3.97	2.41	6.38
TOTAL	58 000				

Source: Turpie et al. (2001).

BOX 3.3 MEASURING THE VALUE OF WATER ABSTRACTION EXTERNALITY OF CULTIVATED FORESTS

The cultivation of exotic tree species such as pine and eucalyptus in industrial plantations is considered a major source of pressure on South Africa's scarce water resources. While forest plantations do not directly compete with other economic sectors for water, they however cause excessive abstraction of rainfall water and hence reducing run off and availability of water for downstream users. Reduction in stream flow affects many economic sectors such as irrigation farming and maintenance of ecosystems and wildlife resources. It also introduces additional economic costs such as the need to invest in expanding existing and developing new water supply sources. Reductions in run-off (stream flows) in excess of the original natural vegetative cover (grassland) due to afforestation is considered an environmental externality of cultivated plantations. The social value of this externality is measured as the opportunity cost of water forgone to down stream uses.

As the impacts of reduced run-off on other economic sectors are relatively more difficult to measure, net value-added foregone in irrigated agriculture is used as a proxy to value water abstraction effects. This approach implies that irrigation agriculture is the next-best user of water (that is, generating the highest social returns) compared with other alternative uses. While net value-added forgone in agriculture and other economic activities is already reflected in current measures of output (value-added), the value of affected ecosystem services is typically missing from current income accounts. The difference between value-added (VAD) per unit water abstracted by industrial plantations and that used in irrigation farming was used as the social opportunity cost of water abstraction. The net VAD (NVAD) measure is derived as follows:

$$NVAD = VAD/m^3 \text{ in agriculture} - VAD/m^3 \text{ in plantations}$$

Reductions in run-off following afforestation were calculated using GIS-based forest hydrology models for the major tree species under the different timber production regimes (pulp and sawlog rotations) in different productivity classes (Olbrich and Le Maitre, 1999). Estimates of NVAD per m^3 of water were then multiplied by annual rates of run-off reductions due to afforestation based on changes in standing timber volumes to derive total VAD lost to agriculture as a result of water abstraction (Appendix Table B.4).

The impact of the water abstraction externality is already reflected in increased plantation values and reduced potential production in downstream uses. When VAD per unit of extracted water in plantations exceeds VAD in potential alternative uses, the GDP measure is more than fully compensated for the potential VAD lost downstream. When the opposite holds, then GDP is reduced from its potential level. One should also remember that the environmental value of ecosystem services lost is not reflected in the current SNA. In which case this measure of NVAD forgone underestimates the opportunity cost of reduced stream flow. However, lost NVAD in agriculture provides an estimate of how VAD in industrial forestry is currently overestimated as a result of run-off reductions due to afforestation. This lost value to agriculture of abstracted water amounted to 0.85 per cent and 24.08 per cent of VAD in agriculture and forestry respectively (Hassan, 2002).

In principle all the benefits derived from the use of F&WL goods and services need to be accounted for in the current account. However, different treatments are required in adjusting measures of output and income (GDP) for different benefits depending on the type and nature of the goods and services enjoyed and the purpose for which they are used. For instance, indirect environmental benefits and ecological services that contribute to increased or reduced output in other sectors are already accounted for through the manifestation of such impacts on the affected sectors and activities. An example is the benefit of watershed protection services of forests realized as higher output of the agricultural sector as potential damage leading to reduced output is avoided. However, this value is not attributed to the natural resource sectors supplying these intermediate services. Consequently value-added in receiving sectors is overestimated and the economic contribution or value of supplying natural resource sectors is not recognized. To avoid double counting, care must be taken in adjusting the SNA measures of value-added for such intermediate use values.

3.3   ASSET VALUES AND DEPRECIATION OF FOREST AND WOODLAND RESOURCES

As discussed in Chapter 1, the new SNA (UN, 1993) expanded its assets' boundary to include natural capital that fits the modified definition of economic assets. This modification allowed the inclusion of F&WL resources that are owned (individually or collectively) and can generate economic benefits. Accordingly both cultivated and natural (uncultivated) forests that are exploited for economic use qualify respectively, as produced and non-produced economic assets (UN, 2001). This definition excludes F&WL resources that are conserved or inaccessible for economic use. In the SEEA however, this category constitutes what is defined as non-economic environmental assets. This category of assets is distinguished from non-produced economic assets as providing environmental services such as waste and pollution deposition, habitat and nutrients supply and not the tangible natural resources or raw materials provided by the latter for use as inputs in production or for final consumption.[3] All the biomes of F&WL in South Africa are exploited for economic benefits and hence qualify as produced and non-produced economic assets except for the 9 per cent portion conserved of NFWDL and fynbos which fall under the environmental assets category of the SEEA.

The SEEA distinguishes between and separates land assets (forest land) from the biological resource assets on forest land (for example animals and plants living and growing in the forest). Other forest assets include all produced capital assets such as structures, roads and equipment erected on forest lands (UN, 2001). While biological resource assets such as timber accounts measure the state and change in standing volumes of the resource, land asset accounts are particularly useful for monitoring land use changes. Timber asset accounts are in general essential for determining carbon absorption capacity. However, the social value of carbon sink benefits (demand side) of F&WL resources is not included in the SEEA as carbon is accounted for as part of the emissions accounts to link its social costs to source (or supply) sectors and not for valuing the benefits of absorbing carbon in sink (or demand) sectors.

Physical Assets' Accounts for F&WL in South Africa

Physical assets accounts have been compiled for both timber and carbon stocks of F&WL resources in South Africa. Since fynbos carbon storage densities are relatively small and non-permanent, carbon stocks were developed only for CPLNT and NFWDL resources. Methods and approaches used for constructing the physical assets accounts are discussed below and detailed accounts tables are presented in the appendices.

Timber stock accounts

Cultivated plantations (CPLNT).   Physical accounts were constructed for the extraction, use and consequent changes in standing stocks of CPLNT by species and wood products for the 1980/81–95/96 period (Appendix Table B.2). Timber production (regeneration) as addition to standing timber volumes was based on results of complex forest growth simulation models. The information used for compiling these accounts came from various sources. Factual information on annual harvesting, replanting, new afforestation and damage caused by natural factors, such as fire and pests, were compiled from annual statistics published by the Department of Water Affairs and Forestry (DWA&F). This same source provides detailed information on areas under plantations of different species and rotations by age class. Average mean annual increment (MAI) on total areas under all age-groups (for example not controlling for tree age effects on yield) again by species and rotation was also applied as a simple alternative to growth simulation models. Ignoring tree age effect on timber yield (MAI method) considerably overestimates growth by 32 per cent per year, on average over the study period. This is a clear evidence of the importance of considering more accurate measures of growth and accumulation in timber stocks.

CPLNT timber stocks show a steady upward trend over the whole period of study, indicating that additions to timber volumes due to growth, afforestation and replanting exceeded growth in harvesting and damage effects, leading to net positive accumulation of stocks. It is shown in Hassan (2002) that new afforestation and replanting of industrial timber followed market signals as conveyed by the timber products relative prices. As the relative price of pulp to sawlogs began to decline after 1989, areas cultivated to sawlog rotations started rising and approaching new cultivation for pulp rotations by 1996, closing down the initial gap between standing stocks of timber managed for pulp and sawlogs.

Natural forest and woodlands (NFWDLN).   Standing biomass of wood in the NFWDLN biome was determined using a modelling approach, which provided an above-ground woody biomass figure of 683 million tons. Mean above-ground annual production was taken as 3.4 per cent of standing biomass (Shackleton, 1997), generating 23 million tons. Net change in the stock of standing timber volumes was then derived from this estimate of annual yield by subtracting damage due to natural factors (10 per cent), annual conversion or transformation to other land uses (1 per cent) and calcu-lated annual harvest volumes (4.775 million tons). This gave a net positive change (accumulation) in standing aboveground timber stocks of 9.296 million tons, implying growth higher than abstraction and damage. However, this national average masks important spatial variations in net accumulation. In many parts of the country, the NFWLN resource is under severe pressure and experiencing unsustainable patterns of extraction. Moreover, while the national average indicates growing volumes of biomass, the land area covered by NW&F continues to shrink as a result of steady conversion into agricultural and other land uses. Accordingly attention should be paid to site-specific and regional variations in terms of conserving and sustaining the revealed high value of this resource.

Fynbos vegetation.   No comprehensive data exist on the area of fynbos vege-tation types that have been transformed by development or ploughed for agri-culture, and estimates differ substantially. This study adopted the latest estimates by Low and Rebelo (1996), which uses Moll and Bossi's (1983) vegetation map coverage of the transformed areas (areas from which native vegetation cover has been removed). Most habitat transformation within the Cape Floral Region has been the removal of *renosterveld* over the past few centuries. However, there has been a recent increase in areas being ploughed for the cultivation of fynbos species for the ornamental flower industry. Replacement of natural vegetation with monocultures, or near monocultures, significantly affects biodiversity, and is hence considered to result in loss of natural vegetation, as with any other crop. Significant reductions in plant species richness have been observed in tilled as opposed to untilled mountain fynbos systems (Davis, 1990). Overgrazing, especially in eastern grassy

BOX 3.4 MEASURING THE WOOD BIOMASS AND CARBON DENSITIES OF CULTIVATED FORESTS

Timber Biomass

Empirical timber growth and yield models (Hassan, 2002) were employed to simulate timber yield for the two most common tree species in South Africa by age group and type of rotation. Data for the base year (1980/81) were used to calculate timber yield and growth over production cycles of all tree species under the pulp and sawlog rotations commonly practiced in South Africa. In calculating changes in physical stocks, harvesting was deducted from mature trees' volume and harvested volumes were converted into area equivalents accordingly (using per hectare volume of standing timber at maturity). Damage data, on the other hand, was available in areas and not allocated by forest age. Therefore damage effects were converted into volume equivalents and reduced using the average standing volume for the respective year. Additions were made of growth calculated using the above timber growth models applied to all age-groups of all tree species standing in the base year (1980/81). Replanting of harvested land and new afforestation entered as the zero–one age-group for the respective year in the growth calculations.

Carbon Densities

The following dynamic method is used to estimate carbon densities stored in standing CPLNT. Methods that use final (peak) carbon densities at maturity or the mean carbon storage over the full rotation are simple static alternatives to the dynamic method (Christie and Scholes, 1995).

$$S_t = \sum C_{tj} A_{r-t,j} - C_g A_r \qquad (1)$$

Where:

S_t is net difference in total C stored in year t in tons C
C_{tj} is C density per ha of plantations of age t and type j
$A_{r-t,j}$ denotes area of type j planted in year $r-t$

C_g is C density per ha of the preceding land use and
A_t measures area of previous vegetation type at time r (time of conversion).

To avoid double counting, the study calculated C densities using annual net growth (net depletion) of standing forest stocks in the respective year for different age classes in the specific forest rotation type (Hassan, 1999). That means timber volumes harvested or damaged in year t are reduced from growth and new afforestation in the subsequent year (t+1).

The same timber growth functions used above were employed to estimate growth in standing timber volumes at different ages. The calculated timber volumes in m^3/ha were then converted to cabon densities in tons C/ha using the following conversion function (Christies and Scholes, 1995):

$$C = V_s {}^* D_w {}^* F_c / F_s \qquad (2)$$

Where:

C is tree biomass C density in tons C/ha
V_s is stem wood volume in m^3/ha
D_w is density of wood in Mg/m^3
F_c is the fraction of oven-dry mass that is carbon
F_s is the fraction of whole tree biomass per ha in stemwood

Estimates of the above model parameters for different plantation species and rotations common in South Africa were taken from Christie and Scholes (1995). Carbon densities of the original vegetation (montane grassland) replaced by industrial plantations was estimated to be 6 tons C/ha. This multiplied by areas converted into industrial forestry (as new afforestation) was then deducted from annual carbon densities stored in plantations.

fynbos as well as fires that frequently occur are also important factors that can lead to local extinction of certain plant species (Richardson et al., 1992; van Wilgen et al., 1992).

Within the fynbos vegetation, change in quality is mainly due to invasion by alien plants, which is considered the greatest threat to fynbos biodiversity including certain rare habitat types such as wetlands. This study divided the remaining, untransformed area of fynbos vegetation types into five categories of quality, based on levels of infestation by alien species. The following categories of alien infestation were used: zero (0 per cent alien cover), occasional (<5 per cent cover), scattered (5–25 per cent cover), medium (25–75 per cent cover) and dense (>75 per cent cover). The area of each vegetation type that fell into each quality category was determined using geographic information systems (GIS) coverage of alien infestation (Fairbanks et al., 1996) intersected with Low and Rebelo's (1996) vegetation coverage for the Western Cape, where about 80 per cent of the fynbos biome is found.

Carbon stock accounts

Atmospheric carbon is absorbed by plant vegetation in the form of stored carbon (C). Different vegetation types have different storage densities. Carbon sink functions of forest resources have been treated as a stock variable. Accordingly, similar to the case of timber, net accumulation in carbon stocks was calculated for making the necessary adjustments to Net National Product and asset accounts. This treatment assumes that climate-sensitive industries (for example agriculture) derive indirect benefits from carbon sequestered in F&WL mitigating the climate change impacts of a higher concentration of atmospheric carbon and its negative environmental consequences. Net change in the carbon densities of standing stocks of CPLNT and NFWLND resources were derived. Carbon storage in forests can be estimated either for the standing biomass of trees or for the semi-permanent timber products extracted from standing tree stocks.[4]

Cultivated plantations (CPLNT).   The total biomass of CPLNT is higher than that of the montane grasslands it usually replaces, which in turn means higher storage of carbon. Accordingly this study calculated the incremental (net) carbon storage of CPLNT as the difference between carbon densities in the two vegetation types. Various methods were used in the literature to calculate carbon storage densities (IPPC/OECD, 1994; Harmon et al., 1990; Schroeder, 1992; Winjum et al., 1993). This study employed a dynamic method, which provides for variability in carbon densities of forest biomass of different age groups to calculate carbon storage in CPLNT.

Carbon densities stored in CPLNT in South Africa averaged 4.41 million tons C/annum over the study period excluding total stock at the base year 1980/81 (Appendix B tables). The study computed an amount of 3.94 million tons C stored in industrial plantations in 1990 which compares well with an independent earlier estimate of 3.69 million tons C for the same year by Christie and Scholes (1995). According to Christie and Scholes (1995) this carbon stock absorbs about only 4 per cent of total CO_2 emissions in the country.[5]

Natural forest and woodlands (NFWDLN).   The carbon content of above- and below-ground wood stocks of NFWDLN was taken as 45 per cent (Scholes and Walker, 1993). Based on the above derived wood biomass stock estimates, the total annual sequestration of carbon by NFWDLN was esti- mated to be 11.046 million tons (Appendix B tables). This corresponds to a carbon density value of 31 g $C/m^2/yr$, which is comparable with the conserv- ative estimate of 30 g $C/m^2/yr$ (excluding soil carbon) determined by Scholes and van der Merwe (1996). It must be noted that this rate of carbon uptake will not continue indefinitely at any single point and will decline as any woodland approaches a steady state. However, frequent disturbances generally prevent woodlands from attaining a steady state (such as fires or harvesting) although they also result in the release of carbon stored in the wood.

Monetary Asset Accounts and Depreciation of Forest and Woodlands

As discussed in Chapter 1, determining values for all entries in the physical accounts is the basic challenge of constructing monetary accounts. While market prices ruling at the time of transaction (or their imputed proxies) are used to value current flows of costs and benefits, asset valuation methods are used to measure values of resource stocks. The resource rent is typically derived as the measure of standing resource asset value. Both the resource rent as well as the user cost of El Serafy (1989) are also employed to value deple- tion of resource assets. Valuation of assets is used to adjust the capital account (assets balance sheets) of the SNA, whereas measures of asset depletion are needed to adjust the current account for depreciation of natural capital in deriving the correct NDP figures. Monetary asset accounts are developed in this section to value changes in the F&WL resource stocks described above and adjust conventional national accounts measures of true income and wealth for their depletion.

Valuing timber assets
As argued in Chapter 1, the discounted sum of the stream of resource rents generated by the resource over its life span (production cycle) is the theoreti- cally most correct method of valuing resource assets. However, among the various methods of asset valuation introduced, the net price method (NPM) which measures the stumpage value of trees (current resource rent), is the most commonly used technique for valuing timber stocks in the empirical literature. The NPM calculates asset values (V) as the simple product of the stumpage value (measured as net prices, that is selling price P minus marginal or aver- age per unit costs C) times the standing volume of timber stocks Q at every time period t (for example $V_t = (P_t - C_t) * Q_t$). This expression, however, was shown to yield incorrect measures of asset values, especially in the case of

renewable assets such as biological resources, which naturally regenerate and grow.

Because renewable biological resources such as trees complete a growth cycle over a length of time before reaching maturity, their standing stock at any point in time consists of a mixture of different age-groups. This is typical to wood resources, where there is a long lag between planting or regeneration and maturity for harvesting. Accordingly the NPM, which does not distinguish between age-groups in terms of maturity (quality) and hence value, and applies one price to all standing timber volumes, may generate biased esti-mates of the values of renewable assets. As net prices reflect values of mature timber harvested and traded in the market, they are considered inappropriate to use for valuing immature timber that is not immediately available for use. This is because of either a quality differential or the opportunity cost (time value) of the need for immature timber to grow to maturity. An alternative more accurate method for calculating timber asset values was derived based on the present value criteria (Vincent and Hartwick, 1997).

The correct asset value method (AVM) provides for variations due to natural regeneration and time to maturity of a tree (for example to reach the age or quality for which current timber prices are paid). To allow for the age effect (remaining time in years to maturity $t–T$) in the case of forest resources a distinction is made between the value of mature (V_T) and immature (V_t) forests as follows:

$$V_T = (P_T - C_T) * Q_T / [1 - (1+r)^{-T}] \qquad (3.1)$$

$$Vt = (P_T - C_T) * Q_T * (1+r)^{t-T} / [1 - (1+r)^{-T}] \qquad (3.2)$$

T is terminal time, which is the time of maturity (or rotation length) for F&WL resources (mature and ready for harvesting). Hence V_T is the asset value of mature trees (for example V_0, or capitalized value at initial period) and V_t is the capitalized value of immature forest assets. Q_T is the harvest volume at maturity (optimal rotation). P_T and C_T, respectively, are per unit resource price and per unit extraction costs at maturity. The above formulation of net accu-mulation allows for addition to timber stocks through growth in immature forests G_t and reductions due to harvesting of mature timber D_T.[6]

It is clear that both equations (3.1) and (3.2) will yield higher asset values, respectively, for mature and immature trees than the simple NPM product expression $(P_t - C_t) * Q_t$ (due to the additional discounting terms). This implies that applying the NPM will undervalue standing timber stocks of a growing wood resource such as forests[7] (Vincent and Hartwick, 1997). To use the AVM for deriving asset values one needs information on the age structure of the forest, the optimal rotation age (T) and the discount rate in addition to the stumpage value (resource rent) needed for the NPM. As all the required data were available in the case of CPLNT, both the AVM and the NPM were applied and compared. However, for lack of necessary information on age structure and the irrelevance of optimal rotation age for the case of the unmanaged open access harvesting from NFWDLN, the CAV method could not be applied and only the NPM was used to value NFWDLN timber assets. Also due to the fact that no reliable information was available on standing physical stocks of fynbos, no asset valuation was attempted. However, a more distinct approach was employed to derive estimates of asset depletion values for the fynbos biome. Detailed monetary accounts tables for all F&WL resources are given in Appendix Tables B.4–B.7.

Valuing carbon stocks

While net change in the physical stock of carbon stored in F&WL is not difficult to measure (usually proportional to timber volumes), establishing a value per unit of carbon released or sequestered is the most difficult task in the valuation exercise. The common practice in the literature is to use global value estimates such as those generated by climate change impact models (Nordhaus, 1994). In countries where an environmental carbon charge is levied, such as Sweden, the user charge is applied (Hulkrantz, 1992). As no attempt has been made in South Africa to estimate carbon values, the present study could only borrow and adapt estimates from other parts of the world. Figures used in the literature to value carbon covered a very wide range between US$5 to US$130 per ton of carbon. If one uses Nordhaus's (1994) estimate of 1 per cent of GDP as the climate change damage cost, this will come to the equivalent of US$9 per ton of carbon for South Africa at 1995 prices. The fact that CO_2 contributes about 60 per cent of total greenhouse gas emissions in South Africa (Rowlands, 1996; Scholes and van der Merwe, 1995), leads to a carbon value of US$5.4/ton for South Africa at 1995 prices. This compares well with Nordhaus's (1994) global estimate of US$5.2/ton of carbon in 1994. The present study used the US$5.4/ton estimate to value carbon stocks in both CPLNT and NFWDLN.

Accounting for depreciation of forest and woodland resources

The compiled monetary asset accounts were used to derive estimates of asset depletion (or net accumulation) for adjusting the SNA measures of sustainable income (NDP). From the above physical and monetary accounts it is clear that the physical stocks and values of timber assets have been appreciating (net addition) in the case of CPLNT and NFWDLN. The reverse however, is true for fynbos resources (net depletion). The correct measure of asset valuation (AVM) estimates applied to the case of CPLNT was employed to calculate net accumulation in timber for the cultivated forest sector. Net accumulation (depletion) of asset values (D_t) in this case is derived simply as the difference between asset values estimated for each two consecutive periods (for example V_t and V_{t+1}):[8]

$$D_t = V_{t+1} - V_t \qquad (3)$$

Net accumulation in timber values of CPLNT in 1998 (R1.09 billion) amounted to 0.15 per cent of the GDP, 3.2 per cent of total value-added in agriculture, forestry and fisheries combined and 63.4 per cent of value-added generated in the CPLNT sector (Table 3.2).

On the other hand the NPM measures of average stumpage prices (resource rents) were applied to the cases of NFWDLN and fynbos resources. This yielded a total positive net accumulation (appreciation) in NFWDLN timber asset values of R7.09 billion, which amounted to more than fourfold the contribution of forestry to GDP and about 21 per cent of the value-added in the combined agriculture, forestry and fisheries in 1998. Net annual change in carbon stocks stored in CPLNT was equivalent o about 7 per cent of its officially recorded contribution to GDP in 1998. NFWDLN contributed about 21 per cent of the recorded value-added of CPLNT in 1998 in net carbon stock accumulations.

As mentioned earlier, lack of reliable information on depletion of fynbos resources by area or volume precluded the compilation of timber or carbon assets accounts. This was not thought to be of significance since fynbos is not an important source of timber products like CPLNT and NFWDLN and has relatively smaller biomass densities and hence carbon storage values. However, as seen above, fynbos resources provide many highly valuable goods and services, the supply of which is seriously degraded by alien plant invasion. Accordingly depreciation of fynbos asset values due to quality degradation, which reduces the capacity of the resource to supply the same stream of net benefits from the goods and services it provides, was derived. This was measured as the loss of potential fynbos values due to quality degradation rather than physical depletion of the resource stocks.

The method used to derive depreciation in fynbos asset values is presented in Box 3.5. The net effect of alien invasion of fynbos resources led to a depreciation in its asset value of R0.62 billion in 1998 prices (Table 3.2). This was equivalent to 36 per cent of the recorded contribution of CPLNT to GDP. In spite of the depreciation in fynbos resources, building up of timber stocks, especially in NFWDLN, is the main source of net accumulation, contributing 94 per cent of the total annual change in the value of F&WL assets.

Table 3.2 *Net change in asset values of F&WL resources in South Africa (R billion in 1998 prices)*

Types of values	Cultivated forest	Natural woodlands	Fynbos	Total	Total (%)
GDP				**741.6**	
Contribution of agric., CPLNT & fisheries				34.10	
Contribution of cultivated forest (CPLNT)				1.72	
Net change in total asset values	**1.21**	**7.45**	**-0.62**	**8.05**	**100%**
Net annual change in timber stocks	*1.09*	*7.09*	*-0.62*	*7.57*	*94%*
% of GDP	0.15	0.96	0.08	1.02	
% of agric., CPLNT & fisheries	3.20	20.79	1.80	22.12	
% of CPLNT	63.37	412.24	36.04	440.12	
Net annual change in carbon stocks	*0.12*	*0.36*	NA	*0.48*	*6%*
% of GDP	0.02	0.05	NA	0.07	
% of agric., CPLNT & fisheries	0.35	1.06	NA	1.41	
% of CPLNT	6.98	20.93	NA	27.91	
% of total change in asset values	**15**	**93**	**-8**	**100**	

Note: NA: not available.

BOX 3.5   MEASURING THE IMPACT OF ALIENS'
INVASION ON THE POTENTIAL VALUE
OF PRISTINE FYNBOS

This study assumed that the potential yield of pristine fynbos goods and services is affected by aliens only through a reduction of the area in which the indigenous species can grow. Accordingly a percentage decrease in fynbos yield potential proportional to the percentage cover of aliens was calculated for each category of alien infestation. More specifically this meant that there is negligible change under conditions of light (occasional) infestation but that only 87.5 per cent of the value remains in scattered infestations (12.5 per cent cover), 50 per cent in areas of medium infestation (50 per cent cover) and 12.5 per cent in densely infested areas (87.5 per cent cover) (Appendix B).

The total flow of benefits (VAD) from fynbos calculated in section 3.2 above for the entire vegetation (X_v*A) is therefore made up of the following aggregate of contributions from fynbos areas under all levels of infestation ($X_i^* a_i$):

$X_v * A = \sum_i X_i * a_i$ Where X_v is the average VAD per ha across the entire vegetation and A is the total area under fynbos. X_i and a_i are, respectively, VAD per ha and area of fynbos under infestation level category i (no to light infestation, scattered infestation, medium infestation and dense infestation). The above assumption of proportional reduction in potential fynbos values to degree of infestation means that X_i can then be defined in terms of the value of pristine fynbos (X):

$X_i = \lambda_i * X$ Where λ_i is the percentage decrease in fynbos value for infestation level category i, for example 0 per cent, 12.5 per cent , 50 per cent and 87.5 per cent. Substituting in the above equation, we get:

$X_v * A = \sum_i a_i * \lambda_i * X$ Where X is the VAD from pristine fynbos. The value of pristine fynbos can thus be estimated by solving for X in the above equation.

$X = (X_v * A) / (\sum_i a_i^* \lambda_i)$

As we know X_v, A, a_1 to a_4 (areas under the four levels of infestation – Appendix B) and λ_1 to λ_4, one can derive X and, consequently the loss (depreciation) of potential fynbos values for each infestation level group (D_j). Note that from the above $D_i = a_i * (X - X_i) = a_i * X * (1 - \lambda_j)$. Derived estimates of the depreciation of fynbos asset values are given in Appendix B.

Calculating Loss of Water Yields as a Result of Alien Invasion

This study made an attempt to estimate the loss of water runoff caused by different levels of infestation and the consequent effect on total value of water yielded by fynbos ecosystems. Based on forest hydrology models described in Chapman et al. (1995) and Le Maitre et al. (1996) the mean annual runoff of the fynbos biome (with minimal vegetation cover), was calculated to be 231mm (2310 m³/ha) for an average rainfall year for the Western Cape. The biomass of a 7.5-year stand of fynbos comprising 70 per cent short ericoid-restioid fynbos and 30 per cent tall moist fynbos (Van Wilgen et al., 1996), and of a 7.5-year-old stand of alien trees was calculated as 2810g.m⁻² and 10 459 g.m⁻², respectively (g.m⁻² measures dry mass in grams per square metre). Therefore, a heavily invaded area has an additional biomass of 7649 g.m⁻² compared with a pristine catchment. For a 10 000 ha catchment, the loss of available water attributed to alien vegetation can be estimated using the equation: [$Q = 0.0238*B$], where Q is the reduction in annual streamflow (mm) and B is the aboveground biomass (g.m⁻²) (Van Wilgen et al., 1998). Thus the additional biomass created by aliens in heavily infested areas results in streamflow reduction of 182 mm, reducing overall catchment yield by 18.2 million cubic metres (Mm³) from 23.1 Mm³ to 4.9 Mm³ (Turpie et al., 2002). This water loss is for an area having 100 per cent alien vegetation cover. Assuming that the above-ground biomass of alien vegetation is proportional to cover, unit area water loss from alien plants for different infestation cover classes is calculated below. The monetary values are calculated based on a water price of R0.72/m³ derived as the opportunity cost of water in the Western Cape (Turpie et al., 2002).

Amount and value of water lost as a result of alien invasion cover based on estimates of a total catchment yield of 2310 m³/ha/year for a 10 000 ha catchment.

Infestation level	% cover	Mean % cover	Water yield m³/ha/year	Water loss [% of total 2310 m³]		Value of loss (R/ha/year)
Zero/Light	0–5	2.5	2260	50	[2.2%]	36.00
Scattered	5–25	15	2040	270	[11.7%]	194.40
Medium	25–75	50	1400	910	[39.4%]	655.20
Dense	> 75	87.5	721	1590	[68.8%]	1144.80

3.4 REVISING NATIONAL ACCOUNTS FOR THE CONTRIBUTION OF FOREST AND WOODLAND RESOURCES

In this section, flow benefits and asset values of F&WL resources reported in the previous sections are incorporated in the SNA revising both GDP, the measure of current economic activity, and NDP, the measure of economic activity net of changes in assets (Table 3.3). The total addition to GDP is R3.707 million, which is about 0.5 per cent of the officially reported GDP in 1998 (Table 3.3a). Virtually all of this value (98 per cent) is provided by NFWDLN. The entire value of flow benefits from NFWDLN of R 3.634 million (Table 3.1) should be added to GDP. Although fynbos contribute more than 15 per cent of the total flow benefits in Table 3.1, they contribute only 2 per cent of the revision to GDP in Table 3.3. The contribution to revising GDP is smaller because most of the fynbos values reported in Table 3.1 are already included in the national accounts, though not attributed to fynbos resources. The largest contribution of fynbos, the support of pollination, is already included in the national accounts indirectly, under agricultural production. With a more refined accounting system, the delivery of the pollination service from fynbos to agriculture would be represented. While this practice would not change the total amount of GDP, it would change the distribution of GDP, slightly lowering that of agriculture and increasing that of forestry. The same holds for the 26 per cent flow benefits of CPLNT in Table 3.1. As mentioned above, this is mainly because the largest contribution of cultivated forests comes from commercial logging activities, the value of which is already accounted for in the national accounts. The water abstraction externality is already reflected in GDP, which is lower than potential GDP because of the reduced output of downstream users of water.

From the value for direct consumptive use values of fynbos, the national accounts already include everything except wild figs and about 10 per cent of the rest; this amount of R11 million is added to GDP. The remaining values

Table 3.3   Adjusting national accounts for the missing values of F&WL resources in South Africa

	R million at current 1998 prices
A. Adjustments to GDP:	
Official GDP	**740.581**
Flow values of F&WL resources missing from GDP	
Cultivated forests	
Natural forests and woodlands	3.634
Direct consumptive use values	2.613
Indirect use values (livestock)	1.021
Fynbos	73
Direct consumptive use values (sour figs)	11
Direct non-consumptive (recreation) values	12
Indirect use values (livestock)	7
Non-use values	43
Total missing values	**3.707**
Total GDP adjusted for missing F&WL resources values	**744.288**
B. Adjustments to NDP:	
Official NDP (GDP-Depreciation)	**645.929**
NDP based on adjusted GDP	649.636
Net accumulation in asset values of F&WL resources	8.046
Assets values	7.566
Carbon values	480
Total NDP adjusted for net accumulation in F&WL resources	**657.682**
% of Original Unadjusted NDP	*102%*

generated by fynbos are included in whole (non-use value, R43 million) or in part (50 per cent of livestock grazing and non-consumptive use values) depending on the extent to which they are already included in the national accounts.

The asset accounts of the national accounts of South Africa have not included forests of any sort, commercial or natural, so not only is GDP in need of revision, but the net asset accumulation component of NDP also needs to be adjusted. Total net accumulation of R8.046 million consists of two components: the change in asset value (R7.566 million) plus the value for carbon sequestration (R480 million) reported in Table 3.2. Because NDP is equal to GDP minus depreciation, revised NDP should include both the revisions to GDP as well as the revisions to the asset accumulation figures. This makes the revised NDP R657.682 million, which is nearly 2 per cent more than the officially reported NDP of R645.929 million.

3.5 CONCLUSIONS AND POLICY IMPLICATIONS

Employing a natural resource accounting framework, this chapter has revealed that the current SNA in South Africa highly underestimates the contribution of F&WL resources to income and wealth. This is because many direct and indirect economic and environmental benefits derived from F&WL resources, particularly the non-traded goods and services of natural forests and woodlands, are not captured in the conventional measures of production (income) and wealth. The flow and asset values of F&WL resources missing from the national accounts were established leading to a significant upward revision of GDP and NDP. The forest resource accounting exercise covered values of services critical for agricultural production such as pollination as well as water yield and carbon sequestration functions, the value of which is usually not credited to the F&WL resource sectors. It is essential to trace the origins of such services so that we do not inadvertently degrade or destroy the resources providing them.

Results of the analysis also indicated a low potential for cultivated plantations to play an effective role in managing the carbon budget of the country for lower atmospheric carbon balances, compared with alternative strategies employing instruments targeting source sectors (for example clean development technologies). On the other hand the more extensive NFWDLN, currently exploited under open-access regimes have a higher potential as a carbon sink option for South Africa. Moreover the country's fynbos biome, which is a highly valuable biological resource, is seriously threatened by the steadily growing pressure from increased commercialization, invasion by alien species, conversion to agriculture and extensive open-access extraction. This points to the importance of more careful utilization of these resources and the implied trade-offs between sustenance of sensitive environmental functions and increased economic benefits from harvesting.

While commercial cultivated plantations in South Africa are managed under private ownership and fully integrated in the market, there are no clear policies for rent capture from the use of forest land,[9] which by definition accrues to private timber production and processing sectors. In fact, forest plantation companies could be enjoying some direct or indirect subsidy schemes that increase profitability and hence companies' 'quasi-rents', which in many cases encourages inefficiencies in timber production and processing activities (Day, 1998). On the other hand, old-growth natural forests and woodlands that are not conserved and accessible are in most cases exploited as an open-access resource with no fees or royalties collected on their extraction. However, the extractive agents that capture the rent are in most cases the households living within or near the resource. Nevertheless, lack of property rights reduces incentives for these households to conserve forests. It is therefore important to introduce institutional mechanisms that define and establish individual or collective rights to managing these resources to ensure sustainable use.

While the same also applies to wild fynbos velds that are not conserved, fynbos products are largely extracted for commercial purposes (the flower industry), whereas NFWDLN products are mainly directly harvested by rural households for their own use. The rent from wild fynbos velds is accordingly captured by private commercial firms. Similar to the case of commercial logging of natural forests, poor capture of resource rents in such cases provides higher incentives (above normal profits) for more conversion, commercialization or excessive harvesting of fynbos resources.

NOTES

1. Whereas cultivated forests introduce a negative externality through water abstraction, natural vegetations such as fynbos are considered a source of water supply. The value of this water service lost as a consequence of degradation of fynbos resources is derived as an asset value loss in Section 3.3.
2. Approximated by the value of milk, meat, manure and other livestock products and services such as ploughing and transport (Shackleton et al., 2001).
3. Significant variations currently exist between countries in terms of how close their forest accounting practices follow or deviate from the SEEA guidelines (UN, 2001).
4. A minimum life cycle of 20 years is considered as a permanent sink of carbon for carbon-containing products (IPCC/OECD, 1994).
5. These estimates excluded carbon in root biomass, which is estimated to be equivalent to 15 per cent of aboveground biomass (Christie and Scholes, 1995), and did not account for soil carbon.
6. This formulation assumes a linear cost function (for example marginal and average costs are equal) and that all standing trees are harvested at the optimal rotation age T. It also assumes constant prices and logging costs and hence does not account for holding gains or losses (change in value of asset due to price movements). See Vincent and Hartwick (1997) for alternative more complex expressions for calculating net accumulation inclusive of holding gains or losses.
7. The NPM produces unbiased estimates only in the case of what is known as a 'normal forest' (where there are equal areas under each age class) and optimal harvesting (Vincent and Hartwick, 1997).
8. Vincent and Hartwick (1997) also derived the correct versions of the NPM and El Serafy user cost measures of depreciation, which can be used directly and require less data.

9. It is important to distinguish between timber resources of old-growth forests that are purely natural resources and timber harvested from managed second-cut or cultivated plantations that is a produced resource or economic good.

REFERENCES

Chapman, R., D. Scott and D. le Maitre (1995), 'Hydrological impacts of aliens in fynbos catchments', in C. Boucher and C. Marais (eds), *Managing Fynbos Catchments for Water*, FRD Programme Report 24.

Christie, S.I. and R.J. Scholes (1995), 'Carbon Storage in Eucalyptus and Pine Plantations in South Africa', in *Environmental Monitoring and Assessment*, 38: 231–41.

Cowling, R.M. and D.M. Richardson (1995), *Fynbos: South Africa's Unique Floral Kingdom*, Cape Town, Fernwood Press.

Davis G.W. (1990), 'Commercial wildflower production in the fynbos biome and its role in the management of land-use', unpublished PhD Thesis, Botany Department, University of Cape Town, Rondebosch, South Africa.

Day, B. (1998), 'Who's collecting the rent?: taxation and super-profits in the forest sector', Environment Department Working Paper, Washington, DC, World Bank.

Department of Water Affairs and Forestry (1996), *Commercial Timber Resources and Round Wood Processing in South Africa*, 1980/81–1995/96 Series, Pretoria, South Africa.

Department of Water Affairs and Forestry (1997), *South Africa's Forestry Action Programme, National Forestry Action Programme*, Pretoria, South Africa.

DWA&F *see* Department of Water Affairs and Forestry.

Ellery, W.N., R.J. Scholes and M.T. Mentis (1991), 'An initial approach to predicting the sensitivity of the South African grassland biome to climatic change', *South African Journal of Science*, 87: 499–503.

El Serafy, S. (1989), 'The proper calculation of income from depletable natural resources', in Y. Ahmed, S. El Serafy and E. Lutz (eds), *Environmental Accounting for Sustainable Development*, Washington, DC, World Bank.

Fairbanks, D.H.K. and M.W. Thompson (1996), 'Assessing land-cover map accuracy for the South African land-cover database', *South African Journal of Science*, 92: 465–70.

Harmon, M.E., W.K. Ferrell and J.F. Franklin (1990), 'Effects of carbon storage of conversion old-growth forests to young forests', *Science*, 240: 699–702.

Hassan, R.M. (1999), 'Correcting measures of national income and wealth for environmental values: the case of water abstraction and carbon sink externalities of cultivated forests in South Africa', *Southern African Forestry Journal*, 184 (March): 1–11.

Hassan, R.M. (2002), 'Values of cultivated forests missing from national income and wealth measures', in R.M. Hassan (ed.), *Accounting for stock and flow values of wooded land resources: methods and results from South Africa*, CEEPA Monograph 1, Centre for Environmental Economics and Policy in Africa (CEEPA), University of Pretoria, Pretoria (Forthcoming).

Hulkrantz, L. (1992), 'National account of timber and forest environmental resources in Sweden', *Environment and Resource Economics*, 2: 283–305.

IPCC/OECD (Intergovernmental Panel on Climate Change/Organization for Economic Co-operation and Development) Joint Programme (1994), 'IPCC Draft Guidelines for National Greenhouse Gas Inventories', *IPPCC/OECD Joint Programme, Paris.* 3 volumes.

Le Maitre, D.C., B.W. van Wilgen, R.A. Chapman and D. McKelly (1996), 'Invasive plants and water resources in the Western Cape Province, South Africa: modelling the consequences of a lack of management', *Journal of Applied Ecology*, 33: 161–72.

Low, A.B. and A.G. Rebelo (1996), *Vegetation of South Africa, Lesotho and Swaziland*, Pretoria, DEAT.

Moll, E.J. and L. Bossi (1983), 1:250000 scale map of the vegetation of the Fynbos Biome – maps 1–9, Ecolab, University of Cape Town, Rondebosch, South Africa.

Nordhaus, W.D. (1994), *Managing the Global Commons*, Cambridge, Massachusetts Institute of Technology Press.

Olbrich, B.W. and D. Le Maitre (1999), 'Forestry', Chapter 6 in B. Olbrich and R. Hassan (eds), 'A comparison of the economic efficiency of forest plantations and irrigated agricultural crops. Case study: the crocodile catchment, Mpumalanga', Report No. K5/666, Water Research Commission, Pretoria, South Africa.

Rebelo, A.G. (1987), 'Management implications', in A.G. Rebelo (ed.), *A Preliminary Synthesis of Pollination Biology in the Cape Flora*, South African National Scientific Programmes Report No. 141.

Richardson, D.M., I.A.W. Macdonald, P.M. Holmes and R.M. Cowling (1992), 'Plant and animal invasions', in R.M. Cowling (ed.) *The Ecology of Fynbos – Nutrients, Fire and Diversity*, Cape Town, Oxford University Press.

Rowlands, I. (1996), 'Going with the floe: South Africa and global climate change. Social Policy Series', *Policy: Issues and Actors*, 9 (2).

Scholes, R.J. and D.O. Hall (1996), 'The carbon budget of tropical savannas, woodlands and grasslands', in A.I. Breymeyer, D.O. Hall, J.M. Melillo, and G.I. Agren (eds), *Global Change: Effects on Coniferous Forests and Grasslands*, London, Wiley, pp. 69–100.

Scholes, B. and M.L. van der Merwe (1995), 'South African green house inventory', CSIR Report FOR-DEA 918, CSIR, Pretoria, South Africa.

Scholes, R.J. and M.L. van der Merwe (1996), 'Sequestration of carbon in savannas and woodlands', *Environmental Professional*, 18: 96–103.

Scholes, R.J. and B.H. Walker (1993), *An African Savanna: Synthesis of the Nylsvley Study*, Cambridge, Cambridge University Press.

Schroeder, P.E. (1992), 'Carbon storage potential of short rotation tropical tree plantations', *Forest Ecology and Management*, 50: 31–41.

Shackleton, C.M. (1997), 'The prediction of woody productivity in the savanna biome, South Africa', PhD thesis, University of the Witwatersrand, Johannesburg, South Africa 204 pp.

Shackleton, C., R. Hassan, M. de Wit, S. Shackleton and R. Beukman (2002), 'The contribution of natural woodlands and forests to national income and economic welfare', in R.M. Hassan (ed.), *Accounting for stock and flow values of wooded land resources: Methods and results from South Africa*, Centre for Environmental Economics and Policy in Africa (CEEPA), University of Pretoria, South Africa.

Turpie, J., B. Heydenrych and R. Hassan (2002), 'Accounting for fynbos: A preliminary assessment of the Status and economic value of fynbos vegetation in the western cape', in R.M. Hassan (ed.), *Accounting for stock and flow values of wooded land resources: Methods and results from South Africa*, Centre for Environmental Economics and Policy in Africa (CEEPA), University of Pretoria, South Africa.

United Nations (1993), *Integrated Environmental and Economic Accounting.* Studies in Methods, Handbook of National Accounting, Series F, No. 61, New York.

United Nations (2001), *Integrated Environmental and Economic Accounting 2000*, Draft, available through the UN website: www.un.org.

Van Wilgen, B.W., W.J. Bond and D.M. Richardson (1992), 'Ecosystem management', in R.M. Cowling (ed.), *The Ecology of Fynbos: Nutrients Fire and Diversity*, Cape Town, Oxford University Press.

Van Wilgen, B.W., P.R. Little, R.A. Chapman, A.H.M. Görgens, T. Willems and C. Marais (1998), 'The sustainable development of water resources: history, costs and benefits of alien plant control programmes', draft Report, Environmentek, CSIR, Pretoria.

Vincent, J.R. and J.M. Hartwick (1997), 'Accounting for the Benefits of Forest Resources: Concepts and Experience', Report commissioned by the FAO Forestry Department, Food and Agricultural Organization (FAO), Rome (Draft).

Von Maltitz, G.P. and R.J. Scholes (1995), 'The burning of fuelwood in South Africa: when is it sustainable?' *Environmental Monitoring and Assessment*, 38: 243–251.

Winjum, J.K., R.K. Dixon and P.E. Schroeder (1993), 'Forest management and carbon storage: an analysis of 12 key forest nations', *Water, Air and Soil Pollution*, 70: 239–57.

APPENDIX B: DETAILED FOREST ACCOUNTS FOR SOUTH AFRICA

Table B.1   Distribution and extent of woody resources in South Africa[1]

Vegetation type	*Kwazulu-Natal*		Northern		Eastern Cape	
	000 km²	Conserved (%)	000 km²	Conserved (%)	000 km²	Conserved (%)
Forests	**6.53 (30)**	–	**0.94 (4)**	_	**5.3 (25)**	–
Cultivated	5.30 (37)	–	0.7 (5)	–	1.6 (11)	–
Natural	**1.23 (17)**	**25.1**	**0.24 (3)**	**51.8**	**3.7 (52)**	**7.1**
Afromontane	0.79 (13)	16.4	0.24 (4)	51.8	2.8 (48)	8.7
Coastal	0.04 (4)	27.4	0.0 (0)	–	0.9 (96)	–
Sand	0.35 (100)	44.6	0.0 (0)	–	0.0	–
Thicket	**7.99 (19)**	**1.5**	**0.0 (0)**	–	**28.4 (68)**	**4.3**
Woodlands	**51.4 (12)**	**8.7**	**118.2 (28)**	**12.4**	**17.4 (4)**	**0.33**
Fynbos	**0.0 (0)**	–	**0.0 (0)**	–	**9.9 (13)**	**21.4**
Grassy fynbos	0.0 (0)	–	0.0 (0)	–	5.7 (96)	16.7
Other fynbos	0.0 (0)	–	0.0 (0)	–	4.2 (6)	27.5

Note: (1) Figures in brackets denote percentage of total area under the respective vegetation type (e.g. % of row totals).

Source: Cultivated forest data from DWA&F (1997) and the rest adapted from Low and Rebelo (1996).

Western Cape		Mpumalange		Other Provinces		Total	
000 km²	Conserved (%)	000 km²	Conserved (%)	000 km²	Conserved (%)	000 km²	Conserved (%)
2.6 (12)	–	6.17 (29)	–	0.0 (0)	–	21.5	–
0.9 (6)	–	5.80 (41)	–	0.0 (0)	–	14.3	–
1.7 (24)	25.7	0.37 (4)	40.1	0.0 (0)	–	7.2	18.1
1.7 (24)	25.7	0.37 (6)	40.1	0.0 (0)	–	5.9	17.6
0.0	–	0.0 (0)	–	0.0 (0)	–	0.9	9.5
0.0	–	0.0 (0)	–	0.0 (0)	–	0.4	44.6
5.6 (14)	9.9	0.0 (0)	–	0.0 (0)	–	41.9	4.4
0.0	–	28.08 (7)	38.5	202.5 (49)	9.6	417.6	9.3
60.1 (78)	11.5	0.0 (0)	–	6.6 (9)	0.1	76.7	11.5
0.10 (4)	0.2	0.0 (0)	–	0.0 (0)	–	5.9	16.2
60,0 (85)	11.5	0.0 (0)	–	6.6 (9)	0.1	70.8	11.1

Table B.2   Stock accounts for cultivated forests in South Africa for 1981–96 (volume in million m³ and areas in 000 ha)

Year	Opening stocks m³	ha	Additions [a] m³	Harvesting m³	Damage m³	Closing stocks m³	Stock Changes Growth Model m³	MAP [b] m³	Deviation (%)
1980/81	137.680	1122.3	29.117	11.66	0.80	154.3	16.7	15.9	-4.61
1981/82	154.346	1075.0	27.028	12.54	0.82	168.0	13.7	16.3	16.26
1982/83	168.008	1093.3	26.810	11.96	0.63	182.2	14.2	18.1	21.49
1983/84	182.231	1107.6	26.697	11.58	1.36	196.0	13.8	19.4	28.98
1984/85	195.994	1139.3	26.769	12.70	0.85	209.2	13.2	20.4	35.30
1985/86	209.217	1174.6	27.023	13.43	1.90	220.9	11.7	20.2	42.14
1986/87	220.913	1194.8	27.645	14.40	1.91	232.2	11.3	21.0	45.99
1987/88	232.246	1224.0	29.520	14.96	0.74	246.1	13.8	23.4	40.85
1988/89	246.070	1257.5	30.799	14.68	1.00	261.2	15.1	25.4	40.59
1989/90	261.187	1299.4	32.332	16.00	2.59	274.9	13.7	24.4	43.73
1990/91	274.931	1323.0	33.747	16.59	0.84	291.2	16.3	28.3	42.39
1991/92	291.243	1400.1	34.437	15.83	1.93	307.9	16.7	29.5	43.57
1992/93	307.917	1420.7	38.074	15.83	2.98	327.2	19.3	29.4	34.48
1993/94	327.185	1417.7	40.173	14.34	3.66	349.4	22.2	30.8	27.91
1994/95	349.364	1412.3	41.616	16.75	3.13	371.1	21.7	29.8	27.04
1995/96	371.099	1409.4	42.422	17.96	1.51	394.1	23.0	31.8	27.76
Average per annum									32

Notes:
a   Includes growth, replanting and new afforestation.
b   All results reported in the table come from calculations based on using empirical timber growth models, except those in column MAI showing stock changes results derived by using the average mean annual increment (MAI) for the various tree species in different rotations.

Table B.3   The original area of fynbos in the Western Cape classified by quality categories reflecting various impact levels of infestation by alien species[a]

| Fynbos type | Remaining | | | | | | Transformed |
	No infestation	Occasional infestation	Scattered infestation	Medium infestation	Dense infestation	Total	
Mountain	890 738	1 052 519	177 724	76 799	74 952	2 272 732	145 068
	(36.8)	(43.5)	(7.4)	(3.2)	(3.1)		(6)
Grassy	2094	0	0	0	17 682	19 776	824
	(10.2)	(0)	(0)	(0)	(85.8)		(4)
Laterite	144	1 423	319	21 634	4209	27 729	33 891
	(0.2)	(2.3)	(0.5)	(35.1)	(6.8)		(55)
Limestone	32 839	3 880	77 925	44 991	44 426	204 061	10 740
	(15.3)	(1.8)	(36.3)	(20.9)	(20.7)		(5)
Sand plain	28 868	22 300	70 276	33 822	974	156 240	364 560
	(5.5)	(4.3)	(13.5)	(6.5)	(0.2)		(70)
Strandveld	40 438	64 967	26 809	44 460	19 561	196 235	105 665
	(13.4)	(21.5)	(8.9)	(14.7)	(6.5)		(35)
TOTAL	995 121	1 145 089	353 052	221 706	161 804	2 876 773	660 748

Notes: Quality classes reflecting the degree of infestation by alien vegetation are described as pristine (un-invaded), occasional (<5% alien cover), scattered (5–25% cover), medium (25–75% cover) and dense (>75% cover). Figures in parentheses represent percentages of the total original area in the Western Cape.

Source: Turpie et al. (2001).

Table B.4 *Value of water abstraction externality due to run-off reduction with afforestation (1980/81–95/96)*

Year	Volume of standing timber (million m³)				Total run-off reduction (million m³)			Water value lost[a] R million	GDP %	VAD in Agricult[b] %	VAD in Forestry %
	Pulp – soft	Pulp – hard	Sawlog – soft	Sawlog – hard	Pulp	Sawlog	Total				
1980/81	17.18	25.04	49.35	46.10	76.91	233.95	310.86	19.48	0.03	0.49	18.30
1981/82	19.46	30.25	53.93	50.70	89.93	256.05	345.98	24.41	0.03	0.48	15.98
1982/83	21.50	35.01	57.31	54.18	101.75	272.46	374.21	29.73	0.04	0.66	18.42
1983/84	23.60	40.28	60.75	57.60	114.46	289.01	403.47	36.09	0.04	0.78	11.73
1984/85	25.71	45.86	63.74	60.69	127.66	303.52	431.18	43.43	0.04	0.69	25.15
1985/86	27.54	51.63	66.41	63.64	140.52	316.74	457.25	51.86	0.04	0.75	25.70
1986/87	28.72	57.15	68.90	66.14	151.51	328.75	480.26	61.33	0.04	0.70	25.83
1987/88	29.59	63.05	70.86	68.75	162.32	339.00	501.32	72.09	0.04	0.68	25.56
1988/89	30.84	69.75	73.63	71.85	175.25	352.75	528.00	85.49	0.04	0.73	30.33
1989/90	31.92	77.97	76.15	75.16	190.04	365.83	555.87	101.34	0.04	0.74	21.22
1990/91	32.91	85.38	78.35	78.29	203.44	377.57	581.01	119.27	0.05	0.92	20.88
1991/92	34.18	94.69	80.48	81.90	220.30	389.64	609.93	140.99	0.05	0.91	26.02
1992/93	35.34	103.69	83.47	85.41	236.48	404.68	641.16	166.88	0.05	1.21	30.47
1993/94	36.93	113.40	87.29	89.57	254.68	423.48	678.15	198.75	0.05	1.17	37.46
1994/95	40.67	123.17	90.96	94.57	277.88	442.79	720.67	237.82	0.06	1.26	28.71
1995/96	42.48	134.53	94.43	99.67	299.06	461.48	760.54	282.60	0.07	1.43	23.53
Average								104.47	0.05	0.85	24.08

Notes:
[a] Net potential VAD lost to irrigation agriculture due to abstraction of water by plantations.
[b] Includes agriculture, forestry and fisheries.

Table B.5 *Provincial and national direct use value estimates (1998 Prices)*

	ECP[a]	KZN[a]	Northern Province	Rest of SA	Total SA
Total area (ha million)	17.050	9.495	12.231	83.411	122.187
Original wooded area (ha million)	4.94	6.09	11.851	23.794	46.675
% Transformed					
L&R	46.1	66.2	40.2	50.8	49
Land cover	14	14	14	14	14
Average	30.1	40.1	27.1	32.4	31.5
% Conserved	3.1	8.2	12.4	9.6	9.6
Accessible wooded area (ha million)[b]	3.3	3.2	7.2	13.8	27.5
% of Total land area[c]	19.36	33.70	58.87	16.55	22.51
Rural population (million person)	3.666	4.603	2.473	7.393	18.135
User population (million person)[d]	0.710	1.551	1.456	1.224	4.082
Total use value (R million)	396.180	1 528.914	842.573	865.956	3 633.623
Harvest value (R/ha)[e]	120.06	477.79	117.02	62.75	132.13
Harvest rate (t/person)[f]	0.885	1.190	0.780	0.952	–
Total harvest volume (million ton)[g]	0.628	1.846	1.136	1.165	4.775
Harvest rate (t/ha)[h]	0.190	0.577	0.158	0.084	0.174

Notes:
[a] ECP and KZN refer to Eastern Cape and KwaZulu Natal provinces, respectively.
[b] Potential accessible calculated as original wooded area minus transformed and conserved.
[c] Accessible wooded area as a percentage of total land area.
[d] Equals to rural population multiplied by the percent of total land area that is accessible wooded land.
[e] Calculated as total use value divided by accessible wooded area.
[f] Only volumes of fuelwood, construction and fencing timber were considered from Table 3.2.
[g] Equal to ton/person multiplied by user population.
[h] Calculated as total harvest divided by accessible wooded area.

Table B.6 National non-use value estimates (1998 prices)

	Total in million units
Annual biomass production (million ton)	
Above ground	23.224
Below ground	19.032
Total	42.256
Annual biomass withdrawal (million ton)	
Damage (herbivory, fire, etc.)[a]	4.226
Harvesting[b]	4.775
Conversion/degradation[c]	8.709
Total	17.710
Net change in biomass (million ton)[d]	24.546
Net change in carbon stock (million ton)[e]	11.046
Value of carbon sink (R/ton)	32.76
Total value of carbon stock (R million)	361.867
Net change in above-ground biomass (million ton)[f]	9.296
Average value of standing stock (R/ton)[g]	762.82
Total value of asset depreciation (R million)[h]	7091.175

Notes:
[a] Natural damage caused by herbivory, fires, etc. as 10% of total annual biomass production.
[b] Annual total harvesting of timber resources calculated in Table 3.5.
[c] Conversion/transformation to other land uses taken as 1% loss of total standing biomass.
[d] Annual production minus total withdrawal.
[e] 45% of biomass.
[f] For calculating depreciation in timber stocks, only aboveground volumes were considered.
[g] Total direct use value per ton from Table 3.5.
[h] Value per ton multiplied by net change in aboveground standing stocks.

Table B.7 Estimates of value flows derived from fynbos resources in the Western Cape Province at 1997 prices (VAD in R/ha) by vegetation type and quality (decreasing with increased level of invasion by alien plants)

Veg type	Products/services	Zero/light infestation 0–5% cover	Scattered infestation 5–25%	Medium infestation 25–75%	Dense infestation >75%
Mountain fynbos	Consumptive use value	20.16	17.64	10.08	2.52
	Indirect use value (bees)	78.99	69.11	39.49	9.87
	Non-consumptive use value	12.61	11.03	6.31	1.58
	Non-use (existence) value	14.18	7.09	1.77	0.00
	Total	**139.88**	**117.52**	**65.07**	**15.86**
Laterite fynbos	Consumptive use value	368.48	322.42	184.24	46.06
	Indirect use value (bees)	856.81	749.71	428.41	107.10
	Non-consumptive use value	12.61	11.03	6.31	1.58
	Non-use (existence) value	12.99	6.50	1.62	0.00
	Total	**1522.32**	**1327.16**	**756.29**	**188.67**
Limestone fynbos	Consumptive use value	116.00	101.5	58.00	14.50
	Indirect use value (bees)	1700.01	1487.51	850.01	212.50
	Non-consumptive use value	12.61	11.03	6.31	1.58
	Non-use (existence) value	14.18	7.09	1.77	0.00
	Total	**1924.62**	**1679.17**	**957.44**	**238.95**
Sand plain fynbos	Consumptive use value	0	0	0	0
	Indirect use value (bees)	871.37	762.45	435.69	108.92
	Non-consumptive use value	12.61	11.03	6.31	1.58
	Non-use (existence) value	14.18	7.09	1.77	0.00
	Total	**896.97**	**779.98**	**443.61**	**110.50**
Strandveld fynbos	Consumptive use value	8.77	7.67	4.39	1.10
	Indirect use value (bees)	883.24	772.83	441.62	110.40
	Non-consumptive use value	12.61	11.03	6.31	1.58
	Non-use (existence) value	14.18	7.09	1.77	0.00
	Total	**923.43**	**803.13**	**456.84**	**113.81**

Table B.8 Net national product adjusted for net accumulation in timber and carbon stocks (SA 1980/81–1995/96)

Year	Conventional NNP	Net accumulation of carbon stocks					Net accumulation of timber and carbon		NNP adjusted for timber and carbon values (R million)
		Volume (million Mg C)	Value (R Million)	NNP (%)	Agriculture (%)	Forestry (%)	Value in R million	% of NNP	
1980/81	46 617	50.87	184.2	0.40	4.64	136.2	184	0.40	46 801
1981/82	53 263	18.47	85.76	0.16	1.68	46.0	310	0.58	53 573
1982/83	58 285	2.70	13.80	0.02	0.31	7.1	371	0.64	58 656
1983/84	66 235	3.28	18.71	0.03	0.40	6.0	456	0.69	66 691
1984/85	77 508	3.44	21.70	0.03	0.34	9.6	542	0.70	78 050
1985/86	86 817	3.46	24.26	0.03	0.35	8.9	620	0.71	87 437
1986/87	98 900	3.45	26.78	0.03	0.31	8.3	631	0.64	99 531
1987/88	117 815	3.15	27.10	0.02	0.26	7.2	730	0.62	118 545
1988/89	140 545	3.68	35.15	0.03	0.30	9.3	830	0.59	141 375
1989/90	166 839	3.94	42.17	0.03	0.31	7.2	916	0.55	167 755
1990/91	192 849	1.25	12.24	0.01	0.09	2.0	987	0.51	193 836
1991/92	221 908	2.55	33.16	0.01	0.21	5.0	1546	0.70	223 454
1992/93	249 668	1.71	25.07	0.01	0.18	3.5	1219	0.49	250 887
1993/94	281 339	4.04	68.30	0.02	0.40	8.3	1241	0.41	282 480
1994/95	312 463	6.08	116.49	0.04	0.62	11.9	1249	0.40	313 712
1995/96	365 698	4.96	105.87	0.03	0.53	8.8	1454	0.40	367 152
Average		4.41	52.55	0.03	0.42	10.5		0.56	

Table B.9 Estimates of lost value flows derived from fynbos resources in the Western Cape Province at 1997 prices (VAD in R/ha) by vegetation type and quality (increasing with increased level of invasion by alien plants)

Veg type	Products/services	Zero/light infestation 0–5% cover	Scattered infestation 5–25%	Medium infestation 25–75%	Dense infestation > 75%
Mountain fynbos	Consumptive use value	0	2.52	10.08	17.64
	Indirect use value (bees)	0	0.09	0.37	0.64
	Non-consumptive use value	0	1.58	6.31	11.03
	Non-use (existence) value	0	7.07	12.41	14.18
	Water yield values	36.00	194.4	655.20	1144.80
	Net depletion	**36.00**	**205.67**	**685.11**	**1188.33**
Laterite fynbos	Consumptive use value	0	46.06	184.24	322.42
	Indirect use value (bees)	0	0.47	1.88	3.29
	Non-consumptive use value	0	1.58	6.31	11.03
	Non-use (existence) value	0	7.07	12.41	14.18
	Water yield values	36.00	194.4	655.20	1144.80
	Net depletion	**36.00**	**249.98**	**861.62**	**1498.48**
Limestone fynbos	Consumptive use value	0	14.50	58.00	101.50
	Indirect use value (bees)	0	1.28	5.13	8.97
	Non-consumptive use value	0	1.58	6.31	11.03
	Non-use (existence) value	0	7.07	12.41	14.18
	Water yield values	36.00	194.4	655.20	1144.80
	Benefits of alien plants	0	0	−139.47	−244.07
	Net depletion	**36.00**	**219.27**	**599.33**	**1039.49**

Table B.9   continued

Veg type	Products/services	Zero/light infestation 0–5% cover	Scattered infestation 5–25%	Medium infestation 25–75%	Dense infestation >75%
Sand plain fynbos	Consumptive use value	0	0	0	0
	Indirect use value (bees)	0	0.84	3.35	5.85
	Non-consumptive use value	0	1.58	6.31	11.03
	Non-use (existence) value	0	7.07	12.41	14.18
	Water yield values	36.00	194.4	655.20	1144.80
	Net depletion	**36.00**	**203.93**	**677.45**	**1176.18**
Strandveld fynbos	Consumptive use value	0	1.09	4.39	7.67
	Indirect use value (bees)	0	0.79	3.19	5.58
	Non-consumptive use value	0	1.58	6.31	11.03
	Non-use (existence) value	0	7.07	12.41	14.18
	Water yield values	36.00	194.4	655.20	1144.80
	Benefits of alien plants	0	0	–154.96	–271.19
	Net depletion	**36.00**	**205.02**	**526.92**	**912.73**

4. Fisheries accounts: management of a recovering fishery

Glenn-Marie Lange

4.1 INTRODUCTION

The world fish catch has roughly tripled over the past few decades from 40 million metric tons in 1961 to just under 120 million tons in 1998 (Figure 4.1). Fish are an important source of protein, consumed either directly as food, or as fishmeal input in livestock production and aquaculture. Despite this enormous increase, per capita fish consumption (including fishmeal used as animal feed) has not changed that much, increasing roughly 50 per cent from a global

Catch: millions of tons
Use: kg per person

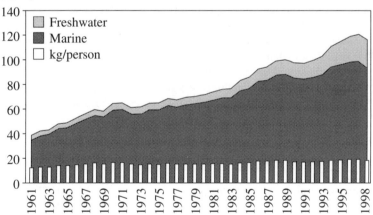

Note: Data for fish catch include both aquaculture and capture fisheries.

Source: Data based on (FAO, 2001a), Population Dept. of Commerce, United States Census Bureau (2001).

Figure 4.1   World fish catch and per capita consumption, 1961–98

average of 13 kg per person in 1961 to 19 kg in 1986, where it has remained since then, with some annual fluctuations. Although aquaculture has grown rapidly, capture fisheries still provide most of the world's fish catch.

This rapid increase in fish production has put enormous pressure on the world's fish stocks and the majority of fisheries are either at or beyond sustainable exploitation. While total catch measured in tons has grown over time, what the aggregate figures do not show is the replacement of high-value fish by less desirable, lower-value fish due to depletion of the stock of high-value fish. According to the Food and Agriculture Agency (FAO), as recently as 25 years ago roughly 40 per cent of fish stocks were well managed (exploited less than maximum sustainable yields), 50 per cent were fully exploited and less than 10 per cent were at risk (exploited beyond the maximum sustainable yield) (Table 4.1). By 1999, only 25 per cent could be considered well managed and 28 per cent were at serious risk. All of the world's major fishing areas are affected to some degree by overexploitation.

Most of the world's fisheries generate no rent because rent is dissipated on excess capacity or overfishing. Poor management has been identified as the major source of overexploitation, especially policies that have subsidized the industry and promoted overcapacity. FAO calculated the gap between estimated fishing revenues and costs – the implicit global fishing subsidy – to be US$54 billion in 1989, of which US$30 billion was capital costs (FAO, 1993). Further work by Milazzo (1998) confirmed the high level of subsidies, but produced a lower estimate: US$15–20 billion for revenue of US$80 billion. Neither of these studies considered additional costs incurred by governments in managing fisheries. Especially pernicious are policies of some countries that subsidize distant water fleets, which have overexploited the fisheries of other countries and the high seas.

In a global context, Namibia's fisheries policy stands out, in many respects, as a model. Struggling to recover from severe overexploitation prior to its

Table 4.1   Exploitation of fish stocks in relation to maximum sustainable yield (%)

Degree of exploitation of fish stock	1975	1999
Well managed:		
Under maximum sustainable yield	40	25
Fully exploited	50	47
At risk:		
Exploited beyond maximum sustainable yield	10	28

Source: Based on FAO (2001b).

independence in 1990, Namibia has developed a strong fishing industry that not only operates without subsidies, but actually pays part of the resource rent to government. The cost of managing the fisheries is recovered by fishing taxes and the observer system to enforce quota allocations is paid for by the private sector. In contrast to many other countries, there is general acceptance by the Namibian fishing industry of these fees and taxes.

Namibia's Fisheries

Namibia has one of the world's richest fisheries based on a productive eastern ocean boundary upwelling system, the Benguela ecosystem, which extends more than 2000 km from the Cape of South Africa past Namibia and up to southern Angola (Moorsom, 1984). As surface water is drawn away from the coast, there is a constant upwelling of cold, nutrient-rich water, which provides rich feeding grounds for marine life, especially along the Namibian coast. However, marine populations are sensitive to minor changes in environmental conditions and can fluctuate significantly. The diversity of species in this ecosystem is low but the abundance is very high, which is ideal for commercial fishing.

Namibia's fisheries are predominantly large-scale commercial operations with a small recreational fishing industry. Unlike many countries with rich fisheries, small-scale, non-commercial fishing did not develop in Namibia, largely due to geographic and climatic considerations. Namibia's coast has always been sparsely populated because it is a desert region. In addition, the coastal waters are quite rough and provide few good harbours, especially for the small craft that have formed the basis for small-scale indigenous fishing industries in many other countries (O'Toole, 1998).

The commercial fisheries are dominated by three species: hake (*Merluccius capensis* and *Merluccius paradoxus*), horse mackerel (*Trachurus capensis*) and pilchard (*Sardinops ocellatus*). Anchovies (*Engraulis capensis*) were important in earlier decades, but the stock has been so depleted that it is no longer a major component of the catch. Other commercial species include rock lobster (*Jasus lalandii*), monkfish (*Lophius vomerinus*), kingklip (*Xiphiurus capensis*), sole (*Austroglossus microlepis*), snoek (*Thyrsites atun*), tuna (*Thunnus alalunga, Thunnus obesus*) and deep sea crabs (*Chaceon maritae*). Since 1990, hake has accounted for an average of about 50 per cent of the value of output, horse mackerel 20 per cent, and pilchards another 16 per cent, though there has been considerable variation from one year to the next depending on the state of the fish stocks and the TAC. In recent years deep-water fishing has developed, mainly orange roughy (*Hoplostethus atlanticus*) and alfonsino (*Beryx splendens*), accounting for as much as 16 per cent of the value of output (MFMR, 1999).

Prior to independence in 1990, Namibia was administered by South Africa. During that time, Namibia exercised some control over the inshore fisheries within a 12-mile territorial limit, mainly rock lobster and pelagic fish, but the offshore fisheries were not subject to any effective control. The International Commission on South East Atlantic Fisheries (ICSEAF) set total allowable catches (TACs) and country quotas for the more lucrative demersal and mid-water fisheries in Namibia's offshore waters. ICSEAF did not attempt to enforce these limits and the South African administration was unable to exercise any control over the offshore fisheries because no country recognized South Africa's authority to claim a 200-mile EEZ (Exclusive Economic Zone) for Namibia.

Outside the 12-mile limit, Namibia's fisheries operated essentially as open-access fisheries and, as a consequence, were severely depleted (Figure 4.2). The combined biomass of the three major commercial species fell from a peak of nearly 14 million tons to around 2 million tons, where it has remained during the 1990s. The offshore fisheries were dominated by foreign fleets, particularly those of Spain, South Africa and the former USSR. The Spanish and former USSR fleets targeted hake and horse mackerel, respectively. The

Thousands of tons

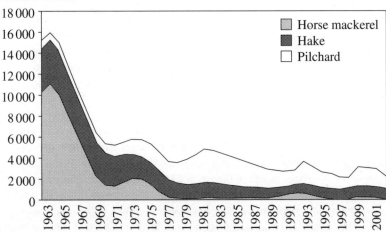

Note: Figures represent fishable, adult biomass. Figures prior to 1990 were estimated using different methods and are not entirely comparable with figures after 1990.

Source: Based on data from Lange and Motinga (1997) and Marine Research and Information Centre, MFMR (2001).

Figure 4.2　Stock of major commercial fish species in Namibia, 1963–2000

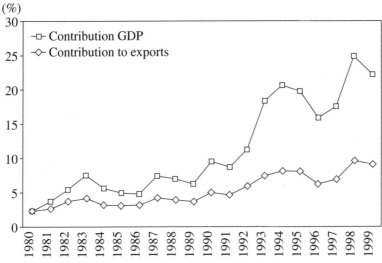

Source: calculated from CBS (1999a, 2000)

Figure 4.3   Contribution of fisheries to GDP and exports in Namibia,
1980–99

Namibian-based fisheries operations were dominated by a tightly knit cartel of South African companies whose main interest was the pelagic fishery (Moorsom, 1984). There were only two significant independent Namibian companies and a number of other very small Namibian operators received a small proportion of the quotas (Manning, 1998). With an apartheid system like South Africa's, the majority of Namibians were excluded from participation in the industry.

At the peak of production in the 1960s and 1970s, the Namibian fisheries sector, consisting then of only the pelagic and the rock lobster fisheries, contributed about 10 per cent to GDP and 15 per cent to exports (Moorsom, 1984, p. 27). However, the economic contribution of the fisheries collapsed thereafter, falling to 2 per cent of GDP and exports by 1980, which reflected both the decline in fish stocks and the uncontrolled operation of foreign fleets (Figure 4.3).

After independence, Namibia established control over its 200-mile EEZ and a new fisheries policy was introduced by the Ministry of Fisheries and Marine Resources (hereafter referred to as the Ministry of Fisheries) to ensure sustainable management of fisheries and to ensure that exploitation of fisheries would benefit all the Namibian people. To ensure sustainability, annual TACs are set for the major commercial species. To ensure that Namibians benefit economically, quota levies were introduced to recover resource rent (with subsidies for Namibians) and criteria for allocation of rights of exploitation were established that favoured Namibian ownership, especially Namibians previously excluded under the South African regime. Policies also created incentives to establish a fish processing industry, which is viewed as a major potential source of economic growth for the future.

Under this system, a remarkable transformation of the industry has been achieved in a relatively short time. The fish stocks have stabilized and government is hoping they will eventually recover to previous, higher levels. Fisheries have also increased their economic contribution, accounting for 9 per cent of GDP and 30 per cent of exports in 1998 (CBS, 1999a). Employment in the industry more than doubled between 1991 and 1998 (MFMR, 1999). The Namibian industry operates without subsidies and has increased its contribution to state revenue dramatically after independence, rising from virtually nothing to Namibia $93 million (US$18m) in 1998 (CBS, 2000). This last point is all the more remarkable because of the global trend for massive government subsidies for the fishing industry in most countries (FAO, 1993; Kaufman and Green, 1997; Milazzo, 1998).

Despite the goal of Namibianization, a major force in the fishing industry is still the large, foreign-owned companies and those previously established Namibian companies, which benefited from discriminatory practices before independence. The continuing role of foreign companies is not surprising because it is not possible for a small country like Namibia to quickly develop the expertise and capital required to operate large commercial fisheries. Foreign investment and partnerships are necessary to support development of Namibia's fishing industry. However, monitoring of the industry and periodic review of policy to assess whether it is making progress toward the development of a genuinely Namibian fishing industry has been a policy concern.

Fish have become one of Namibia's most valuable economic assets and proper management is essential. Government must balance the pressure from industry for higher TACs, and with it the danger of further collapse, against the goal of rebuilding the fish stock by restraining fishing activity to prudent levels. An economic assessment of the value of the fish stock, the economic loss incurred through overexploitation and depletion of the stock, and the potential value of the stock under different management regimes is an essential tool for government. This assessment is provided by environmental accounts for fisheries.

This chapter presents the fisheries accounts for Namibia and describes their use to assess the management of the industry. It begins with a brief description of current Namibian fishing policy. This is followed by a section that describes the methodology and the data sources used to construct the accounts. The fourth section presents the physical and monetary accounts. Section 4.5

discusses the policy implications based on an analysis of the resource rent. The final section provides concluding remarks and policy recommendations.

4.2   NAMIBIA'S FISHERIES POLICY

After independence, Namibia adopted a constitution with strong support for sustainable development, requiring

> that ecosystems, essential ecological processes and biological diversity are main-
> tained and living natural resources are utilised on a sustainable basis for the benefit
> of Namibians, both present and future (Government of Namibia, 1990, Art. 95(1))

A White Paper presented the policy for development of the fisheries sector under the new constitution. It identified two main objectives for fisheries management:

1. to establish sustainable management of fisheries and rebuild the seriously depleted fish stocks to previous higher levels;
2. to maximize benefits for Namibians from the fisheries sector, especially those previously excluded from the industry as a result of discriminatory laws and practices (Government of Namibia, 1991).

Sustainable management and restoration of the stocks are to be achieved through a strictly enforced TAC each year. Namibia has an adaptive management system in which the TACs for the major commercial species are adjusted each year in response to changes in the fish stock. The Ministry of Fisheries biologists recommend a TAC to the Sea Fisheries Advisory Council for a given year based on their assessment of the stock. The Sea Fisheries Advisory Council, with representatives from both the government and the private sector, advises the Ministry of Fisheries on a TAC for each species. As in many countries, there has often been disagreement between Ministry of Fisheries biologists and the industry over the state of the fish stocks and what the TAC should be. The Minister makes the final decision on TAC. Progress has been made in halting further depletion of the fish stocks, though the expected recovery of fish stocks to the high levels seen in previous decades has not occurred. In part this may be due to adverse environmental conditions in the 1990s, although some fisheries biologists have argued that a complete cessation of fishing for a period of time may be necessary for the recovery of some fisheries.

Several steps have been taken to address the second objective, maximizing benefits for Namibians. Fisheries policy aims to increase the contribution of fisheries to national development by creating a Namibian-based fishing industry that would increase incomes for Namibians, create employment on vessels and onshore fish processing plants, and collect resource rent to support development in other sectors of the economy. Export earnings would be raised by encouraging the export of value-added fish products and by the development of new overseas markets for Namibian fish products. A further objective is to improve nutrition and food security through increasing the supply and promoting the consumption of fish in Namibia and in neighbouring states.

Post-independence fisheries policy is described in the Sea Fisheries Act of 1992 and more recently in the Marine Resources Act of 2000, which came into effect in August 2001. The key to the success of the fisheries policy is the quota system. The quota system operates according to the following principles:

1. The TAC is divided into quotas, which are issued on an annual basis to holders of rights of exploitation for seven species: alfonsino, hake, horse mackerel, orange roughy, pilchard, red crab and rock lobster. Observers are present on all boats to ensure compliance.

2. Rights of exploitation are assigned for a period of 4, 7 or 10 years on the basis of criteria designed to encourage the participation of previously excluded Namibians (these criteria are described in the text below). The Marine Resources Act of 2000 introduces two major revisions to assignment of rights of exploitation. First, the period for which rights are assigned have been extended to 7, 10, 15 and 20 years in order to accommodate the industry's need for a longer planning period. Second, long-term rights will no longer be awarded to foreign companies unless they form joint ventures with Namibian companies.

3. Quotas are not transferable, although, with Ministry approval, there may be leasing for a season.

4. Quotas are awarded for one species; any other species that is caught is considered by-catch and is subject to high fees. (Observers are present on all vessels to prevent dumping of by-catch.)

5. Quota fees are levied for major commercial species: hake, pilchard, horse mackerel, tuna and crab (Table 4.2). The levies must be paid for the entire quota allocated to a company and accepted by it, even if the company does not land the entire quota. The ministry is considering levying quota fees to other managed fish as well. In addition, by-catch fees are levied to discourage excessive by-catch.

6. Rebates for quota levies are given on the basis of Namibian ownership and the contribution to the development of a Namibian fishing industry (see Table 4.2 and discussion in the text below).

To generate greater benefits for previously excluded Namibians, 'newcomer' Namibian companies that were not in the industry before independence were

Table 4.2   Quota levy rates by fishery and ownership (Namibian $ per ton of fish)

A.   1991–98

	Ownership of company and vessel			
	Foreign	Namibian -based[b]	Namibian[a]	Other considerations
	$	$	$	
Hake	800.00	600.00	400.00	$200 rebate for onshore processing
Pilchard	N/A	150.00	100.00	$25 rebate when processed onshore for fish meal
Horse mackerel	62.66	46.90	31.30	$15.65 rebate if landed in Namibia
Tuna[c] (pole and line)	400.00	300.00	200.00	$100 rebate if landed or processed in Namibia
Tuna[c] (longline, sashimi)	1 200.00	N/A	N/A	
Crab (red)	556.00	556.00	556.00	
Crab (spider)	225.00	225.00	225.00	

B.   1999

All quota levies increased by 10%.

C.   2002*

All quota levies expected to be increased by 50% over 1999 values.

Notes: *new quota levies not yet finalized.
[a] Namibian owned defined as Namibian-majority ownership, Namibia-flagged vessel, and more than 80% of the crew is Namibian.
[b] Namibian-based defined as foreign-majority ownership, Namibia-flagged vessel, and/or less than 80% of the crew is Namibian
[c] No quotas are set so a catch levy is charged.

Source: MFMR (1997, 2000).

given preference in allocation of rights of exploitation. Companies are selected on the basis of managerial and technical competence and, in addition, on the basis of characteristics which promote Namibianization of the industry, such as employment of Namibians, purchase of vessels and establishment of onshore processing plants. Foreign companies operating in the past that did not make a substantial commitment to Namibianization did not have their rights of exploitation renewed. However, no formal system of weighting for these factors has been established.

The assumption that underpins this approach is that formal ownership automatically brings with it control over economic benefits and, therefore, allocating fishing rights to Namibian-owned companies will ensure that the rent associated with the rights will accrue to Namibians. At the same time, government recognized that the industry could not change overnight and continued to grant quotas to some of the big foreign companies that had made a substantial commitment to developing a Namibian industry. For example, Pescanova SA, the largest multinational Spanish fishing company, established a large processing plant in Lüderitz, Namibia's southern port, and was granted about 19 per cent of the hake quota in 1997, the largest single share awarded (MFMR, 1999). Treatment of foreign companies changed under the new Marine Resources Act 2000 to further encourage Namibianization; as of 2001, rights will only be awarded to foreign companies if they have formed joint ventures with Namibian companies

Although quota leasing for a season is in principle allowed, little official leasing has gone on in the past and quotas have been, in effect, non-transferrable. That is because in awarding a right of exploitation, the capacity to fish is one of the primary considerations and leasing a quota has been viewed as an indication that a company is not capable of fishing. Non-transferable quotas are generally viewed as economically less efficient than transferable quotas because such a system does not allow companies the flexibility to adjust catch to vessel capacity (Arnason, 1992; Hannesson, 1993). For example, the TAC awarded in a given year may be substantially lower than a company's vessel capacity. It would be more efficient for that company to sell its TAC to another company that also has excess capacity so that a single company could catch the combined TAC more efficiently, operating at full capacity. This inefficiency results in a loss of income, though the size of this loss may vary depending on the nature of the fishery and the number of companies involved.

The government decided to make the quotas non-transferable in order to nurture the newly established Namibian industry and the Namibian jobs this would create. It recognized that Namibian newcomers would have difficulty competing with established fishing companies, who have much greater financial resources and management experience. Under that pressure, the newcomers would be tempted to sell their quotas, if allowed. Although this might result in higher incomes generated to a few Namibians, it would undercut the development of a Namibian fishing and fish processing industry and the employment that would generate. In the trade-off between the economic inefficiency of non-transferable quotas and the creation of a Namibian fishing industry fostered by non-transferable quotas, it has been assumed that the inefficiency losses would be relatively small.

A further problem is that quotas that are non-transferable cannot be used as collateral to obtain financing from banks. Lack of credit has been a serious constraint for newcomers, which have been forced to turn to other sources of credit, often the foreign fishing companies that operated in Namibian waters prior to independence. There is clearly a need for substantial investment in the industry, which foreign companies can provide. But the foreign companies are then in a position to stipulate conditions of repayment that include the disposition of the fish and extensive management control, even though the foreign company may be a minority partner. With no other source of finance, Namibian companies are vulnerable to unequal arrangements in which the benefit to Namibians' is greatly reduced. These and other problems arising from fisheries policy in the 1990s are discussed in Manning (1998, 2000).

Several other aspects of the system of quota allocation and the non-transferability of quotas have put additional pressure on Namibian companies to enter into unequal partnerships that reduce the benefit of fishing to Namibians. First, companies are encouraged to purchase vessels as an indication of serious intent in the industry, a factor considered in the allocation of rights of exploitation. This adds considerably to the financing problem and may encourage overcapacity.

Second, once the Ministry of Fisheries offers a company its quota for the year, the company may then accept the full quota, or part of the quota, or reject it altogether. There is considerable pressure on a company to accept the full quota that it is offered. Rejecting the quota could lead ultimately to a withdrawal of the right of exploitation, as it would indicate an incapacity to participate in the industry. Accepting a smaller quota may lead the Ministry to regard that company as only having capacity to deal with a smaller quota, resulting in the Ministry offering a smaller quota to the company in future years. In addition, a company must pay the quota levy for the entire quota whether or not it eventually catches that amount. In practice, this policy has been modified so that in years when less than 80 per cent of the TAC is caught, quota fees must be paid only on the amount of fish actually caught.

Although it is possible to lease quotas, there is no formal market for leasing and most of the leasing that does occur has taken place informally (Manning 1998). Leasing has been discouraged. Government specifically wanted to prevent the emergence of 'paper quotas', where Namibian companies merely rented their quotas without gaining real expertise in fishing.

The government does support Namibian companies by providing substantial rebates on quota fees for Namibian ownership, employment of Namibians on fishing vessels and establishment of onshore fishing processing plants (Table 4.2). For most fish subject to quota levies, the subsidy to fully Namibian companies is 50 per cent. The rebates for Namibian ownership created incentives for foreign companies previously operating in Namibian waters to reorganize in order not only to better qualify for allocation of rights of exploitation, but also to qualify for these rebates. In ways described in Manning, (1998, 2000) it has been possible for a foreign company to qualify as Namibian without necessarily ensuring that control and profits would actually accrue to Namibian partners.

Fisheries policy was designed to promote the development of a Namibian fishing industry and in many respects it has been a success. As seen in Figure 4.2, the contribution of fisheries to GDP and exports increased enormously, as did Namibian employment. Fish processing increased from only a few canning factories in 1990 to 20 by 2000. Foreign companies continued to play a major role in the fishing industry, providing much-needed finance, technical expertise and international distribution networks, but Namibian participation increased significantly.

Despite the policy's success, there is growing concern that ten years after independence too much of the economic benefit still accrues to foreign companies. This is especially serious since government has allowed the real cost of quota levies to fall over time, in effect allowing most of the substantial resource rent from fisheries to accrue to the private sector. The quota fees were set in 1991 and were not changed until 1999, when they were increased by only 10 per cent despite significant inflation and a decline in the exchange rate over the decade. Quota levies will be increased again in the near future, probably by 50 per cent, although the exact amounts have not yet been finalized (Wiium and Uulenga, 2001).

In 2000, there was a major revision in fisheries policy in order to address this concern. The Minister announced that rights of exploitation would only be awarded to Namibian companies and that any foreign company that wished to participate in Namibian fisheries must have a Namibian partner. Foreign companies protested that this amounted to a forced partnership in which the Namibian partner provides only the fishing right while the foreign partner provides everything else (Steenkamp, 2001). Since quotas are still not freely tradable, there is no efficiency gain. The intention is to improve the bargaining power of Namibian companies to ensure that more of the rent accrues to Namibians rather than to foreign companies.

4.3   METHODOLOGY AND DATA SOURCES

Fish resource accounts are based on the SEEA (UN, 2001) and a more specialized manual for fisheries that addresses some of the issues unique to compilation of fisheries accounts (FAO and UN, forthcoming). A number of countries have constructed accounts for fish or are planning to do so in the near future (Table 4.3). Relative to other resources, fisheries accounts are not constructed

Table 4.3   Countries compiling accounts for fisheries

	Physical	Monetary
Regular compilation by statistical offices		
Norway	X	X
Namibia	X	X
Canada*	X	X
United Kingdom*	X	X
Occasional studies		
Iceland	X	X
Philippines		X
Korea		X

Notes: * countries planning to introduce fisheries accounts.
The list includes only countries for which accounts were constructed within government offices and does not include one-time academic or other studies.

by many countries. In part, that may be because fisheries are not economically significant in most countries. In addition, the compilation of fisheries accounts presents greater challenges than other resources: fish cannot be directly observed the way forest resources can, multi-species fisheries are affected by complex predator–prey interactions, there are often large inter-annual variations, and fish may migrate out of territorial waters.

Fish accounts are part of aquatic resources in the SEEA (System of Environmental and Economic Accounts) which include freshwater and marine resources, cultivated and non-cultivated. Namibia has important artisanal freshwater fisheries in the northern part of the country, as well as small amounts of cultivated marine resources, such as seaweed and shellfish. However, the most important resources are the marine capture fisheries, mainly hake, pilchard and horse mackerel. Accounts have only been constructed for these three species so far. In future work, other aquatic resources will be included, starting with those that are subject to controls by the Ministry. The recreational fishing sector is important for tourism, and there are some conflicts with commercial fishing policy. However, its estimated value is less than 5 per cent of the commercial industry (Kirschner et al., 1999; Zeybrandt and Barnes, forthcoming), so it is not included in the fisheries accounts at this time.

Physical Accounts

As with all asset accounts, fish accounts are constructed for opening stocks, changes that occur during the accounting period and the closing stock.

Changes that occur during the year consist of catch, recruitment, mortality and other volume changes. Other volume changes can include factors such as the migration of fish stock out of the country's territorial waters due to environmental events. In practice, there is not enough information to quantify all the different sources of change so the changes are collapsed into two categories: 'Catch' and 'Other volume changes'. For long-lived species like orange roughy, it would be useful to construct stock accounts by age class, as is done for forestry. Norway and Iceland have constructed stock accounts by age class (Sorenson and Hass, 1998), but this has not been possible in Namibia.

The treatment of migratory and straddling stocks in the accounts is not always well defined. Where straddling stocks are jointly managed, the partner countries set TACs and assign shares of the TAC to each country. In such cases, a country's share of TAC may be used to assign it a share of the associated stock (FAO and UN, forthcoming). Some of Namibia's fish are migratory within the Benguela marine ecosystem, especially in response to environmental disturbances. However, the circumstances under which fish migrate are not well understood and there is no agreement yet for joint management among the three countries sharing the ecosystem. A regional fisheries management body, South East Atlantic Fisheries Organization (SEAFO), is being set up but does not yet play a management role. Consequently, Namibia estimates its own fish stock, but without a separate estimate for migration, a factor that may account for some of the large inter-annual fluctuations.

Stock sizes are estimated using virtual population assessment models combined with two independent survey approaches for each species (Namibia Foundation, 1998, pp. 10–11). Direct survey methods provide one approach: swept-area trawl surveys for hake, and acoustic surveys for horse mackerel and pilchard. Analysis of commercial landings for catch, effort and biological information such as age structure provide additional information. There are a number of limitations to these methods. First, observed fish catch may be subject to high-grading or under-reporting which distorts the true age structure. In addition, the models relating the age distribution of a fish catch to underlying populations are themselves subject to considerable uncertainty. There is also uncertainty about the relationship between spawning stocks and recruitment of juveniles. Recruitment can be affected more strongly by environmental factors than by the size of the spawning stock. There is also not enough information to distinguish between the impact of harvesting on fish stock and the impact of environmental changes.

Monetary Accounts

As described in Chapter 1, the value of fish, like any other asset, is the net present value of the stream of income (rent) it is expected to generate in the future. Constructing monetary accounts has two components: (1) defining how rent is to be calculated, and (2) making projections about the future rent a fishery is likely to generate. Both these components raise unique challenges for fisheries.

Measuring resource rent

Rent is defined as the value of production minus the marginal exploitation costs. When markets are lacking, rent is often measured with the residual approach explained in Chapter 1. However, for fisheries managed under an individually tradable quota (ITQ) system such as Iceland or New Zealand, a market for quotas may develop that, under the right circumstances, reflects the rent. In Namibia, there are three sources of data available that could potentially be used to calculate rent, two based on the residual approach, and a third based on an unofficial price for the rental of the quota.

Residual approach:
1. national accounts, which provide information for the entire fisheries sector since 1980 as well as detailed statistics for each fishery since 1990;
2. annual survey of fishing companies, which provides information about income, revenue, assets and catch for each company in 1994, 1995, and 1996;

Market-price approach:
3. quota trading prices for hake based on a survey of unofficial trading in the hake fishery in 1995.

The advantages and disadvantages of each approach are discussed below.

The chief advantage of the first source of data, the national accounts, is that it is comprehensive, covering all fisheries and all years, although data for the years before 1990 are incomplete and cannot be used reliably. The classification of fisheries consists of: pelagic (mainly pilchard), demersal (mainly hake), midwater (mainly horse mackerel), deep-water tuna (pole and long-line), linefish, rock lobster, crab, and other fish. Production data are provided by the Ministry of Fisheries based on industry surveys landings and fish prices for a large number of differentiated fish products.

The problem lies in the estimation of intermediate costs and value-added. These figures are estimated based on constant, average production costs estimated by a model developed by the Ministry of Fisheries (MFMR and CBS, no date). On average, intermediate costs, mainly fuel, account for about 40 per cent of the value of output. Because there are no reliable data on labour costs, value-added is evenly split between compensation of employees and gross operating surplus in all fisheries.

For a stable fishery, the assumption of cost proportions that do not vary over time may provide a reasonable approximation. However, Namibia's fisheries have been subject to significant fluctuations, which would cause production costs to fluctuate as well. Environmental disturbances, which are not uncommon, can reduce catch rates by as much as 50 per cent. Consequently, production costs may be underestimated in a bad year and overestimated in a good year. The national accounts include information about the stock of fixed capital for the fishing industry as a whole, but do not estimate the capital stock and capital costs in each fishery.

The annual survey of fishing companies, established in 1994, provides detailed information about income, expenditures, capital assets, fish catch, employment and ownership. These data have the advantage over national accounts of providing actual income and expenditure data for individual companies in a given year. In fact, the survey instrument was originally designed to help improve the national accounts as well as to provide the Ministry of Fisheries with useful information. Survey responses were collected for three years: 1994, 1995 and 1996. However, fishing companies have challenged the legality of the survey and results for 1997 and 1998 were only recently obtained. In addition, no attempts have yet been made to verify the survey responses and very little data cleaning has been performed. Data have only been processed for hake in 1995 and for all fish in 1997 and 1998. These factors severely limit the usefulness of the survey for the years for which data have been collected. While the company survey would provide an ideal data source, there is not yet information for a long enough period to use these data to estimate rent. However, the survey does provide useful insights into the fishing industry.

The third approach to measurement of resource rent is the price at which fish quotas are traded. Quota trading prices are a good measure of the value of fish where there is a competitive market for fish quota. Generally, quota trading represents a sharing of rent between the holder of the quota and the buyer, and only occurs when rents are high enough to cover both the 'normal' profit each party would require to do business, plus transactions costs associated with the trade. In a competitive market, such as might occur under ITQ management regimes, transactions costs may be quite low. However, transactions costs are usually higher when the market for trading quota is not well developed. Other conditions can also distort quota trading prices, such as unequal power between buyers and sellers. Since there is no official market for trading of quota, imperfect market conditions exist and the trading prices for quota under these conditions do not necessarily reflect the rent generated in the industry.

Even though quotas are officially non-transferable (except under very limited circumstances), a survey of the Namibian hake fishery in 1995 by Manning (1998) found trading was taking place. However, the lack of officially sanctioned quota trading not only distorts the market, but also makes it less reliable as a source of data for valuation. The deals often take place with secrecy and there can be no official verification of quota prices, making this a less than ideal source of data.

Despite the conceptual advantages of using trading prices for hake quotas, or the survey of fishing companies, the national accounts have been used for constructing the fish accounts because they are the only data source that can provide policy-makers with comprehensive accounts for all fisheries over all the years since independence. An assessment of sustainability cannot be provided on the basis of the data for two or three years; rather, it is the trend over time that is useful for policy-makers and for that reason data from the national accounts have been used.

In actual implementation of rent calculations from national accounts data, average cost is used rather than marginal cost because data about marginal cost are not generally available. Rent was calculated for each fish stock (hake, pilchards, horse mackerel) using the general formula for residual value given in Chapter 1 (the time subscript is omitted for clarity of presentation):

$$RR_i = TR_i - (IC_i + CE_i + CFC_i + NP_i)$$

$$NP_i = i \times K_i$$

Where

RR = resource rent
TR = total revenue
IC = intermediate consumption
CE = compensation of employees
CFC = consumption of fixed capital
NP = normal profit
i = the rate of return on fixed capital
K = the value of fixed capital stock in the fishery
for each fishery, i, where $i = 1,2,3$ for hake, pilchards, horse mackerel, respectively.

All figures are provided from the national accounts except for i, the opportunity cost of capital. There is little long-term borrowing in the fishing industry that might indicate an appropriate cost of capital for that sector. The Ministry of Fisheries recommended that a 30 per cent return on fixed capital should be used because unpredictable environmental disturbances make fishing is a very high-risk activity. This is much higher than is used for most calculations, and higher than the 10 per cent rate used for calculating the value of sub-soil assets in Namibia (see further discussion of this issue in Chapter 2). Rent calculations were made for two rates of return to fixed capital: 20 per cent and 30 per cent.

In calculating fisheries resource rent, the boundary between the fishing and fish processing industries was relaxed. This was done for two reasons. First, much of the fish is processed offshore on factory trawlers whose continuous-process operation make the separation of fishing from fish processing some-what arbitrary. In 1998, the figures for hake were 40 per cent processed offshore and 60 per cent processed onshore (Uulenga, 1999). Second, there is a high degree of vertical integration in the industry, which makes the separa-tion very difficult. The combination of a primary industry and its immediately downstream processing industry is common practice in accounting for forestry (Eurostat, 2000).

Estimation of rent requires a figure for fixed capital stock for each fishery. The national accounts do not provide the distribution of fixed capital across different fisheries, so capital stock was allocated to each fishery in proportion to their values of output. While this may not be realistic, it is the best estimate that can be made at this time.

As mentioned in Chapter 1, there are several factors that can cause the private costs of extraction to differ from the social costs. Of all the factors mentioned, only one is significant for fisheries in Namibia: resource manage-ment costs incurred by government. A preliminary study of these costs has been made by Wiium and Uulenga (2001), although there is not attempt to disaggregate costs by fishery.

Measuring asset value: projecting future resource rent
The value of each fish stock is the net present value of the rent it will gener-ate in the future. The present value calculations require projections of future prices, technology, costs of production, fish stock levels and resource exploita-tion paths. Future stock levels depend partly on fisheries policies and partly on environmental conditions and their impact on fish stocks, which are difficult to forecast. The economics of fishing also depends on fisheries policy: a more efficient fishery generates higher rent and is of greater economic value. In the absence of alternative information, common practice has been to assume that the current year's prices, technology, and production costs remain constant in the future. The calculation then relies on the remaining variables, levels of stock and exploitation.

Prediction of future stock levels is much more difficult with marine capture fisheries than with other renewable resources, like forests, because there is a high degree of uncertainty resulting from poorly understood dynamics of many fish populations and of large marine ecosystems. In some relatively well-understood fisheries, a bioeconomic model can be used to assess the likely future stocks, costs of fishing and rent under different management regimes. If government is clear about its management objectives, the model can be used to assess the value of the fish stock with reasonable accuracy. Such a model was used, for example, to assess the value of Iceland's fisheries (Danielsson, 2000).

It is exceedingly difficult in the Benguela ecosystem to assess the biological status of Namibia's fish stocks and to determine whether they will, in the long term, remain at current levels increase to previous higher levels, or collapse further. Each of these possibilities has different implications for future rent and the value of the asset. If fish stocks remain constant, then rent and asset value will remain constant. If there is a recovery from depletion and fish stocks increase, the rent will increase over time and the present value of the asset is much higher, than under the constant-stocks assumption. If, on the other hand, fish stocks decline, then the asset value will be much lower.

Despite the Ministry of Fisheries' goal of restoring the fish stock to previous higher levels, there is little evidence that this objective will be achieved in the near future. Indeed, as the next section will show, some of the major fish stocks ended the decade lower than they began in 1990. Hence, it may be considered optimistic to assume that the stocks have stabilized at current levels and will generate the same rent in the future. Under this assumption, the net present value formula takes the following form:

$$V_t^i = \frac{Rent_t^i}{r}$$

Where

V^i = the value of the resource stock at the close of the period
$Rent^i$ = the total rent
r = the discount rate
for each fishery, i, where $i = 1,2,3$ for hake, pilchard, horse mackerel, respectively.

While the fluctuation of rent over the past ten years shows that this is an unrealistic assumption on a year-to-year basis, this assumption is used for lack of any other information at this time. The issue of alternative values for the stock under alternative assumptions, especially alternative management regimes and a partial recovery of fish stocks, is discussed later. A social discount rate of 10 per cent is used, a rate which is commonly employed by a number of governments in southern Africa for project evaluation.

4.4   PHYSICAL AND MONETARY ACCOUNTS FOR FISH

Physical Accounts

The physical accounts for hake, pilchard and horse mackerel are shown in
Table 4.4 for the years 1990 to 2000. Full accounts cannot be constructed prior
to 1990 because foreign operators, who dominated the industry at that time,
were not required to report their catch. It is notable that net annual change has
been positive, on balance over the ten-year period, only for hake, which ended
the decade 30 per cent higher than in 1990. Fishable biomass of pilchard was
less than half its magnitude at the beginning of the decade. The pilchard fishery, in particular, has been subject to large fluctuations, all but disappearing in
1996. The government has attributed this primarily to regular but unpredictable environmental disturbances in the Benguela system and the consequent temporary migration of fish to Angolan waters (MFMR, 1997; O'Toole,
1998). Even horse mackerel, which improved during the late 1990s, fell below
the 1990 level in 2000.

*Table 4.4   Physical accounts for hake, pilchards and horse mackerel in
Namibia, 1990–2000 (thousands of tons)*

A.   Hake

	Opening stock	Net annual change	Catch	Other volume changes	Closing stock
1990	906	45	55	100	951
1991	951	120	56	176	1072
1992	1072	40	87	127	1112
1993	1112	−18	108	90	1094
1994	1094	−4	112	108	1090
1995	1090	28	130	158	1118
1996	1118	41	129	170	1159
1997	1159	35	110	145	1194
1998	1194	−5	141	136	1188
1999	1188	−2	161	159	1186
2000	1186	−17	160	143	1170

Table 4.4 continued

B. Pilchard

	Opening stock	Net annual change	Catch	Other volume changes	Closing stock
1990	500	160	89	249	660
1991	660	−19	68	49	641
1992	641	−210	82	−128	431
1993	431	−216	116	−100	215
1994	215	−90	115	25	125
1995	125	−120	95	−25	5
1996	5	145	2	147	150
1997	150	150	32	182	300
1998	300	−25	65	40	275
1999	275	−50	42	−8	225
2000	225	−135	27	−108	90

C. Horse mackerel

	Opening stock	Net annual change	Catch	Other volume changes	Closing stock
1990	1450	−100	409	309	1350
1991	1350	750	434	1184	2100
1992	2100	−300	426	126	1800
1993	1800	−300	479	179	1500
1994	1500	−100	360	260	1400
1995	1400	−200	314	114	1200
1996	1200	−200	319	119	1000
1997	1000	800	306	1106	1800
1998	1800	0	258	258	1800
1999	1800	−50	288	238	1750
2000	1750	−500	320	−180	1250

Source: Marine Research and Information Centre (2001).

The physical accounts for fish show a great deal of inter-annual variation in levels of stock, indicating how difficult it is to manage Namibia's fish stock. Pilchard is particularly volatile: the TAC doubled from 1990 to 1994, then fell by more than 80 per cent in the following two years, before increasing again in 1998. Hake has gradually increased, except for small dips in 1994–5 and again in 1999–2000. Horse mackerel first increased gradually until 1994, then decreased.

An examination of trends in biomass, TAC and catch for each fishery provides an indication of the response of fisheries managers to changes in fish stock (Figure 4.4). Pilchard biomass increased slightly in the early 1990s and

A. Pilchard

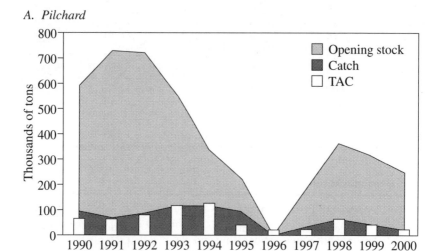

B. Hake

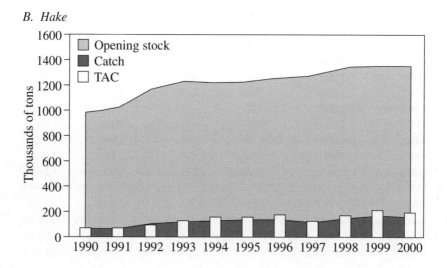

C. Horse mackerel

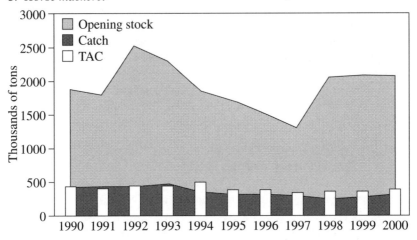

Source: based on data from Marine Research and Information Centre (2001).

*Figure 4.4   Biomass, TAC and catch for major commercial species,
1990–98*

then crashed precipitously, all but disappearing by 1996. Interestingly, TAC and catch continued to increase, even as the biomass was falling, until 1995 when the TAC was reduced by more than two-thirds. Fishing companies experienced considerable economic hardship and claimed that the pilchard had not been depleted, but had only migrated to Angolan waters. The fishing vessels went to Angolan waters, which accounts for the above-TAC catch in 1995. TAC for hake were initially set at a low share of fishable biomass and gradually increased over the decade as the stock grew. When horse mackerel stocks began to fall, TAC and catch were reduced soon after, though not by as much as the drop in the biomass.

Monetary Accounts

The rent is shown for two different assumptions about the cost of fixed capital, the 30 per cent return which the Ministry of Fisheries believes is appropriate, and a 20 per cent return which is closer to interest rates paid by other industries, though still high (Table 4.5). The effect of the lower rate of return on rent estimates is relatively small: rent is lowered by an average of 13 per cent, which indicates that the fishing industry is not as capital-intensive as other resource-based industries like mining. This result should be treated with caution because of the shortcomings of the capital stock data. However, the

analysis for hake fishing in 1995, based on the survey of fishing companies
which includes information about the value of assets, also showed relatively
low sensitivity to the rate of return used, which suggests that the result
obtained from the national accounts data may not be that misleading.

Pilchard generated the most rent at the beginning of the decade, but was
eventually surpassed by hake. This is not surprising since Namibia already had
an established pilchard fishery prior to independence and only achieved
control over the other fisheries over the 1990s. The rent per ton for hake has
been steadily rising, reflecting both improvements in the industry and also the

*Table 4.5   Resource rent for pilchards, hake and horse mackerel, 1990–98
(in millions of Namibian dollars)*

A.   Resource rent assuming a 30% cost of fixed capital

	Pilchard	Hake	Horse mackerel	Total rent
1990	114	24	8	147
1991	61	26	26	114
1992	124	22	14	160
1993	184	48	27	259
1994	211	132	31	374
1995	184	177	31	392
1996	–4	155	36	187
1997	85	226	37	347
1998	136	601	79	816

B.   Resource rent assuming a 20% cost of fixed capital

	Pilchard	Hake	Horse mackerel	Total rent
1990	117	27	9	153
1991	65	30	30	125
1992	135	36	20	192
1993	201	68	37	306
1994	229	159	40	429
1995	201	209	39	449
1996	0	192	51	243
1997	95	261	49	406
1998	150	640	91	881

Source: Author's calculations based on data from the Central Bureau of Statistics and assumptions described in the text.

devaluation of the Namibian dollar over time, which has a major impact on earnings because most Namibian hake is sold to the lucrative European market. Pilchard has shown the greatest volatility of rent over the decade. Rent became negative in 1996 when virtually no pilchard was caught that year and the industry suffered considerable losses. Horse mackerel, though harvested in higher volumes than either of the others, generates the least rent. The unit rent for horse mackerel has been positive, but an order of magnitude lower than hake and pilchards.

The monetary accounts, showing the value of the fish stock in current prices and in constant 1998 prices (real asset values are calculated using the 1998 unit rent for each species), are given in Table 4.6 assuming a cost of fixed capital of 20 per cent. Over the past decade, there has been a remarkable 61 per cent increase in the real value of fish stocks from Namibian $5463 million to Namibian $8813 million in 1998, even though there was a decline in physical stocks of pilchard and horse mackerel over that period. This increase in value is attributable to the increase in the stock of hake as well as management and economic factors that have improved the rent-generating capacity of fish.

There are considerable differences among the fisheries with hake clearly dominating fish wealth. By 1998 hake generated real rent per ton of Namibian $2057 and had increased its share of fish wealth from 43 per cent to 73 per cent in real terms. The growing importance of hake is mirrored by the declining importance of pilchard. Pilchard rent per ton declined by 20 per cent to Namibian $1055 in 1998, and its share of fish wealth declined from 35 per cent to 17 per cent. Even though the physical volume of horse mackerel is many times larger than that of hake or pilchard, its value is relatively small. The real rent per ton generated by horse mackerel had increased in the 1990s, but in 1998 it was still only Namibian $142; its share of fish wealth declined from 22 per cent to 10 per cent in 1998.

The emergence of hake as the most valuable fish stock represents a success for government policy which targeted the development of the hake fishery, controlled almost entirely by foreigners prior to independence. This turnaround in the fishing industry also indicates how management can have a profound impact on the economic value of a fishery. This issue will be revisited in a discussion of the economic efficiency of the industry, and the potential value of fish under alternative management regimes.

Private Value Versus Social Value of Namibia's Fisheries

In calculating the resource rent and the value of fisheries, only the private costs are generally taken into account. Several factors can cause the social costs of harvesting to diverge from the private costs (see Chapter 1), and for fisheries, resource management costs are potentially significant. Wiium and

Environmental accounting in action

Table 4.6   Monetary accounts for hake, pilchards and horse mackerel in
*   Namibia, 1990–98 (millions of Namibian $)*

A.   Asset value in current prices

	Pilchard	Hake	Horse mackerel	Total rent
1990	1168	268	90	1526
1991	646	304	301	1250
1992	1348	365	204	1916
1993	2008	683	365	3056
1994	2292	1591	402	4285
1995	2011	2089	389	4489
1996	3	1918	509	2431
1997	950	2615	493	4057
1998	1500	6402	911	8813

B.   Asset value in constant 1998 prices

	Pilchard	Hake	Horse mackerel	Total rent
1990	1935	2334	1195	5463
1991	1478	2380	1268	5126
1992	1783	3709	1244	6737
1993	2522	4585	1399	8506
1994	2522	4757	1066	8345
1995	935	5527	908	7370
1996	22	5766	938	6725
1997	609	5003	882	6494
1998	1500	6402	911	8813

Notes: Values were estimated for the closing stock using the present discounted value method
assuming a 10% social discount rate and a 20% cost of fixed capital.
Constant price assets calculated using 1998 per unit rent.
Figures may not sum to total because of rounding.

Source: Author's calculations based on Table 4.1, data used to calculate Figure 4.2.

Uulenga (2001) have undertaken a study of resource management costs for the
fishing industry. They consider only the costs incurred by government, excluding support to fisheries management by foreign donors on the grounds that
whereas foreign contributions are useful they may not all be essential for fisheries management. Foreign donor contributions have been significant, but

declining, accounting for 56 per cent of government expenditures in 1996 and 25 per cent in 1999 (Wiium and Uulenga, 2001). Sufficient information is not available for calculations in other years.

Between 1994 and 1999, most of resource management costs, 86 per cent or more, was spent for research, monitoring, control and surveillance. Resource management costs have accounted for anywhere from 10 per cent to 37 per cent of resource rent earned, a not insignificant amount (Table 4.7). Clearly, it is important to account for the full social costs. Even taking into account full management costs, Namibia's fisheries earn high net rents. The second issue regarding management costs is whether fishing taxes and fees fully cover resource management costs. In many countries, fees, if applied at all, rarely cover the costs of management. In Namibia, quota fees have accounted for most of the revenue collected by government. In all years, fees have covered costs, but fees were significantly greater than costs in only three out of the six years for which there is information.

Fisheries as a Share of Namibia's National Wealth

The monetary accounts for fish provide a useful assessment of the economic impact of the changing management strategy and also an indicator of what Namibia stands to lose if the fish stock is depleted. The fisheries accounts also help to provide a more complete picture of Namibia's national wealth, which is necessary for sustainable macroeconomic management. As a share of total, real wealth, fisheries accounted for 14 per cent in 1998, up from 12 per cent in 1990, surpassing the share of minerals, which is now less than 5 per cent of national wealth. Total wealth is discussed further in Chapter 6.

4.5   POLICY IMPLICATIONS FOR FISHERIES RESOURCE MANAGEMENT

In managing a public resource like marine fisheries, government policy can be guided by either of two alternative objectives: the promotion of commercial exploitation to maximize resource rent, or the promotion of a combination of socio-economic objectives in which economic efficiency plays a more limited role. Some countries may adopt a mix of these policy objectives for different fisheries. Namibian policy has primarily adopted the first objective, commercial exploitation. Namibian policy also has socio-economic goals, notably the Namibianization of the fishing industry, as well as a more general, but somewhat vague, objective of utilizing this national resource for the broader benefit of all Namibians. Namibia seeks to achieve these socio-economic objectives within an economically efficient, commercial fishing industry. As

Table 4.7 Fisheries resource management costs and revenues received, 1994–99

A. Resource management costs incurred by government

	1994	1995	1996	1997	1998	1999
Monitoring, control, surveillance	47%	58%	65%	59%	59%	52%
Research	44%	31%	25%	31%	29%	34%
Other	9%	10%	10%	10%	12%	14%
Total	100%	100%	100%	100%	100%	100%
Total in millions of Namibian $	52.1	54.3	69.3	73.9	82.4	66.0
Resource mgmnt costs as % of rent	14%	14%	37%	21%	10%	NA

B. Taxes and fees paid by fishing industry

	1994	1995	1996	1997	1998	1999
Total in millions of Namibian $	131.8	111.1	72.0	91.0	97.3	119.6
Ratio of fees to management costs	2.53	2.05	1.04	1.23	1.18	1.81

Notes: *less than 1%
NA: not available
Resource management costs do not include contributions by foreign donors.
Taxes and fees include quota levies, by-catch fees, Sea Fisheries Fund levies, license fees and observer fund fees.
There is not enough information to calculate resource management costs prior to 1994, or to determine the cost associated with each fishery.

Source: Based on data from Wiium and Uulenga (2001) and Table 4.5 for resource rent.

the discussion in section 4.2 indicated, designing policy to achieve both objectives is difficult. In this section, the fisheries resource accounts are analysed to provide insight into the economic efficiency of the industry and the extent to which the groups targeted by policy are actually benefiting from exploitation of fisheries.

Resource Rent and Economic Efficiency

The Namibian fishing industry generates substantial amounts of resource rent. Recognizing that marine fisheries are a public resource from which the public should benefit, the government established a system of quota levies in order to recover this rent (see section 4.2). The quota levies go into government's general revenue fund where they can potentially be used to support economic development that would benefit all citizens. (There is a separate, much smaller fee levied on major commercial species on a volumetric basis, the Sea Fisheries Fund, which is earmarked to pay for research necessary for the proper management of fisheries.) The general economic importance of rent recovery was described in Chapter 1. Full recovery of fisheries resource rent is important for several reasons (see Lange and Motinga, 1997 for further discussion of these issues):

1. Recovery of rent contributes to the sustainable management of fisheries by increasing the cost of fishing, which lowers the economic incentives for overfishing and depletion of the resource.
2. Set at the appropriate level, levies create incentives for the most economically efficient (most profitable) level of fishing, based on both biological and economic criteria.
3. Recovery of rent promotes equity by paying the owner of this resource, the state, for utilization of its asset. These revenues can then be used for development that benefits all Namibians, not just the small minority involved in the fishing industry.

Although large rents are generated by fisheries, relatively little rent is being collected by government (Figure 4.5, Table 4.8). In the early 1990s when quota levies were first established, more than 50 per cent of the rent was recovered by government. This share is small in comparison to the share of rent recovered from mining (see Chapter 2), but the poor state of the fisheries made fishing appear risky, as discussed in section 4.3, and the newly independent government of Namibia wanted to encourage foreign investment so it allowed a substantial portion of the rent to accrue to the private sector. The share has since dropped precipitously to 26 per cent in 1997 and only 11 per cent in 1998. By 1998, over N$700 million in rent went to the private sector.

millions of Namibian $

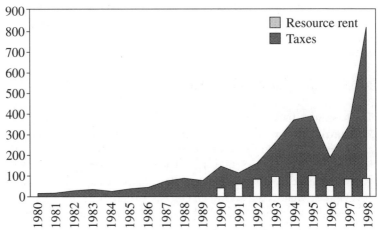

Source: Rent obtained from Table 4.5; taxes obtained from MFMR (1995, 1996a, 1996b, 2000).

Figure 4.5 Resource rent and taxes from fisheries in Namibia, 1980–98

The percentage of rent accruing to the private sector has been highest in the pilchard fishery and lowest for horse mackerel. In some years, rent was not sufficient to pay for the taxes and the percentage accruing to the private sector was negative (hake in 1993 and pilchards in 1996).

There are several reasons for the low recovery of rent in Namibia. One problem is the failure to index the quota levies to inflation and the depreciation of the Namibian dollar. The quota levies were increased by 10 per cent in 1999, but this is a small adjustment in relation to inflation during the 1990s. All but a small portion of fish is exported and revenues are paid in international currencies, so most rent is earned in foreign currency. The Namibian dollar has fallen more than 50 per cent against major international currencies over the decade, so, in effect, the value of the tax in Namibian dollars, relative to the rent in foreign currency, has fallen by an equivalent amount. This is a common problem faced by many countries that may find it politically difficult to adjust taxes for inflation unless an inflation component is built into the initial tax law.

An additional source of declining rent recovery stems from the subsidies provided to encourage Namibianization of the industry. There has been a gradual transition of company ownership from foreign ownership to those qualifying as Namibian (Manning, 1998; 2000) in response to government policies. With quota levy subsidies of as much as 50 per cent, there is a strong incentive for foreign companies to qualify. For example, on a hake quota of 1500 tons, the median allocation for frozen hake in 1997, a company would save

Table 4.8   Resource rent accruing to the private sector, 1990–98

A.   Total taxes paid
(millions of Namibian $)

	Pilchard	Hake	Horse mackerel	Total
1990	NA	NA	NA	44
1991	NA	NA	NA	64
1992	NA	NA	NA	87
1993	11	60	25	96
1994	15	72	28	115
1995	6	67	25	98
1996	1	38	13	53
1997	5	58	16	79
1998	9	57	19	85

B.   Percentage of rent accruing to the private sector

	Pilchard	Hake	Horse mackerel	Total
1990	NA	NA	NA	70
1991	NA	NA	NA	44
1992	NA	NA	NA	46
1993	94	–	8	62
1994	93	45	10	68
1995	97	62	19	74
1996	–	76	63	68
1997	94	74	58	74
1998	93	91	76	89

Notes: '–' indicates negative rent for that year
Taxes are not broken down by species for 1990–92
Taxes include quota levies and Sea Fisheries Fund Levies, but not other fees.
NA: not available.

Source: Rent obtained from Table 4.5; taxes obtained from MFMR (1995, 1996a, 1996b, 2000).

Namibian $330 000 in quota fees by qualifying as Namibian based, and Namibian $660 000 by qualifying as Namibian owned. This could be viewed as a positive development in Namibianizing the industry. However, Manning has documented how foreign companies could qualify as Namibian simply by having a Namibian address, or a partner whose only contribution is his or her Namibian citizenship in order to take advantage of the quota subsidy. Under such circumstances, much of the economic benefit would accrue to foreign companies rather than government's intended beneficiaries, Namibian companies.

It has been argued that low rent recovery is necessary to promote the development of a Namibian industry because, although the average industry profits are high, the Namibian newcomers do not fare as well as the established companies, a topic discussed in the next part of this section.

Because taxes do not recover much of the resource rent, the system of quota levies does not contribute in a strong way to sustainability, economic efficiency, or equity in the fishing industry. However, despite a low rate of resource rent recovery, Namibia is doing extremely well by international standards. As noted in the introduction, global fishing is marked by inefficient production and large subsidies. By contrast, Namibia's fishing industry operates at a profit, receives no subsidies and contributes to government revenues. The Norwegian fishing industry, for example, operated at a loss, earning negative rents until 1995 (Figure 4.6). It survived only because of large subsidies provided by the Norwegian government, although this policy has changed in more recent years with the expansion of aquaculture (Milazzo, 1998). The Philippines, another country with fisheries accounts, estimates that its fishing industry operates at a profit and generates positive economic rent, but the rate of rent recovery is quite low, averaging only 11 per cent over the period 1988 to 1994 (Lange, 2000). Iceland's fisheries, a major economic activity, appear to be operating profitably but do not pay any taxes on rent that is earned (Danielsson, 2000).

Millions of NOK

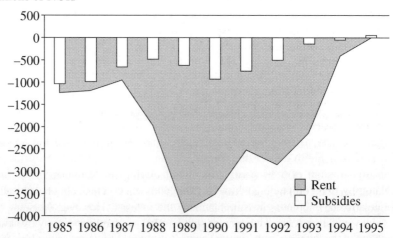

Source: Lindholt (2000), Sorenson and Hass (1998), Statistics Norway (2000).

Figure 4.6   Resource rent and subsidies to fisheries in Norway, 1985–95

Economic efficiency: potential vs. actual value of assets

Resource management can be evaluated in terms of economic efficiency to determine if alternative policies might increase the income generated and, hence, the economic value of a resource. Inefficiency can occur because of overcapacity, either vessel capacity or fish processing factory capacity. Inefficiency can also occur when there are economies of scale and quota allocations are too small, or when quotas are spread out over inexperienced companies instead of creating incentives so that only the most efficient companies obtain quotas.

The analysis of the Namibian Survey of Fishing Companies indicates substantial variation in the rents earned by company. Despite the problems with the survey data described in section 4.3, there were sufficient data for a reasonable analysis of the hake fishery. Using data from the first survey in 1994, Arnason (1996) found that companies with larger quota allocations tended to generate higher rents per ton of hake than the smaller, mostly newcomer, companies. His analysis suggested that there was overcapacity and inefficiency in the industry.

Analysis of the more complete 1995 survey by Ljung and Sternhufvud (1998) confirmed Arnason's observation. In 1995 survey returns were obtained for 18 companies, comprising 85 per cent of the hake catch. The average rent was estimated at Namibian $785 per ton, but varied enormously among the 18 companies. The data suggest large differences in efficiency: some companies reported negative rents, while others reported rents as high as Namibian $1815 per ton. The rent generated by the three top-earning companies was more than double the industry average rent. The above-average rent-earners were mainly large, experienced operators with good international connections while the lower earners were mainly the smaller Namibian newcomers to the industry. It is also the case that foreign companies may receive substantial direct and indirect subsidies from their home governments, which would reduce their costs and increase the apparent rent.

A study of the South African hake fishery in 1996 by Strydom and Nieuwoudt (1998) supports the evidence of inefficiency in the Namibian hake fishery. Since the hake fisheries are fairly similar in South Africa and Namibia, it is reasonable to expect that difference in rent would be largely attributable to the structure of the industry. The South African hake industry was dominated by two companies, which together controlled nearly 80 per cent of the quota in 1996, creating significant economies of scale, greater economic efficiency and high rents. The average quota rental price for hake in South Africa, where it is legal to rent quotas, was Namibian $1840 per ton (the South African and Namibian currencies exchange on a one-for-one basis). This is much higher than the average rent earned in the Namibian hake industry and is similar to the rent earned by the top Namibian earners.

In an analysis of TAC, fishing capacity and fish processing capacity in the mid-1990s, Manning (1998, 2000) found significant overcapacity in the hake fishery. Part of the reason for excess capacity may be an expectation of high stock levels in future. Another reason for overcapacity lies in the criteria for awarding rights of exploitation. Evidence of serious intent to establish a Namibian industry is one of the criteria and one of the acceptable forms of evidence has been purchase of a vessel or establishment of an onshore fish processing plant. Thus, Namibia's policy may have inadvertently encouraged overinvestment.

The above evidence suggests that Namibia's fisheries could generate even higher average rents under a policy regime that consolidated fishing activities among fewer, more efficient companies. However, although Namibia's fisheries policy seeks to create an efficient fishing industry, employment creation is an important national objective. The national unemployment rate in 1997 was 20–30 per cent, depending on how broadly unemployment is defined (Ministry of Labour, 2001) and greater efficiency in fisheries would have a negative impact on employment, although it is uncertain how great that impact would be.

Norway provides an example of fisheries policy guided by socio-economic objectives, not efficiency. It is an extreme case of economic inefficiency where the economic value of many of its fish stocks was zero. Norway sought to ensure employment in fishing communities as a component of its strategy to promote equitable regional development. For more than 30 years, the government provided subsidies to raise fishermen's incomes to the average level of industrial workers (Milazzo, 1998). Analysis of micro-survey data of Norway's herring fishery found significant differences in rent-earning capacity between large and small fishing vessels, as well as between aquaculture and capture fishing. Generally, the large-scale operations were more efficient and generated positive resource rent, while the small vessels did not. Assuming that most of the fishery could be managed in such an efficient manner, one study of Norway's herring fishery estimated the potential resource rent of one billion Norwegian kroner (study by Flam reported in Sorensen and Hass, 1998). Norway might achieve a higher economic value for fisheries under more economically efficient management, but might sacrifice its socio-economic objectives in doing so.

Another study of the economic impact of alternative fisheries management strategy was carried out by Hutton and Sumaila (2000) for the South African hake fishery. This study used an age-structured bioeconomic model to analyse the economic value of the hake fishery under different combinations of quota allocations to demersal trawling and longlining – two different fishing methods that yield fish with very different market prices, and also have different effects on the fish stock. The results indicated that rent is maximized under the current TAC allocations to each sector, implying that the current government management strategy achieves optimal utilization of resources.

While it is not possible to quantify potential improvements in the economic efficiency of the Namibian fishing industry at this time, these observations raise the likelihood that the potential value of fisheries is much greater than the actual value under current management. It is certainly legitimate for government to follow a policy that promotes greater social equity or employment at the expense of economic efficiency, but it is important that government make this decision fully informed about the economic costs of such a trade-off.

Resource rent and equity: who benefits from Namibian fisheries
There are a number of ways in which different groups may benefit from a successful fishing industry: private companies benefit from profits and resource rent, workers benefit from relatively well-paying employment and the public benefits from resource rent collected by government which can be used to support broad-based national development. Most of the resource rent accrues to fishing companies where it primarily benefits private companies, and to a lesser degree, the small share of workers employed in the industry. It can be argued that it does not matter whether rent accrues to the government or to the private sector as long as it is reinvested to promote further economic growth and employment creation. Some would even argue that it is better for the rent to accrue to the private sector because the private sector would make more productive use of income than the public sector.

In terms of Namibia's objective of utilizing fish resources for the benefit of all Namibians, there are two problems with policy in the 1990s under the Sea Fisheries Act 1992. First, Manning (1998 and 2000) raises the disturbing possibility that much of the uncollected rent has accrued to foreign partners of fishing companies rather than to their Namibian partners. In this case, there is relatively little benefit by any Namibians. The second problem is that only a small number of Namibians have benefited from fisheries exploitation. Because the fisheries are exploited on a commercial basis, relatively few companies are involved, between 150 and 200. Only the Namibian elite who are well educated and have demonstrated business expertise can qualify for rights of exploitation. This excludes the majority of Namibians.

In the past year, government has recognized the first problem and considered a number of ways to ensure that more of the rent accrued to Namibians. Government chose to address the problem by requiring that all foreign companies have a Namibian partner. This will increase the bargaining power of Namibians in joint ventures and hopefully enable them to extract a greater share of the rent from foreign partners in return for providing the quota. The new policy, the Marine Resources Act of 2000, while transferring more of the rent from foreign companies to Namibian companies, does not address the second problem; benefits from fishing will still accrue to a small minority, not the majority of Namibians.

In revising fisheries policy, a number of alternative policies were considered including substantially raising quota levies in order to recover more of the rent, instituting a quota auction, or a system of tradable quotas. Any of these three policies would have resulted in government recovering a greater share of the resource rent. In this way, the benefits from exploiting a national resource could have been used to support national development, such as education, transportation and other public infrastructure, which might have provided greater benefits for the majority of Namibians.

4.6   CONCLUSIONS

Summary

In many respects, Namibia's effort to transform its fishing industry over the past ten years has been a tremendous success: the economic value of fishing has increased; Namibian participation in the industry has increased; the fishing industry operates without subsidies, covers many of the costs of fisheries management, and generates substantial amounts of rent of which at least some of it is returned to government. Few other nations could make such claims. In other respects, however, Namibian has yet to achieve the objectives it has set for itself. Its success in halting depletion of fisheries looked positive at the beginning of the 1990s but is now less certain. Namibia's economic benefits from fishing have increased enormously but these benefits have been concentrated among a small elite; Namibia's success in utilizing this resource for the benefit of the majority of Namibians, admittedly a much more complex task, has been limited.

Fisheries managers now face two major economic challenges:

- the industry does not appear to be operating as efficiently as possible because of excess capacity, exacerbated by unpredictable fluctuations in the fish stock;
- a small group of Namibians and foreign companies remain the major beneficiaries of uncollected rent rather than government's intended target – the majority of previously excluded Namibians.

Namibia's fisheries can potentially generate considerable rent but only about 11 per cent of this rent is now collected by government. Part of the uncollected rent accrues to the private sector, and part may be used to pay the high costs of over-capacity. In the specific years under review in this chapter, excess capacity may have resulted, in part, from unexpected declines in the fish stocks. Excess capacity has resulted in part from government's goal of creating a Namibian industry and the policies used to bring that about.

Government policy makers must balance two sometimes conflicting objectives: how to promote a Namibian-based fishing industry while at the same time promoting economic efficiency which will generate the highest economic returns. In an economy like Namibia's, with high unemployment, it is worth sacrificing some economic gains for greater employment. However, the preliminary analysis presented here indicates that the trade-off between efficiency and the creation of a Namibian industry is not small and so should be weighed carefully, especially with an eye for who actually receives the benefits.

Policy recommendations

The already significant contribution of the fishing industry to the Namibian economy could be improved in two ways: (1) greater attention to the economic implications of fisheries policy, especially the trade-offs between economic gains and other policy objectives of government and (2) greater support of the Namibian industry, in part through closer monitoring of the relationship between Namibian companies and their foreign partners. Some of the specific steps in that direction that could be taken relatively easily include:

- regular analysis of resource rent and capacity utilization by fishery and by company;
- review of the system of rights allocation and quota fees.

Many of the observations about the fishing industry in this chapter are based on information that covers only a few years, or sometimes a single year. While highly suggestive, the assessment cannot be considered conclusive because a longer time series of information is required for accurate assessment of a dynamic fishery like Namibia's, in which the fish stocks fluctuate considerably and unpredictably from one year to the next.

The annual survey of fishing companies is critical to improving the economic assessment of fisheries because of the very detailed information about the state of each fishery it provides. It has only recently overcome the legal challenges and achieved nearly 100 per cent compliance. The survey can provide the data for a dynamic economic analysis of specific fisheries as well as specific groups of companies, such as the newcomer companies, but needs to undergo a rigorous quality review in order to be useful for policy decisions.

The hake quota rental prices in South Africa show that it is possible to generate higher rents than appear to be generated in Namibia at present. Given the low recovery of resource rents from the fishing industry, it might appear that quota levies should simply be raised. However, this could severely damage the small newcomers, the core of the Namibian industry. There are a number of alternative management regimes. For example, ITQ (individual transferable quotas) might solve some of the problems such as overcapacity and the lack of collateral for obtaining finance from conventional sources, though this system also has its problems. A review of options, based on a thorough understanding of the economics of each fishery and each category of company (for example, newcomer versus foreign) would be extremely useful.

Fisheries policy creates incentives for Namibianization of the fishing industry, but does not provide newcomer Namibian companies with sufficient financial, technical and other resources to successfully operate in a truly independent fashion. The need for foreign investment and technology transfer is unavoidable during the process of creating a truly Namibian industry and foreign investment should be encouraged. It is not clear that the new policy, requiring foreign companies to enter into joint ventures, is the best approach. It may well simply create 'paper quotas' with Namibian partners providing nothing but the quota, and foreign companies providing everything else. Concern about this and its effect on investment was raised in a recent article about the industry:

> one caveat is that further foreign investment in onshore white fish processing plants, the main stimulus of industrial growth in recent years, may be adversely affected by government's insistence that the granting of new long term exploitation rights is conditional on the formation of joint ventures with new Namibian entrants, irrespective of their technical and financial capacities. (Steenkamp, 2001, p. 1)

As an alternative government might assist Namibian companies directly to gain expertise in fishing, collecting more of the resource rent in order to fund such support. In some sectors, government has provided extensive financial and technical assistance. For example, farmers have received technical assistance through agricultural extension offices and concessionary financing from the AgriBank. During periods of drought, government has stepped in to assist farmers in various ways. The Namibian fishing industry has not received similar support from the government. In the past there was some discussion of establishing a Fisheries Bank, which would accept the non-transferrable quota as collateral and provide funds at relatively low rates (Namibia Foundation, 1998, p. 25). The government's resistance to subsidizing the industry should be applauded. However, it is difficult for unsubsidized Namibian companies to compete with heavily subsidized foreign companies. A more flexible quota system might provide some measure of support (for example, the ITQ system mentioned earlier can act as collateral for loans). The Ministry of Fisheries has done some internal studies on these issues, but the results have not been publicly released. The process of setting policy for fisheries is not as transparent as it is for other resources in Namibia.

All policy decisions need to be taken in the context of two other factors – how fisheries policy affects the welfare of the majority of Namibians who do not participate in the fishing industry, and the need for regional fisheries management. Many of the poorest Namibians do not benefit directly from the fisheries policy because successful participation in the industry requires a high degree of literacy and business expertise, though they may benefit to the limited extent that Namibian jobs are created in the fishing and fish processing industry. If the allocation of quota results in the privileged in society gaining a disproportionate share of the benefit rather than those most affected by past discriminatory practices, then this may not be an optimal policy, even though a Namibian industry may be created. It might be better for government to recover a greater share of the resource rent which could be used to support development that more directly benefits previously excluded Namibians. The higher quota fees that have been proposed partially address this concern, but still leave most of the rent in the hands of a very small private sector.

Many of Namibia's fish stocks are migratory, sharing the waters of Angola and South Africa as well as the high seas, which are open to many countries, and moving in response to unpredictable environmental changes. Clearly, national fisheries policies cannot be set in isolation from a regional policy. Namibia has taken major steps to address this issue by initiating several regional fisheries organizations and promoting regional co-operation.

REFERENCES

Arnason, R. (1992), 'Theoretical and practical fisheries management', World Bank Discussion Paper No. 217, Washington, DC.

Arnason, R. (1996), 'On the economic state of the demersal and midwater fishing sectors', report to the Ministry of Fisheries and Marine Resources, Namibia.

CBS *see* Central Bureau of Statistics.

Central Bureau of Statistics (1999a), *National Accounts, 1980–1998*, Government Printer, Windhoek, Namibia.

Central Bureau of Statistics (1999b), unpublished data on capital stock by industry.

Central Bureau of Statistics (1999c), unpublished data on fisheries accounts.

Central Bureau of Statistics (2000), *National Accounts 1993–1999*, Government Printer, Windhoek, Namibia.

Danielsson, A. (2000), 'Integrated environmental and economic accounting for commercial exploitation of wild fish stocks', paper presented at the Tenth Biennial IIFET Conference, Corvallis, OR, USA, 10–14 July.

Department of Commerce, Census Bureau (2001), 'Total mid-year population for the world, 1950–2050', http://www.census.gov/ipc/www/worldpop.html.

Eurostat (2000) *Valuation of European Forests – Results of IEEAF Test Applications*, Eurostat, Luxembourg.

FAO *see* Food and Agriculture Organization.

Food and Agriculture Organization (1993), *The State of Food and Agriculture 1992*, FAO, Rome.

Food and Agriculture Organization (1997), 'Review of the state of the world fishery resources, marine fisheries', Fisheries Circular No. 920 FIRM/C920. FAO, Rome.

Food and Agriculture Organization (2001a), Fish catch database, FAOSTAT Fisheries Data, http://apps.fao.org/default.htm.

Food and Agriculture Organization (2001b), *The State of Food and Agriculture 2000*, FAO, Rome.

Food and Agriculture Organization and United Nations (forthcoming), *System of Integrated Environmental and Economic Accounts for Fisheries*, FAO and United Nations, New York.

Government of Namibia (1990), *Constitution of the Republic of Namibia*, Government Printer, Windhoek, Namibia.

Government of Namibia (1991), 'Towards responsible development of the fisheries sector', White Paper.

Hannesson, R. (1993), *Bioeconomic Analysis of Fisheries*, New York, published for the FAO by Halstead Press.

Hass, J. and K. Sorenson (1998), *Norwegian Economic and Environmental Accounts*, Final report to Eurostat, Statistics Norway, Oslo.

Hutton, T. and R. Sumaila (2000), 'Accounting for the value of hake in South Africa', Discussion Paper of the Resource Accounting Network of East and Southern Africa, University of Pretoria, South Africa.

Kaitala, V. and G.G. Munro (1993), 'The management of high seas fisheries', *Marine Resource Economics*, Vol. 8, pp. 313–29.

Kaufman, B. and G. Green (1997), 'Cost-recovery as a fisheries management tool', *Marine Resource Economics*, 12 (1), (Spring): 57–66.

Kirschner, C., A. Sakko and J. Barnes (1999), 'An economic value of the Namibian recreational shore angling fishery', *South African Journal of Marine Science*, 22: 17–25.

Lange, G. (2000), 'Policy uses of the Philippine System of Integrated Environmental and Economic Accounts', report to the Philippines National Statistical Coordination Board, Manila.

Lange, G. and D.J. Motinga (1997), 'The contribution of resource rents from minerals and fisheries to sustainable economic development in Namibia', Research Discussion Paper No. 19, Directorate of Environmental Affairs, Ministry of Environment and Tourism, Windhoek, Namibia.

Lindholt, L. (2000), 'On natural resource rent and the wealth of a nation, a study based on national accounts in Norway 1930–95', Discussion Paper No. 281, Statistics Norway Research Department, Oslo.

Ljung, E. and C. Sternhufvud (1998), 'Assessment of the resource rent in the Namibian fisheries, the case of hake', unpublished Master's thesis, University of Gothenburg, Sweden.

Manning, P.R. (1998), 'Managing Namibia's marine fisheries: optimal resource use and national development objectives', PhD thesis, London School of Economics and Political Science, University of London.

Manning, P.R. (2000), 'Review of the distributive aspects of Namibia's fisheries policy', NEPRU Research Report, NEPRU, Windhoek, Namibia.

Marine Research and Information Centre, MFMR (2001), Unpublished database of fish stocks, catch and TAC, Swakopmund, Namibia.

MFMR *see* Ministry of Fisheries and Marine Resources.

Milazzo, M. (1998), 'Subsidies in world fisheries', World Bank Technical Paper No. 406, Washington, DC, World Bank.

Ministry of Fisheries and Marine Resources (1993), 'Granting of long term fishing rights to 2004', Press Release, 25 October 1993, Government of Namibia.

Ministry of Fisheries and Marine Resources (1995), *Report of the Activities and State of the Fisheries Sector 1993 and 1994*, Windhoek, Namibia.

Ministry of Fisheries and Marine Resources (1996a), *Fishery Statistics 1996*, Windhoek, Namibia.

Ministry of Fisheries and Marine Resources (1996b), *State of the Marine Environment and the Commercially Utilised Living Marine Resources*, Windhoek, Namibia.

Ministry of Fisheries and Marine Resources (1997), *Fishery Statistics 1997*, Windhoek, Namibia.

Ministry of Fisheries and Marine Resources (1999), Unpublished database of fish quota allocations by company.

Ministry of Fisheries and Marine Resources (2000), *Report of the Activities and State of the Fisheries Sector 1997 and 1998*, Windhoek, Namibia.

Ministry of Fisheries and Marine Resources/Central Statistics Office (no date), Basemod, national fisheries database, Ministry of Fisheries and Marine Resources and the Central Statistical Office, Government of Namibia.

Ministry of Labour (2001), *The Namibia Labour Force Survey 1997*, Windhoek, Namibia.

Moorsom, R. (1984), *Exploiting the Sea*, London, Catholic Institute for International Relations.

Namibia Foundation (ed.) (1998), *Namibia Brief*, No. 20, January, The Namibia Foundation, Windhoek, Namibia.

National Statistical Coordination Board (1998), *Environmental and Natural Resources Accounting*, vol. 1 *Philippine Asset Accounts*, and vol. 2, *Environmental Degradation due to Economic Activities and Environmental Protection Services*, NSCB, Manila, Philippines.

National Statistical Coordination Board (1999), Unpublished data about the Philippine asset accounts, taxes on resources, and environmental degradation, NSCB, Manila.

O'Toole, M.J. (1998), 'Marine environmental threats in Namibia', Research Discussion Paper No. 23, Directorate of Environmental Affairs, Ministry of Environment and Tourism, Windhoek, Namibia.

Sorensen, K. and J. Hass (1998), *Norwegian Economic and Environmental Accounts*, Statistics Norway, Oslo.

Statistics Norway (2000), *Natural Resources and the Environment 2000*, Statistical Analyses 34, Statistics Norway, Oslo.

Steenkamp, P. (2001), 'Whitefish processing growth provides stimulus at coast', *Namibian Economist*, 17–23 August, 14 (32): 1.

Strydom, M.B. and W.L. Nieuwoudt (1998), 'An economic analysis of restructuring the South African hake quota market', *Agrekon*, 37(3): 281–95.

Stuttaford, M. (1996), *Fishing Industry Handbook, South Africa, Namibia and Mozambique*, Stellenbosch, South Africa, Marine Information CC.

United Nations, Commission of the European Communities, International Monetary Fund, Organization for Economic Cooperation and Development, and World Bank (1993), *System of National Accounts*, New York

United Nations (2001), *Integrated Environmental and Economic Accounting 2000*, Draft, available through the UN website, www.un.org.

United States Census Bureau (2001), 'World population information', available through website www.census.gov.ipc.www.

Uulenga, A. (1999), 'The Namibia fisheries accounts', presentation at the United Nations Workshop on Environmental Accounting, 7–16 June, New York.

Wiium, V. and A. Uulenga (2001), 'Fisheries management costs and rent extraction, the case of Namibia', unpublished paper for Ministry of Fisheries and Marine Resources.

Zeybrandt, F. and J. Barnes (forthcoming), 'Economic characteristics of demand in Namibia's recreational marine shore fishery', *South African Journal of Marine Science*, 29pp.

5. Water accounts: an economic perspective on managing water scarcity

Glenn-Marie Lange, Rashid Hassan and Moortaza Jiwanji

5.1 INTRODUCTION

Global water demand has grown rapidly over the past few decades due to population growth as well as increasing per capita water demand. Between 1940 and 1990, withdrawals of fresh water increased more than fourfold, despite improvements in water efficiency (WRI, 1996). With the supply of fresh water limited by the dynamics of the hydrological cycle, in which seawater evaporates and falls over land as precipitation, per capita water availability has been declining, resulting in growing water scarcity in many parts of the world. Increased contamination by pollution has further reduced the supply of fresh water and increased the cost of treatment of available supplies. In much of North Africa and the Middle East, water use is more than 50 per cent of annual renewable supply of fresh water (Gleick, 1998). Groundwater depletion is increasing on all continents and many countries rely increasingly on international water sources, creating a potential for conflict over water in the future. In addition, the scientific community expects climate change to have a major impact on the hydrological cycle, in ways that cannot be predicted at this time.

Access to safe drinking water in much of the developing world has improved over the past 20 years and by 1994 nearly three-quarters of this population had drinking water. However, over one billion people still lack safe drinking water, many of them in Africa, where there has been no improvement over time: the share of the population with access to safe drinking water has remained constant at 46 per cent since 1980 (Figure 5.1). Within Africa, of course, there is tremendous variation, and the three countries featured in this book have done much better than the average for the continent. In 1970, before its diamond wealth was developed, only 29 per cent of Botswana's population had safe drinking water, mostly in urban areas. By 1990, the share had

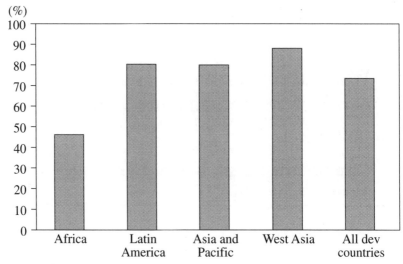

Source: Based on Gleick (1998), Table 7.

Figure 5.1   Percentage of population in developing countries with access to safe drinking water, 1994

increased to 91 per cent, well above the average for developing countries. Historical figures are not available for Namibia and South Africa, but by 1994 57 per cent and 70 per cent of the population, respectively, had access to safe drinking water (Gleick, 1998, Table 5).

Water is often cited as one of the major constraints to development in Namibia, Botswana and South Africa. Of the three countries, Namibia is sub-Saharan Africa's driest country; roughly 80 per cent of its 842 000 km^2 consists of desert, arid and semi-arid land (Brown, 1994; Pallett, 1997). Rainfall is quite low, ranging from less than 25 mm along the western coast to more than 700mm a year in the north-east with a long-term average of about 250 mm per year (Pallett, 1997), less than the minimum amount considered necessary for dryland farming (400 mm a year). Rainfall is not only low but extremely variable and droughts are a common occurrence (Figure 5.2). In addition, Namibia's high temperatures result in high rates of evaporation of rainfall; it is estimated that only 1 per cent of annual rainfall contributes to groundwater recharge and only 2 per cent is retained in reservoirs (DWA, 1991). Botswana has a very similar climate with a somewhat higher average rainfall, 400 mm per year (Pallett, 1997). South Africa is a much larger country with a more varied climate, but its average annual rainfall is still only 500 mm and it is projected to achieve the status of acute water stress in the near future, a situation where

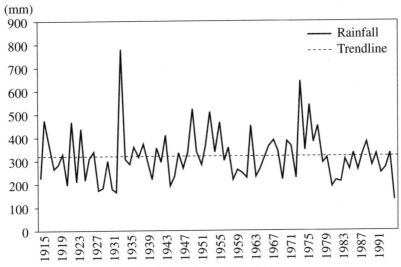

Source: unpublished data from the Weather Bureau of Namibia.

Figure 5.2   Rainfall in Namibia, 1914–94

per capita annual renewable water resources fall below 1000 cubic metres (WRI, 1996).

Water use has grown rapidly over the last 25 years in southern Africa as a result of population and economic growth, increasing pressure on this scarce resource. Water scarcity has international repercussions because every country in southern Africa relies to varying degrees on shared international rivers. Increasing water scarcity and mounting water supply costs require available resources to be used sustainably, equitably and efficiently. In the past, water management authorities approached water scarcity almost exclusively as a supply problem to be solved by feats of engineering. Very little attention was paid to the economic aspects of water use and to managing the demand for water through economic incentives for water conservation. The situation was further exacerbated in South Africa and Namibia by issues of equity, because the apartheid system resulted in unequal development of and access to water resources.

The water accounts presented here for Botswana, Namibia and South Africa provide a unique perspective on the economics of water supply and use, which enable policy makers to monitor not only the physical, but also the economic implications of water supply and water allocation. The economic analysis enables policy makers to make a more informed choice regarding the efficient allocation of water to different economic activities. In addition, the water flow accounts can be combined with economic models to explore the impacts of alternative water policies, such as the impact on water demand of price increases, or the introduction of water conservation technologies. This chapter is based on several major reports: for Botswana, Lange et al. (2001); for Namibia, Lange (1998) and 2002); for South Africa, CSIR (2001). Each of these reports used a range of primary and secondary data, much of which has never been formally published. For a detailed discussion of methodologies, data sources and results, these reports should be consulted.

While previous chapters focused on the asset accounts for resources, this chapter presents the flow accounts because there are insufficient data at this time for water asset accounts. The chapter is organized as follows. The next section provides a brief overview of water policy in each country. Section 5.3 reviews the methodology and major data sources used in the construction of flow accounts. Key aspects of the water accounts are summarized in section 5.4, with a comparative analysis of the three countries. The final section comments on the policy implications of the analysis.

5.2 WATER POLICY IN BOTSWANA, NAMIBIA AND SOUTH AFRICA

In each country, different water institutions, policies and legal rights have been established through a series of laws. Each country has been or is planning to revise water policy, with a new emphasis on economic aspects of water management in supply, allocation and pricing policy. There is no single, central authority responsible for all aspects of water in any of the three countries. Each country has a Department of Water Affairs, but responsibility for management is partly dispersed among other agencies as well. Similarly, there is no central institution responsible for all water supply; rather, a number of different institutions provide water in each country. Some of these institutions rely on relatively large-scale, technologically sophisticated infrastructure for collection and long-distance water distribution networks, while others rely mostly on local, small-scale infrastructure such as local boreholes and small dams. The former generally introduce formal systems of water metering and serve urban areas and the large mining, industrial and commercial activities, whereas the latter generally serve the needs of the rural population and may not keep detailed records about water use.

In each country, self-providers account for a large share of water supply and use. Water authorities have often focused on the formal institutions that provide water to other users, leaving the self-providers relatively lightly monitored and regulated. Consequently, a large share of water use may occur outside the formal management structure and outside the framework of water policy.

In most instances, pricing has not reflected the full financial costs of providing water. The new water pricing policies in Namibia and South Africa call not only for full financial costs (operating plus capital), but full social costs, which include financial costs plus any resource rent generated by water, environmental costs and a scarcity charge. Botswana has partly implemented full-cost pricing and is also gradually moving in that direction.

Botswana

Botswana relies mainly on groundwater and seasonal water collected in a few major dams. Perennial rivers run along part of its north and eastern borders. The major perennial water supply is the Okavango Delta, a unique ecosystem and vast water source. Due to its importance as a major tourist attraction and its designation as a World Heritage Site, Botswana has been deterred from tapping the Okavango Delta as a major water source by international objections to the potential ecological harm it would cause. Although Botswana's total freshwater resources appear vast, the resources available for use are much more limited because of this large ecological requirement.

At independence in 1966, the population of Botswana was very small, predominantly rural and agricultural, and there was little infrastructure of any sort. Most people relied on boreholes or small-scale local dams for water. The rapid growth of the economy after the discovery of diamonds brought a commitment by government to provide basic services, including water supply, to all its population, urban and rural, regardless of cost. Botswana now supplies safe drinking water to over 90 per cent of the population, on par with developed countries.

Botswana's Water Act of 1968 establishes basic policy; a number of other related acts cover specific aspects of water use and supply. All water belongs to the state, which assigns use rights. The Master Water Plan of Botswana (Snowy Mountain Engineering Corporation, 1991) was the basic planning document for Botswana and is about to be updated. A comprehensive Water Act is currently under review but does not strongly reflect the importance of the economics of water. The major water supply institutions in Botswana include:

- Water Utilities Corporation (WUC), a parastatal which provides water to six urban areas mostly from large dams and groundwater.
- Department of Water Affairs (DWA) in the Ministry of Mines Energy and Water Affairs, which provides water to 17 major villages mostly from groundwater but also from rivers along the borders.
- District councils (DC) in the Ministry of Local Government which provide water to more than 200 small villages, mostly from boreholes.

- Users who provide their own water independent of the other three institutions, mainly for mining, livestock, irrigation and wildlife.

As in many countries, Botswana has emphasized engineering solutions to water supply problems, and economics has not played a major role in water policy. WUC, the parastatal, operates on a commercial basis and sets tariffs for full financial cost recovery with a stepped, volumetric tariff and extensive cross-subsidies by type of user. Standpipe water is paid for by the government and provided free to the end-user, although some experiments with pricing are being conducted. Tariffs set by DWA and district councils are heavily subsidized; users with private connections pay for water, but tariffs are set below operations and maintenance costs. Recently DWA has adopted a policy to gradually implement recovery of operations costs, but not full financial costs, let alone full economic costs.

Namibia

Like Botswana, Namibia also relies heavily on groundwater. It has built a number of large dams to collect seasonal water and its only perennial rivers form its northern and southern borders. Until recently, water management was based on the Water Act of 1956, which was written before Namibia achieved independence from South Africa. At that time, water policy was designed to serve the minority of the population involved in commercial farming, mining and the major urban centres; relatively few resources were directed toward the majority of Namibia's rural population. Access to safe drinking water is still considerably lower than in Botswana, even ten years after independence.

In the past, water policy emphasized measures to increase supply as a means to cope with water scarcity, and pricing by the bulk water supplier had little relationship to the cost of providing water. Full financial abstraction costs are paid by self-providers, which include some of the mines and virtually all commercial livestock farmers, although farmers often received subsidies to construct boreholes in the past. As in Botswana, water, in principle, belongs to the state, and is not associated with landownership. However, in some areas property rights have been uncertain or unclear, or government management has been very limited so that water was, in effect, an open-access resource. This has resulted in declining water tables in some major aquifers.

The major institutions responsible for water supply include:

- Namwater, a parastatal, formerly a division of the Ministry of Agriculture, Water and Rural Development (MAWRD), is responsible for bulk water supply. It directly supplies some major end-users such as mines and irrigation schemes, but also supplies municipalities, which then manage local distribution to end-users.

- Rural Water Supply, a division of MARWD which supplies water to rural communities, mainly from local boreholes.
- Users who mainly provide their own water independent of the other two institutions, mainly for mining, livestock and irrigation.

Namibia's water policy has been reoriented since independence, first with the Water and Sanitation Policy (DWA, 1993) and now with a recently drafted, revised Water Act (MAWRD, 2000). The new National Water Policy emphasizes the need to recognize the economic value of water and the use of economic instruments for efficient and equitable water management. Appropriate water pricing is a key component of the new policy, which calls for tariffs that reflect full financial costs, environmental impacts and the opportunity costs of water. In addition, it calls for a tariff structure that will create incentives for water conservation.

Namwater's tariffs have been gradually increased since the early 1990s and will soon reach full financial cost recovery in urban areas, but some commercial farmers still pay well under the full financial cost for irrigation water from Namwater. Separate tariffs had been established for each major water scheme because the cost of providing water varies enormously from one region to another. But this pricing policy may be revised in the future to allow cross-subsidization of different regions.

Most rural communities are provided with water by the Rural Water Supply division of the Ministry of Agriculture, Water and Rural Development. The water policy White Paper states that local communities will eventually take full responsibility for managing and running their own water supply, after extensive training of water-point committees in each village. Under this plan, rural communities will pay the operations and maintenance costs of water supply. However, in some communities, the cost of water is exorbitant and there is as yet no policy for dealing with such costs.

South Africa

In contrast to Botswana and Namibia, South Africa relies mainly on perennial surface water rather than groundwater, and has developed an elaborate system of water storage and inter-basin transfer systems. It has a large number of rivers, some of which are entirely within the country. But the most important rivers, which provide the largest share of South Africa's water, are shared: the Orange, Limpopo and Komati. Like Botswana and Namibia, South Africa until recently relied heavily on engineering solutions to water scarcity with relatively little regard for cost.

South Africa's water policy was similar to Namibia's, designed to serve the minority community, with relatively little service to the rural majority. In one respect, however, South Africa's water policy was quite different: water rights were associated with landownership. The riparian rights principle, which gives exclusive rights to the use of stream water to owners of riparian land (adjoining the river), dominated water entitlements in the past. One result of this system of property rights was to concentrate water rights in the hands of large-scale white commercial farmers. Riparian rights were modified somewhat to accommodate non-riparian demands from industrial and urban users and in recognition of the high variability in the flow patterns of rivers (DWAF, 1986). Nevertheless, riparian rights remained the major determinant of allocation of surface water resources in South Africa and riparian owners have continued to enjoy preferential entitlements.

South Africa's new Water Act (DWAF, 1997) changes the central aspects of the old water policy: it seeks to provide a minimum amount of safe drinking water to all, to establish pricing on the basis of full economic cost (financial cost, plus environmental cost, plus a conservation component to encourage more efficient water use), and makes water the property of the state which can award rights of use with no preference for land ownership.

The major institutions for water supply include:

- Department of Water Affairs and Forestry (DWAF), which oversees the allocation of raw water rights and large capital expenditure projects such as dams and transfer schemes within and between catchments. Decision-making will be decentralized through catchment management agencies (CMAs), water user associations (WUAs), water boards and various local governing bodies (CSIR, 2001).
- Catchment management agencies (CMAs), which are to be established in the near future as water management agencies for each of the 19 defined catchments of South Africa.
- Water user associations (WUA), which are private, cooperative associations of local water users.
- Water boards (WB), which distribute mainly bulk water from national water schemes, and/or groundwater sources to district councils and local authorities.
- District councils and local authorities, which distribute water to end-users in towns and municipalities. They generally buy water from their respective water boards and supplement these supplies through some of their own sources, such as municipal storage dams and groundwater supplies.
- Irrigation boards, which are cooperative groups that manage local water resources for irrigation.

- Users who mainly provide their own water independent of the other institutions, mainly for mining, livestock, and irrigation.

The National Water Act of 1956 set different pricing policies for different sectors of the economy. Generally, agriculture was heavily subsidized, while other sectors were less subsidized. Tariffs for irrigation and stock watering were sometimes set high enough to recover operating costs but not capital costs. One-third of the capital costs of the irrigation boards was formally subsidized, but in practice much more was subsidized as irrigation boards often failed to repay their loans (Hassan et al., 2001). Because water costs form only a small portion of total production costs of industrial and domestic sectors, tariffs for these sectors were, in principle, usually set at full-cost recovery (capital and operating costs) and subsidies were only considered when the unit cost rose above 22 cents/m^3. Different local authorities have established various pricing policies with cross-subsidization to provide a minimum water requirement free or very cheaply to poor households.

5.3 METHODOLOGY AND DATA

Water resources were not treated explicitly in the first, interim SEEA handbook (UN, 1993). Hence, there was less guidance with water accounts than with other components of the SEEA and less experience from other countries to draw on. In the revised SEEA Handbook (UN, 2001), water accounts have received special attention and will be the subject of a future special accounting manual, such as those prepared for fisheries.

Water accounts consist of stock and flow accounts. Water stock accounts report the amount of the total resource and changes in the resource over the accounting period (usually a year, although in the case of surface water, a case can be made for seasonal stock accounts). Stock accounts for water are relatively problematic both conceptually and empirically because of the mobile nature of this resource. Groundwater fits the concept of other resource stocks, such as minerals and forests, although it is often difficult to establish empirically the extent of the stock of groundwater and the amount of fluctuation due to groundwater recharge. Surface water, mainly rivers, does not fit easily into the concept of a stock, being partly a flow and partly a stock concept.

Water flow accounts measure the use of water by detailed economic activities and households. Water is used both directly and indirectly. Direct uses include use for agriculture, manufacturing, services, hydroelectric power production, human consumption and sanitation, recreation and navigation. Indirect uses include transport of water from one place to another, and support of ecosystem health. Because the water flow accounts, like all NRAs, are a set of satellite accounts to the System of National Accounts, they are linked directly to the national accounts through the use of a common classification of economic activities. Although each country follows the same general classification scheme for its national accounts, the International Standard Industrial Classification, this highly detailed classification is implemented at different levels of detail in each country. Consequently, the water use accounts are constructed at different levels of detail in each country.

The few countries that have constructed water accounts have used different methodologies that reflect each country's water issues and available data. Countries that construct water accounts are listed in Table 5.1. France, the first country to construct water accounts, has both stock and flow accounts. France attempted to model all aspects of the hydrological cycle and included extensive water quality accounts in addition to the quantity accounts (INSEE, 1986). More recently, Spain (Naredo and Gascó, 1995), Chile (Meza et al., 1999) and Moldova (Tafi and Weber, 2000) have adopted the French approach,

Table 5.1 Countries that have constructed water accounts

	Stock accounts	Physical flow accounts	Monetary flow accounts	Water quality accounts
France	X	X	cost of providing water	X
Spain, Chile and Moldova	partial	X	cost of providing water	
Germany		X		
Sweden		X	cost of providing water and wastewater treatment	
Denmark		X	cost of providing providing water and wastewater treatment	
Australia	partial	X		
Namibia	partial	X	cost of providing water	
Botswana		X	cost of providing water	
South Africa	partial	X	cost of providing water	

although their accounts are not as extensive. Germany's water accounts grew out of ongoing work to construct material flow accounts and do not include stock accounts (Schoer and Flachmann, 2000). Sweden and Denmark's water accounts are closely linked to the development of the NAMEA, focusing on the use of water by economic activity and the cost of providing and treating this water; they do not have stock accounts. Australia's accounts are based on a pathways analysis of flow accounts, which focus on sources of water as well as where water goes after use by economic activities and households. They do not construct stock accounts (ABS, 2000).

The construction of water accounts for Botswana and Namibia have followed the SEEA approach, which include flow accounts with partial information about stocks or indicators of the state of the stocks. Stock accounts are poorly developed due to lack of data. South African water accounts are derived from the Water Situation Assessment Model for South Africa developed by the Department of Water Affairs and Forestry, which represents an engineering perspective on the hydrological cycle (DWAF, 2000). This has provided more data on stock aspects of the accounts for South Africa, as well as the pathways taken by water from initial source, through all users and final disposition.

The flow accounts for water in southern Africa have focused mainly on the direct use of water by industry and households. Some information has been collected on ecological requirements, but this is not yet a major part of the accounts due to a lack of data. Flow accounts are presented both in physical and monetary form. Physical accounts represent the use of water by detailed economic sector, disaggregated by the natural and institutional sources of water supply. Monetary accounts assess the economic benefits from water use in each sector of the economy, and provide data on costs, revenues and subsidies relating to the supply of water. Detailed accounts for each country are provided in the Appendix C.

Physical Accounts

Physical water accounts for Botswana, Namibia and South Africa are disaggregated both by source of water and by user of water. Sources are disaggregated according to both institutional and natural source; the classification of users is based on the industrial classifications found in the national accounts of each country. The exact classification of the water accounts in each country differs due to differing institutional arrangements for providing water, the relative importance of different natural sources of water, and differing classifications of economic sectors in each country.

Classification of natural and institutional sources of water
Water accounts are disaggregated by both natural and institutional sources. The important natural sources in southern Africa include the following:

- Groundwater: the major source of water for Botswana and Namibia. Groundwater can be classified as fossil and renewable although such a classification cannot be definitively established for these countries at this time. Geographic variations in availability and quality are partially documented but not yet incorporated in the accounts.
- Perennial surface water: perennial rivers are those that run all year and are the major source of water for South Africa. In southern Africa, such rivers usually cross national boundaries and the use of this water is therefore subject to international agreements.
- Ephemeral or seasonal surface water: ephemeral rivers flow only after periods of heavy rainfall. Captured in large dams for distribution as well as in small, on-farm dams for own use, this source forms a major source of water supply in Botswana, Namibia and South Africa.
- Recycled effluent: water that has been used once, treated and reused.
- Return-flow: water that has been used once and returns without human intervention to a surface or groundwater source where it is available for reuse, although it may be of lower quality.
- Other unconventional water sources: water-scarce countries are considering unconventional water sources. For example, Namibia is planning a major desalination plant on the coast and is investigating a small coastal fog-harvesting scheme. Botswana desalinates groundwater in one location.

The first three sources of water are used in all countries in varying proportions. The last three sources do not yet contribute a major share of water supply, although they may be extremely important locally. Recycled effluent is an important source of water in the capitals of Botswana and Namibia, Gaborone and Windhoek, respectively. Return-flow is only significant in South Africa, which has included this source of water in its water accounts. Return-flow is virtually insignificant in Botswana and Namibia because they have such extremely high rates of evapotranspiration.

Institutional sources are those organizations with responsibility to collect water from primary sources and provide it to end-users. The major institutions were described in the previous section on water policy; the classification in use in the water accounts is provided in Table 5.2.

Classification of water users
The classification of users is mainly determined by the classification system a country uses for its national accounts. While the classification system shares a common structure at a very aggregate level, it is disaggregated differently in each country. The most detailed, published national accounts consist of 38 sectors for Botswana, 20 for Namibia and 90 for South Africa.

Table 5.2   Classification of sources of water for Botswana, Namibia and South Africa

	Natural sources	Institutional sources
Botswana	Groundwater Dam storage of ephemeral surface water Perennial surface water Recycled effluent*	Water Utilities Corporation Dept. of Water Affairs District Councils Self-providers
Namibia	Groundwater Dam storage of ephemeral surface water Perennial surface water Unconventional water sources including recycled effluent and desalination*	Namwater Rural Water Supply Self-providers
South Africa	Groundwater Dam storage of ephemeral surface water Perennial rivers Return flow	Dept. of Water Affairs and Forestry Irrigation Boards Water Boards District Councils & Local Authorities Self-providers

Note: *not included in present water accounts but planned for future water work

Source: Botswana: Lange et al. (2001); Namibia: Lange (1998; 2002); South Africa: CSIR (2001).

However, the level of detail provided in each country's classification can be quite different. For example, the national accounts of both Namibia and Botswana distinguish traditional, or own-account, agriculture from commercial agriculture, but the South African national accounts do not. Diamond mining is distinguished from other mining in the national accounts of both Botswana and Namibia, while South Africa distinguishes coal and gold from other mining. South African national accounts have a much more detailed classification of manufacturing than either Botswana or Namibia.

For several reasons, the water accounts sometimes have to introduce additional users into its classification. In some instances that is because the national accounts' classification system is not detailed enough for water policy; for example, the national accounts may not distinguish between rain-fed and irrigated crop production although that is obviously very important for water accounts. In other instances there are important uses of water that do not correspond directly to a single economic activity, for example tourism, which cuts across a number of industries including hotels, restaurants and transportation. Finally, ecological uses of water such as the direct use of water by wildlife or the water requirements for maintaining a healthy ecosystem have no economic counterpart in the national accounts.

The tables in the Appendix C provide the most detailed classifications used in each country; for cross-country comparisons in this chapter, a more aggregate classification must be used for comparable figures across countries. At the most aggregate level, economic users include:

- agriculture: livestock, crops, forestry and fishing
- mining
- manufacturing
- services
- household: urban and rural
- government.

Unaccounted-for water
Unaccounted-for water is calculated as the difference between the annual production of water and the amount that has been billed or otherwise accounted for. It includes both losses during treatment and distribution, as well as other unmeasured use of water. The latter can occur for a variety of reasons, including broken water metres, incorrect reading of water meters and illegal use. It is often very difficult to determine how much each of these factors contributes. Unaccounted-for water, other than leakages, may have an economic use but there is insufficient information to assign it to any particular industry. Measurement of unaccounted-for water is important for two

reasons. First, unaccounted-for water represents a drain on scarce resources, and second, it is a potentially cheap source of additional supply.

The Department of Water Affairs (DWA) in Botswana makes this calculation as part of its water database, and the Water Utilities Corporation of Botswana has provided some estimates of losses, but other institutions in Botswana and in the other countries do not regularly report this figure. Consequently, it has not yet been fully incorporated in the water accounts for the three countries, although it will be addressed in future work.

Monetary Accounts

Physical accounts provide important information, but information about economic costs and benefits of water use is also needed for effective policy. The SEEA provides guidance about several aspects of monetary accounts that can be constructed for resources such as water. The first and conceptually the simplest, the resource management expenditure component of the flow accounts is based on rearranging information that is already included in the conventional national accounts, but is not explicit enough for policy. This component of the monetary accounts for water includes the cost of providing water to each economic sector and the tariffs or other user fees charged to each sector. From this, subsidies – if any – can be calculated.

Equally important are two additional components of the monetary accounts: the economic benefits of water use in each sector, which measure the general contribution of water to socio-economic well-being, and the economic value of water in each sector, which isolates the contribution of water to product value from the contribution of other factors of production, such as labour, capital and other resources (land, minerals, and so on). Water value can be used to assess economic efficiency of the allocation of water. Economic efficiency is based on the concept that water should go to the highest-value producer, a concept being adopted for commercial water uses in the new water policies of all three countries.

Calculation of socio-economic benefits is relatively easy and has a well-developed history in environmental and resource policy analysis. It is described in the SEEA chapter on policy applications of the environmental accounts. Economic valuation, on the other hand, is extremely difficult because the data needed for valuation are often lacking and quite expensive to collect. Many economic valuation techniques exist and the selection of valuation techniques is largely influenced by data availability. The SEEA does not at this time provide much guidance on this component of the monetary accounts.

Analysis of socio-economic benefits

Water consumption for production purposes, such as agriculture and industry, provide economic benefits such as incomes, employment and foreign exchange earnings. While these benefits do not measure the exclusive contribution of water to economic value, they do measure the broadly defined socio-economic benefits from the use of water in one sector relative to another sector, or in one region of a country relative to another, or one country relative to another. This allows policy makers to address questions such as how many jobs would be lost if water were redirected from agriculture to other sectors? The accounts can provide two kinds of indicators useful to policy makers. One approach is based on the environmental-economic efficiency, or 'eco-efficiency', profiles developed by the OECD and others (OECD, 1993). Eco-efficiency profiles juxtapose, for example, the national shares of water use by each industry with the industry's share of income or employment. This provides an indicator of each industry's environmental burden compared to its economic contribution.

A second indicator is calculated as the ratio of water use to economic contribution, which is most often measured by value-added, but can also be measured using output or employment:

$$B_i = \frac{VA_i}{W_i}$$

Where

B = socio-economic benefit of water use in sector i
VA = value-added generated by sector i
W = cubic metres of water used in sector i

This indicator, value-added per cubic metre of water input, has the advantage of summing in a single indicator both the economic benefits and the environmental burden. This makes it possible to compare the economic performance with respect to water use of different sectors across countries, the performance of the same sector in a given country over time, or benefits across regions or across countries. Such figures have a long history in environmental economics, especially in energy and pollution analysis, and are used for benchmarking industry performance (for an application to air pollution, see Hass and Sorenson, 1998).

In Botswana, the socio-economic benefits of water are calculated for the amount of national income and employment per cubic metre of water input in each sector. South Africa and Namibia only calculate the national income indicator at this time because sufficient data about employment are not available.

While the socio-economic benefit, B_i, measures the direct income generated by water use in a sector, there may be additional benefits, upstream and downstream from the direct user. For example, agricultural production directly generates income and employment, but may also support food processing activities that in turn generate additional income and employment. Models based on hybrid IO tables (mixed unit, monetary and physical tables) are used to measure the total (direct + indirect) impact of water use in a given sector. So far, this kind of analysis has only been carried out for one agricultural area within South Africa, the Crocodile River catchment (Hassan et al., 2001).

These socio-economic measures provide an indication of opportunity cost of a given allocation of water by sector. Opportunity cost compares the benefits of using water in one sector to the benefits of the next-best alternative use of water in another sector. In providing scarce water to one industry, for example, there is less available for other industries. For this component of the monetary accounts, opportunity cost is the comparison of the benefits ratio in one sector to other sectors, or the economy-wide average. For instance, water used in agriculture may generate a lower value-added per cubic metre of water input than mining or tourism.

There are a number of drawbacks to this approach. First, opportunity cost assessment assumes that it is possible to easily reallocate water among users. When using water accounts at the national level, this assumption may require transferring water over large distances and is most appropriate for South Africa, with its extensive water transfer infrastructure. The assumption is less useful for Namibia and Botswana, where transactions costs of reallocating water may be quite high. In addition, economic benefit measured by sectoral value-added is generated by a combination of all the factors of production: labour, capital and natural resources such as water. A high value-added per sector means that water use in a given sector is valuable, but the value cannot be attributed solely to water. A good example is diamond mining: this activity generates very high value-added in Botswana (see Chapter 2), but this value-added cannot be attributed to water; rather it results almost entirely from diamonds. Nevertheless, when facing a water scarcity, this simple analysis indicates that, all else being equal, water will generate greater income if allocated to diamond mining than if allocated elsewhere in the economy. Future work will develop spatially disaggregated water accounts at the district level where comparisons of the benefits of water use among sectors are more appropriate.

Economic valuation
Water supply usually has the characteristics of a natural monopoly and competitive markets for water often do not exist so it is not possible to observe a market-determined price for water. The exceptions to this include, for example, tradable water rights in parts of Australia and the United States and local water vending in cities in some developing countries. If markets for water

exist then the marginal value of water can be derived from an estimated demand curve. However, in the absence of water markets, valuation techniques must be used such as hedonic pricing or the production function approach (for a summary of such techniques see, for example, Easter et al., 1997 or Young, 1996). Preliminary studies in South Africa and two agricultural case studies in Namibia have been undertaken using such methodologies (Brunnström and Strömberg, 2000; Hassan et al., 2001; Lange et al., 2000; Lindgren, 1999). However, the work is not far enough developed to generalize to the water accounts at this time.

Delivery cost, revenues and subsidies
This component of the monetary accounts assigns to each industry the cost of delivering water and the user charge (if any) paid by that industry, and calculates the subsidy as the difference between the two. Most of these data are already included in the national accounts, but in a form that cannot be easily identified or used. For example, the total cost of delivering water from a parastatal like WUC or Namwater can be determined by the institution's total costs in a given year. However, the parastatal delivers water in many regions under different water supply schemes, at different costs to different industries, so the total expenditures of the parastatal cannot be reliably used to determine delivery costs to individual industries. Similarly, it may not be easy to determine total water delivery costs for a government agency if these expenditures are mixed in with ministry expenditures for other activities not directly related to water supply. The same is true for self-providers, who rarely maintain complete records of water supply costs independent of other business costs. Substantial additional work is required to develop these monetary accounts from existing data.

Data availability for both costs and revenues in the three countries is fairly limited. Delivery cost data, where available, only include financial costs, and sometimes only the operating and maintenance costs, but not the capital costs. The lack of data exists despite the new water pricing policies in Namibia and South Africa that call not only for full financial costs, but full social costs.

Data Sources

The data sources and major limitations are summarized for each country in Boxes 5.1–3. The share of total water use provided by each supplier gives an indication of the impact of data problems for each supplier on the national water accounts. In Botswana, reliable records of metered water use are only available from WUC, DWA and mining, which account for about 35 per cent of total water use. In Namibia, records of metered water use are available from Namwater, which accounts for 41 per cent of water use. Because the water accounts for South Africa are based on a complex database constructed for the

BOX 5.1   BOTSWANA: SUMMARY OF WATER DATA SOURCES AND DATA PROBLEMS

A.   WATER UTILITIES CORPORATION: 16% of water use in 1996

Data Source:
Unpublished data base of customer billing records;
Unpublished data base of water use and tariffs by customer type and by tariff band

Major Problems:
Some discrepancies between billing records and published figures for water use

B.   DEPARTMENT OF WATER AFFAIRS: 8% of water use in 1996

Data Source:
For each major village, unpublished databases with the following information:
Production, Consumption, and Losses; Consumption by economic sector; Expenditures and Revenues

Major Problems:
Missing data for water use in some villages in early years;
Extensive missing data for Expenditures and Revenues
Incomplete record of operations and maintenance costs, no information about capital costs

C.   DISTRICT COUNCIL WATER FOR SMALL VILLAGES: 18% of water use in 1996

Data Source:
Per capita water use derived from one month of metered water use in each village, used to derive average daily use per person and applied to village population in all years

Major Problems:
Information for only one year. No information about how much water is used for domestic consumption, schools and clinics, offices, local government, livestock water and other uses. No information about costs or revenues

D. SELF-PROVIDERS (mainly mining, irrigation, livestock watering): 58% of water use in 1996

Data Source:
Livestock: estimated on the basis of numbers of livestock and daily water requirements.
Irrigation: figure for 1990 from Water Master Plan.
Diamond mining: reported use from Debswana for 1996–98 only. Earlier figures from Water Master Plan
Other mining: copper/nickel & soda ash from WUC records; coal from Water Master Plan

Major Problems:
No reliable livestock figures 1991–4.
Actual livestock and irrigation water use unknown.
No information about costs of providing water

BOX 5.2   NAMIBIA: SUMMARY OF WATER DATA SOURCES AND DATA PROBLEMS

A. NAMWATER: 41% of water use in 1996

Data Source:
Unpublished data base of water supply; water cost by supply scheme, and tariffs by supply point

Major Problems:
Limited information about use by detailed economic sector, final costs and final tariffs because most water delivered to end-user by municipalities

B. RURAL WATER SUPPLY: 19% of water use in 1996

Data Source:
Livestock: estimated on the basis of numbers of livestock and daily water requirements
Rural domestic use: estimated on the basis of population and per capita consumption figure from engineering design guidelines

Major Problems:
Actual use by livestock and population unknown
Delivery costs unknown

C. SELF-PROVIDERS (mainly mining, irrigation, commercial livestock): 40% of water use in 1996

Data Source:
Livestock: estimated on the basis of numbers of livestock and daily water requirements.
Irrigation: partly metered, partly estimated from area under irrigation and average water requirements
Mining: industry surveys

Major Problems:
Actual livestock and irrigation water use unknown.
No information about costs of providing water

BOX 5.3 SOUTH AFRICA: SUMMARY OF WATER DATA SOURCES AND DATA PROBLEMS

A. DWAF: 43% of water use in 1996

Data Source:
DWAF's WSAM (2000a). Combination of hydrological models at quaternary catchment level and aggregate information for bulk water supply. Bulk water tariffs and cost by water supply scheme from DWAF's handbooks

Major Problems:
Not based on records of metered use by detailed industry. Data missing for 3% of water management areas, calculated as a residual

B. IRRIGATION BOARDS: 31% of water use in 1996

Data Source:
Estimated from area and crop under irrigation with average water requirement per hectare

Major Problems:
No metered data

C. WATER BOARDS: 8% of water use in 1996

Data Source:
Total water use and tariffs obtained from Annual Reports of Water Boards

Major Problems:
Water use by detailed user not available

D.   DISTRICT COUNCILS and LOCAL AUTHORITIES: 4% of water use in 1996

Data Source:
Sales of water provided by Statistics South Africa. Converted to physical volumes using average tariff

Major Problems:
Tariffs differ by customer so use of an average tariff to derive physical volumes distorts actual usage by sector

E.   SELF-PROVIDERS (mainly mining, irrigation, livestock watering): 15% of water use in 1996

Data Source:
Livestock: estimated on the basis of numbers of livestock and daily water requirements.
Irrigation: partly metered, partly estimated from area under irrigation and average water requirements
Mining: industry surveys

Major Problems:
Actual livestock and irrigation water use unknown.
No information about costs.

Department of Water Affairs and Forestry, the share of data derived from metered records, or from other sources and methods, cannot be determined at this time.

In all three countries, self-providers are responsible for a great deal of water use – in Botswana, more than half. Typically, there are no records of water use and little information about the financial costs of providing water, although in most instances, self-providers do pay the full financial costs and are not subsidized. There are some exceptions to this, for example, Botswana's diamond mining industry reports annual water use to the Department of Water Affairs. The largest single user of water in each country, agriculture, also goes mostly unmetered. Estimates were made for livestock based on standard assumptions, that is, number of livestock and daily water requirements. Irrigation water use is sometimes metered, but is often estimated on the basis of area under irrigation and average water use per hectare.

The information about delivery costs and tariffs is more limited than the volume data. In most instances where there is water metering, there is also information about costs and tariffs. This is not, however, the case for DWA in Botswana. The data for Namwater in Namibia are also incomplete because much of the local reticulation is provided by municipalities which set end-user tariffs; this information is not currently available although a system is being put in place to collect this information in the future.

5.4   PHYSICAL AND MONETARY ACCOUNTS FOR WATER

A summary of the water accounts for Botswana, Namibia and South Africa are presented in this section. More detailed water accounts are provided in Appendix C and the full accounts can be found in the reports for each country cited at the beginning of this chapter.

Physical Accounts

Annual water use in the three countries for 1996 was the lowest in Botswana, at 142 million cubic metres, and the highest in South Africa at 14 830 million cubic metres. Most of this difference can be attributed to the larger population and economy of South Africa. On a per capita basis, water use is much more similar among the three countries, although the ranking of water intensity is still the same. Botswana has the lowest per capita use of water at 95 cubic metres per person. Namibia's water use is about 65 per cent higher at 157 cubic metres of water per person, and South Africa remains the highest at 365 cubic metres per person, almost four times that of Botswana (Table 5.3).

As in most countries, agriculture is the single largest user of water and ranges from 48 per cent in Botswana to 73 per cent in South Africa. Excluding agricultural use, the levels of per capita water use are more similar among the three countries. Per capita consumption is 49 cubic metres in Botswana and about 40 per cent higher, at 69 cubic metres in Namibia. South Africa is still higher at 98 cubic metres per capita, which is double the use in Botswana. Clearly, agriculture is a key to understanding the difference in water use among the three countries.

The structure of water use is somewhat similar among the three countries, except for agriculture. Agricultural water use dominates all three countries, but, as noted above, is much lower in Botswana (48 per cent) than in Namibia (58 per cent) or South Africa (73 per cent). Water is used in agriculture for both crop irrigation and livestock but in Botswana there is relatively little irrigation, only about 1000 hectares under irrigation in 1996, compared with over 7 000

Table 5.3   Water use by sector in Botswana, Namibia and South Africa, 1996

	Botswana	Namibia	South Africa
Total water use (million m³)	142	256	14 830
Per capita water use (m³ per person)	95	157	365
Per capita water use excluding agriculture (m³ per person)	49	69	98
Percentage distribution by sector			
Agriculture	48	58	73
Mining	11	10	3
Manufacturing	1	2	1
Trade, Services, Government	9	3	9
Households	31	29	13
Total	100	100	100

Source: Adapted from CSIR (2001), Lange and Hassan (1999) and Lange et al. (2001).

hectares in Namibia and 1.2 million hectares in South Africa. Consequently, only 13 per cent of total water use was for crop irrigation in Botswana, while in Namibia and South Africa, crop irrigation accounted for 34 per cent and 53 per cent respectively (Lange et al., 2001; Lange and Hassan, 1999; CSIR, 2001). The rest of agricultural use in each country is accounted for by live-stock watering.

Following agriculture, households constitute the second-largest user of water in all three countries. In fact, in Botswana it appears to be the fastest-growing sector in terms of water use: household water use rose by 21 per cent between 1993 and 1998 while total water use increased by only 5 per cent (Table C2). There is also a large difference between rural and urban household consumption. For example, in Namibia urban households comprise only 29 per cent of the population, but consume more than three times as much water as rural households in communal areas (Table C4). In Namibia, there is a separate estimate for household water use on commercial farms, which includes a significant amount used by farmers and farm work-ers for gardening and household use. Similarly in South Africa, household use of water in urban areas is significantly higher than rural households (Table C7).

In the non-agricultural economy, mining, dominated by diamond mining, is the largest user of water in Botswana and Namibia, 11 per cent and 10 per cent respectively of total use for these countries, but only 3 per cent in South Africa. Manufacturing use of water is very low in Namibia and Botswana, 2 per cent and 1 per cent respectively. Even in South Africa, industrial water use is less than 2 per cent despite the more industrialized and diversified structure of the South African economy. Water use in the manufacturing sectors in all three countries is dominated by the food processing industries. The service and government sectors account for a small share of water in Namibia, although this may reflect problems with the data. In Botswana and South Africa, water use by these sectors, and especially by government, is high: 5 per cent and 9 per cent respectively. Furthermore, water use by the Botswana government has increased significantly since 1993 to 1998 from 5 per cent to nearly 7 per cent of total use.

Both Botswana and Namibia rely primarily on groundwater for most of their water needs, 59 per cent and 50 per cent of total water use in 1996 respectively (Table 5.4). Use of groundwater is particularly high in rural areas, which is hardly surprising given the paucity of surface water in these countries. Groundwater is the cheapest and most reliable source of water because it can be sourced at the point of use and is not solely dependent on rainfall in a given year. There is very little information about groundwater reserves and recharge rates, so it is not possible to assess precisely the extent to which these countries are using renewable groundwater or depleting fossil groundwater. However, water authorities monitor borehole levels in certain areas and define a depletion problem as a case where the borehole level declines continuously

Table 5.4   *Water use by source in Botswana, Namibia and South Africa, 1996 (%)*

	Botswana	Namibia	South Africa
A. Natural source			
Groundwater	59	50	2
Perennial rivers	20	30	59
Dam storage of ephemeral surface water	21	20	39
Total	100	100	100
B. Institutional source			
Self-providers	58	41	9
Government (mostly to rural areas)	26	19	79
Private companies and parastatals	16	40	12
Total	100	100	100

Notes: Government suppliers include DWA in Botswana, Rural Water Supply in Namibia, and DWAF and irrigation boards in South Africa
Private companies and parastatals include WUC in Botswana, Namwater in Namibia and water user associations, water boards and local authorities in South Africa.

Source: Adapted from CSIR (2001), Lange (1998 and 2002) and Lange et al. (2001).

for five years, even after good rainfall. Under this definition, unsustainable depletion of groundwater accounted for about 5 per cent of total water use in Namibia in 1996.

Of the remaining water, Namibia relies more heavily on perennial rivers, which form its northern and southern borders, than Botswana does. In contrast to Botswana and Namibia, South Africa obtains 98 per cent of its water from rivers and only 2 per cent from groundwater. Dam storage accounts for 39 per cent of water use and perennial rivers for 59 per cent. Much of South Africa's surface water is shared with neighbouring countries, so South Africa's water supply is highly dependent on negotiations over regional allocation of these shared waters, notably with Lesotho.

The types of institutional suppliers vary across the three countries but self-providers, those institutions that abstract water for their own consumption, such as livestock farmers and mining, are a significant source of water in all three countries. This is especially so in Botswana where self-providers account for 58 per cent of water use in 1996. Nearly two-thirds of self-providers' water is for livestock, the remaining is for mining and irrigation. In South Africa and Namibia self-providers also use water mainly for livestock, irrigation and mining.

Unaccounted-for water

Unaccounted-for water consists of leakages in the system between the production and metered use by the end-user, and water use that is unrecorded for other reasons described in section 5.3. It is not possible to completely eliminate such losses and a leakage rate of 10 per cent is considered reasonably good (M. Sumser, pers. comm.). Although there are not yet sufficient data to include unaccounted-for water in the water accounts, each country has attempted to gather some information about its magnitude.

In Botswana, unaccounted-for water is reported by the two institutions that meter water use: WUC, which serves the six largest towns, and DWA, serving the 17 major villages (Table 5.5). Losses for WUC have declined, mainly due to infrastructure improvements in Gaborone, the capital of Botswana, which accounts for roughly half of WUC water use. In 1997 WUC began a programme to repair leakages, which resulted in a dramatic reduction in the loss of water from 30 per cent in 1997 to 9 per cent in 1999. The other five towns served by WUC still have high rates of unaccounted-for water, and in some towns these rates have been increasing over time.

The average rate of unaccounted-for water supplied by the DWA to Botswana's 17 major villages is quite high, although it appears to have declined over time, from 28 per cent in 1993 to 24 per cent in 1998. Within this average, loss rates for each of the villages vary enormously: in 1993, Letlhakane registered a questionably low rate of 6 per cent while Ramotswa registered a high of 35 per cent. These figures, however, are probably less reliable than the WUC

Table 5.5   Unaccounted-for water in Botswana (as % metered water use)

	1993	1997	1998	1999
WUC				
Average of all 6 towns served by				
WUC	NA	21	16	15
Gaborone	NA	30	14	9
DWA				
Average	**28**	**23**	**24**	**NA**
Village with highest loss	49	36	35	NA
Village with lowest loss rate	6	3	12	NA

Note: Figure for WUC calculated as the weighted sum of unaccounted for water for each town.
NA: not available.

Source: Adapted from Lange et al (2001).

figures because the record-keeping of DWA, in the past, has not been as rigorous as that of WUC, which is subject to external audits every year.

High rates of unaccounted-for water have also been reported for Namibia (van der Merwe et al., 1998) and South Africa (CSIR, 2001). These reports indicate that unaccounted-for water is a widespread problem throughout southern Africa. For countries with abundant water supplies, the marginal benefit from reducing losses may be fairly low, but in water-scarce countries such as the three discussed here, reduction of unaccounted-for water has been identified as one of the cheapest ways to increase water supply (Arntzen et al, 1998; van der Merwe et al., 1998).

Monetary Analysis and Accounts

Several aspects of the monetary accounts have been at least partially constructed and analysed. Each of the three countries have calculated the economic benefits of water use by sector in terms of sectoral value-added per cubic metre of water input as described in section 5.2. Monetary accounts have also been partially constructed for the three countries, depending on the data available: the cost of delivery of water by sector, water tariffs paid by sector and subsidies received by sector.

Economic contribution of water
The overall economic contribution of water, measured as GDP per cubic metre of water input, is highest in Botswana at 124 pula per cubic metre, and the

Table 5.6   *National income generated per cubic metre of water used by sector in Botswana, Namibia and South Africa, 1996 (pula per cubic metre of water used)*

	Botswana	Namibia	South Africa
GDP per m^3 of water input	124	45	25
GDP per m^3 of water input excluding agriculture	158	108	87
Agriculture	9	6	2
Mining	420	54	61
Manufacturing	437	189	410
Trade, Services, Government	724	542	155

Note: The figures in rand for Namibia and South Africa were converted to the pula at a rate of 0.75 pula per rand.

Source: Adapted from CSIR (2001), Lange and Hassan (1999) and Lange et al. (2001).

lowest in South Africa, 25 pula (Table 5.6). At 45 pula per cubic metre, Namibia is between the two, but closer to South Africa. Removing agriculture, the figures for Botswana and Namibia draw closer together, but at 158 pula per cubic metre of water input, Botswana still generates 50 per cent more GDP per cubic metre of water use than Namibia, and 82 per cent more than South Africa.

There is a tremendous range of economic contribution of water by sector in each country. In Botswana, the value added generated ranges 90-fold, from 9 pula per cubic metre of water in agriculture to 724 pula in the service sectors in 1996; in Namibia the range is similar, from 6 pula to 542 pula. The range is highest, more than 200-fold for South Africa, 2 pula and 410 pula.

Agriculture stands out as the lowest economic contributor in all three countries. This is hardly surprising given that agriculture provides primary products that are highly water-intensive and often relatively low value. On closer inspection of this sector, it becomes apparent that there is great diversity in terms of water use within the sector and that this varies across countries. In Botswana, water use in traditional agriculture, mainly livestock farming, makes a greater economic contribution than in the commercial sector (Table C3). This is because the commercial sector is dominated by irrigation, which is more water-intensive than the traditional sector. This also appears to be the case in Namibia. However, somewhat surprisingly value-added per cubic metre of water used is fairly similar for communal and commercial agriculture in Namibia (Table C6).

As mentioned in the section on methodology, there are some shortcomings to this analysis because the national accounts combine rain-fed and irrigated crop production, so that the value-added for irrigation (which includes rain-fed crops) is, overestimated. This point will be addressed in future work.

The trade, services and government sectors offer the highest returns to national income in Botswana and Namibia, because the production processes are not water-intensive. However, in South Africa, manufacturing is the highest-value use of water, surpassing services and government. Two high-income generating subsectors are especially important in South African manufacturing: electrical machinery and transport equipment. Mining makes a significant value-added contribution in all three countries, and diamond mining contributes the largest value-added in both Namibia and Botswana. In South African mining, coal mining yields the highest value-added per cubic metre in 1998, surpassing gold and other minerals.

The differences among countries at the aggregate level continue at a more disaggregated level. Botswana consistently generates more value-added per cubic metre of water input in all sectors than either of the other two countries. The differences are greatest in mining, where the economic contribution of water in Botswana is seven times that in South Africa: 420 pula and 61 pula, respectively. The high figure for Botswana is due to a combination of factors: the very high value of Botswana's diamonds, and a substantial reduction in the water required for mining. Botswana's diamond mining company, Debswana has introduced extensive water conservation measures. In agriculture and manufacturing, the economic contribution of water in Botswana is four times as great as in South Africa.

While value-added is a powerful indicator of the economic benefit of using water in one sector rather than another, it is not the only consideration. Employment is also an important indicator which policy-makers must take into account. At this time, there are not adequate data to do a full comparison of employment across all countries. However, there is information for Botswana and when employment is added to the socio-economic analysis, the relative benefits of water use by sector changes somewhat. In Botswana, the only country for which this analysis has yet been carried out, mining makes a strong economic contribution in terms of income (35 per cent) but not employment (under 4 per cent), relative to its water use (10 per cent). By contrast, agriculture, which accounted for 48 per cent of water use, generated only 4 per cent of national income but employs 30 per cent of the labour force (defined to include both formal sector employment plus own-account, full-time farmers) (Table C6).

Cost recovery, revenues and subsidies

Data for costs and revenues are not comprehensive in any country, so the monetary accounts are not complete. However, despite the limited data, it can

Table 5.7   Water subsidy by supplying institution in Botswana, Namibia and South Africa

	Degree of subsidy in 1996	% water supplied in 1996
Botswana		
WUC	No aggregate subsidy, but extensive cross-subsidization	16
DWA	3% subsidy of non-energy operations and maintenance costs; 100% of capital costs and energy costs	8
District councils	Close to 100% subsidy, No tariffs for standpipes, Low tariffs only for private connections	18
Self-providers	No subsidy	58
Namibia		
Namwater	87% subsidy for Agriculture, 45% subsidy for Non-agricultural users	48
Rural Water Supply	100% subsidy	10
Self-providers	No subsidy	42
South Africa		
DWAF-CMA	Degree of subsidy not determined at this time	43
Irrigation boards	Degree of subsidy not determined at this time	31
Water boards	Degree of subsidy not determined at this time	8
District councils + local authorities	Degree of subsidy not determined at this time	4
Self-providers	No subsidy	15

Source: Based on CSIR (2001), Lange (2002) and Lange et al. (2001).

be stated with certainty that many users of water do not pay the full financial cost of water (Table 5.7). The major exception to this is the self-providers, who generally pay 100 per cent of their costs account, although even they may have received government subsidies for some of the capital costs in the past.

Botswana provides the least subsidies to water users. Both WUC and self-providers in Botswana cover the full financial cost of water abstraction, accounting for 74 per cent of all water use in 1996. However, WUC implements a complicated system of block tariffs for each of the six major towns served by WUC, which allows for cross-subsidization across different types of customers and according to the volume of water they use. Information about costs for each town is not available so it is not possible to assess whether there is also cross-subsidization by town.

Water supplied in Botswana by DWA and district councils, accounting for 26 per cent of water use, are subsidized to a degree undetermined at this time, but considerable. Both institutions charge only for private connections and standpipe water is provided free. DWA provides some data on the cost and revenues from delivery of water from 1993 to 1998, but there were serious problems with missing data. In addition, the cost data only covered a portion of operating costs, omitting, for example, energy costs for operating boreholes, which is the major source of DWA water. There is no attempt to estimate capital costs by either DWA or district councils. Charges do not cover all the operations and maintenance costs, let alone capital costs. There is also cross-subsidization across villages by both institutions: tariffs are the same in all locations, even though there are great variations in the cost of providing water.

In Namibia, only self-providers pay the full financial cost, accounting for 42 per cent of all water use in 1996. Although Namwater's tariffs have increased substantially in recent years, subsidies to agriculture were still very high in 1996, 87 per cent of total costs, and subsidies to non-agricultural users still averaged 45 per cent. The cost of delivery of water is relatively high because of the highly dispersed population. Namwater's costs for non-agricultural water points ranged from a low of Nambian $0.95 per cubic metre to as much as Nambian $42.35, while tariffs ranged from Nambian $0.30 to Nambian $1.89. In recent years, tariffs have increased faster than costs so that subsidies are gradually coming down. Rural Water Supply was still completely subsidized in 1996 and even in 2000 they have not been able to turn over management of local water supply to many villages. Cost information for Rural Water Supply is not available.

Namibia has a policy of moving gradually toward full-cost recovery for Namwater and recovery of operations and maintenance costs for Rural Water Supply. Namwater's non-agricultural tariffs have been rising by about 20 per cent a year, more in some areas and less in others. Tariffs are set by water scheme to limit cross-subsidization of expensive water supply areas by cheaper ones. Rural Water Supply is running extensive training programmes for water-point management committees in each village, but it is unclear when these committees will be able to fully take charge of water

Table 5.8 *Water subsidies by economic sector in Namibia and South Africa,*
1996

	Subsidy as % of total cost		
	Botswana	Namibia	South Africa
Economy-wide average	**Less than 26%**	**34%**	**86%**
Agriculture	NA	41	97
Mining	NA	7	56
Trade and services	NA	41	56
Manufacturing	NA	45	56
Households	NA	38	56

Note: NA: not available.

Source: Based on CSIR (2001), Lange et al. (2001), Lange and Hassan (1999) and Lange (2002).

supply. Data are not yet available about subsidies by provider for South Africa.

The economy-wide average subsidy in each country follows the same pattern as water use and is inversely related to the economic contribution of water use by sector: in 1996 water subsidies were lowest in Botswana at less than 26 per cent, followed by Namibia at 34 per cent. Water subsidies were highest in South Africa at 86 per cent, where per capita water use is also highest and the economic benefits from water use by sector are lowest. Subsidies by economic sector were calculated for Namibia (Table 5.8). The South African figures were calculated for agriculture and an average figure was calculated for all non-agricultural users. Sufficient data are not yet available to calculate subsidies for Botswana.

In Namibia, only mining paid close to the full costs of water (93 per cent of total costs), mainly because of the predominance of self-providers in this sector. Other sectors received, on average, subsidies in the range of 38 per cent to 45 per cent, but these fairly similar aggregate figures obscure important differences. Among the agricultural subsectors, commercial livestock, watered almost entirely by self-providers, received no subsidies, while irrigated crop production was subsidized at a rate of around 87 per cent. In South Africa, agriculture was even more heavily subsidized than in Namibia, paying only 14 per cent of total costs. Like Namibia, non-agricultural sectors paid much more of the costs of water. Despite the relatively high level of subsidies reported here, subsidies have been declining in Namibia and South Africa, especially for agriculture.

5.5   POLICY IMPLICATIONS

Natural resource accounts for water are particularly important for water-scarce countries, such as many of the southern African countries. Increasing water scarcity and mounting water supply costs make it imperative to use the available resources carefully. The new water policies of Namibia, South Africa and, to a lesser degree, Botswana call for economic efficiency, equity and ecological sustainability in water use, to be achieved in part through pricing reform. Despite the recognition of the need to base water policy on a firm economic basis and, specifically, to reform pricing, there is a striking lack of data upon which to base this pricing policy.

The physical and monetary water accounts offer a unique opportunity for an economic perspective on water supply and use which can assist planners and policy makers to monitor resource trends, resource allocation and user efficiency. Water accounts can indicate where policy objectives have been achieved and where improvements can be made.

The physical accounts can act as an 'early warning' system by indicating which sources of water are in danger of depletion or which sectors are rapidly increasing water use. For example, in Namibia there are serious concerns about groundwater depletion, which has been exacerbated by droughts. Drought reduces the amount of surface water available, which increases the use of groundwater while at the same time reducing the recharge of groundwater sources. While Namibia's commercial livestock numbers declined in the 1990s, livestock numbers in the traditional sector, and their water requirements, have been increasing. The water demands required by different economic growth strategies can be estimated from the water accounts. For example, expansion of the service sector is much better for water resources than agricultural expansion. This allows policy-makers to make a more informed choice regarding the allocation of water to different economic activities, and more broadly, about economic development strategies.

The provision of time series data for year-to-year monitoring is important in such water-scarce countries. For example, the Botswana accounts indicate that between 1993 and 1998 agricultural use of water as a percentage of total use actually declined, whilst household consumption increased. At the macro-economic level total water use per capita and per unit of GDP declined, so that the macro-economic efficiency of water improved by 26 per cent from 1993 to 1998.

Improvement in water productivity can be achieved in two ways:

- Water conservation at the company level can be improved, whereby companies modify processes to produce the same output but with less water. The Debswana diamond mining company in Botswana has been exemplary in its conservation efforts.

• Structural change can improve the economic efficiency of water at the macro level as a result of incentives to encourage growth of less water-intensive sectors and discourage sectors which are highly water-intensive. However, consideration is required when redirecting resources away from sectors that are relevant to broader social objectives such as equity and employment generation in rural areas.

Lessons may also be learned from comparisons with other countries although the interpretation of differences must be done with great care. Much more work needs to be done before the water accounts are as fully comparable across countries as the economic accounts are.

Unaccounted-for water is clearly an important component of the water accounts. Loss rates in Botswana as high as 30 per cent of all water supplied by institutional suppliers are quite alarming. If loss rates are similar for those institutions that do not estimate unaccounted-for water, then a significant amount of water is being lost in a region that is under serious threat of water scarcity. Moreover, efforts to monitor and reclaim the lost water present a relatively cheap, alternative source of water, as the experience of WUC in Gaborone, Botswana indicated.

The monetary accounts – costs, user charges and subsidies – have also proved highly useful for policy. Even though the data for the three countries are far from complete, the evidence suggests that on aggregate full financial costs are not being recovered. This would suggest that as countries move toward full cost recovery, and eventually to full social cost recovery, there may be significant impacts on different sectors of the economy. Without good information about costs and user charges, it is not possible to estimate what the impacts of alternative pricing policies might be. This is a priority area for future work on the accounts. Additional study is needed to determine the economic value of water, and some promising case studies have been undertaken which could provide the basis for more general studies in the future.

While the water accounts of all three countries are preliminary and need improvements, they have already helped to shape policy dialogue in the three countries. Each country has already committed additional resources toward improving the water accounts and incorporating the information in their ongoing policy analyses and reviews. A pilot study is also under way to construct water accounts for international water basins in order to assist in water allocation among nations, for the first time providing an economic perspective on shared water.

REFERENCES

ABS *see* Australian Bureau of Statistics.

Arntzen, J., K. Chigodora, L. Kgathi and E. Segosebe (1998), 'Water demand management, Botswana country study', Final report prepared for the World Conservation Union Regional Programme for Southern Africa.

Artnzen, J., H. Fidzai and K. Chigodora (1999), 'Economic instruments and Botswana's environment', Unpublished report by the Centre for Applied Research, Gaborone, Botswana.

Australian Bureau of Statistics (2000), *Water Accounts for Australia, 1993–93 to 1996–97*, Canberra, Australia.

Brånvall, G., M. Eriksson, U. Johansson and P. Svensson (1999), *Water accounts: Physical and monetary data connected to abstraction, use and discharge of water in the Swedish NAMEA*, Statistics Sweden, Environment Statistics, Stockholm.

Brown, C.J. (1994), *Namibia's Green Plan*, Ministry of Environment and Tourism, Windhoek, Namibia.

Brunnström, E. and L. Strömberg (2000), 'The Value of Irrigation Water Along the Orange River in Namibia', Minor Field Study for a Master's degree from the Department of Economics, Goteborg University, Sweden.

Chenje, M. and P. Johnson (eds) (1996), *Water in Southern Africa*, IUCN–World Conservation Union Regional Centre for Southern Africa, Harare, Zimbabwe.

Council for Scientific and Industrial Research, Environmentek (2001), 'Water resource accounts for South Africa, 1991–1998', Final report to the Natural Resource Accounting Programme of Southern Africa, University of Pretoria, South Africa.

CSIR *see* Council for Scientific and Industrial Research

Department of Water Affairs (1991), *Perspective on Water Affairs*, Windhoek, Namibia, MAWRD.

Department of Water Affairs (1993), *Water and Sanitation Policy*, Windhoek, Namibia, MAWRD.

Department of Water Affairs and Forestry (1986), *Management of the Water Resources of the Republic of South Africa*, Cape Town, South Africa, CTP Book Printers.

Department of Water Affairs and Forestry (1997), 'White Paper on a National Water Policy for South Africa', available from http://www-dwaf.pwv.gov.za/Documents.

Department of Water Affairs and Forestry (2000), Water Situation Assessment Model for South Africa 2000, Version 1f, unpublished database, Pretoria, South Africa.

DWA *see* Department of Water Affairs.

DWAF *see* Department of Water Affairs and Forestry.

Easter, K.W., N. Becker and Y. Tsur (1997), 'Economic mechanisms for managing water resources, pricing, permits and markets', in A. Biswas (ed.), *Water Resources: Environmental Planning, Management and Development*, New York, McGraw-Hill.

Gleick, P. (1998), *The World's Water 1998–1999: Biennial Report on Freshwater*, Washington, DC, Island Press.

Hass, J. and K. Sorenson (1998), 'Environmental profiles and benchmarking of Norwegian industries', *Economic Survey*, January, pp. 28–37, Statistics Norway, Oslo.

Hassan, R., B. Olbrish and J. Crafford (2001), 'Comparative analysis of the economic efficiency of water use in the Crocodile Catchment', Second Draft Report, March 2001.

INSEE (Institut National de la Statistique et des Etudes Economiques) (1986), *Les Comptes du Patrimoine Naturel*, Ministère de L'Environnement, INSEE, Paris.

Lange, G. (1998), 'An approach to sustainable water management in southern Africa using natural resource accounts, the experience in Namibia', *Journal of Ecological Economics*, 26(3): 299–311.

Lange, G-M. (2002 forthcoming), 'Water accounts for Namibia: 1993 to 2000', Research Discussion Paper, Directorate of Environmental Affairs, Ministry of Environment and Tourism, Windhoek, Namibia.

Lange, G. and R. Hassan (1999), 'Natural resource accounting as a tool for sustainable macroeconomic policy: applications in Southern Africa', Policy Brief of IUCN Regional Office for Southern Africa, Harare, Zimbabwe, IUCN–ROSA.

Lange, G., J. MacGregor and S. Masirembu (2000), 'The economic value of groundwater: case study of Stampriet, Namibia', Draft Discussion Paper, Directorate of Environmental Affairs, Ministry of Environment and Tourism, Windhoek, Namibia.

Lange, G., J. Arntzen, S. Kabaija and M. Monamati (2001), 'Botswana's natural resource accounts: the case of water', report to the Botswana Natural Resource Accounting Programme, National Conservation Strategy Agency and Ministry of Finance, Central Statistics Office, Gaborone, Botswana.

Lindgren, A. (1999), 'The value of water: a study of the Stampriet aquifer in Namibia', Minor Field Study for a Master's degree from the Department of Economics, Umea University, Sweden.

MAWRD *see* Ministry of Agriculture, Water and Rural Development.

Meza, F., R. Jiliberto, F. Maldini, A. Magri, M. Alvarez-Arenas, M. García, S. Valenzuela and L. Losarcos (1999), *Cuentas ambientales del Recurso Agua en Chile* (translation, *Environmental Accounts for Water in Chile*), Documento de Trabajo No. 11, Serie Economía Ambiental, Comisión Nacional del Medio Ambiente, Santiago, Chile.

Ministry of Agriculture, Water and Rural Development (2000), *National Water Policy White Paper*, Windhoek, Namibia.

Naredo, J.M. and J.M. Gascó (1995), Las Cuentas del Agua en España (translation, *Water accounts in Spain*), Unpublished report for Ministerio de Obras Públicas, Transportes y Medio Ambiente, Madrid, Spain.

OECD (1993), *OECD Core Set of Indicators for Environmental Performance Review*, Environment Monograph No. 83, OECD, Paris.

Pallett, J. (ed.) (1997), *Sharing Water in Southern Africa*, Desert Research Foundation, Windhoek, Namibia.

Pedersen, L.A. and C. Tronier (2001), *1997 Water Accounts Related to NAMEA*, Statistics Denmark, Copenhagen.

Schoer, K. and C. Flachmann (2000), *Water Flow Accounts as Part of Material and Energy Flow Accounts in Germany*, Federal Statistical Office of Germany, Wiesbaden, Germany.

SMEC *see* Snowy Mountain Engineering Corporation.

Snowy Mountain Engineering Corporation (1991), *Botswana National Water Master Plan*. Report to Government of Botswana, Gaborone, Botswana.

Tafi, J. and J.-L. Weber (2000), 'Inland water accounts of the Republic of Moldova', Draft report to Eurostat, TACIS Project Environment Statistics MD92FR01.

United Nations (1993), *Integrated Environmental and Economic Accounting*, Studies in Methods, Handbook of National Accounting, Series F, No. 61, New York.

United Nations (2001), *Integrated Environmental and Economic Accounting 2000*, Draft available through the UN website: www.un.org.

Van der Merwe, B., B. Groom, S. Bethune, H. Buckle, R. Pietres, M. Redecker, R. Steynberg, L. Hugo and T. Basson (1998), 'Water demand management country study – Namibia', Report to IUCN (World Conservation Union) Regional Office for Southern Africa, Harare, Zimbabwe.

Windhoek Consulting Engineers, Interconsult, Desert Research Foundation of Namibia (1999), 'State of environment report on water in Namibia', Report prepared for the Ministry of Environment and Tourism.

World Resources Institute (1996), *World Resources 1996–1997*, Oxford, Oxford University Press.

WRI *see* World Resources Institute.

Young, R. (1996), 'Measuring economic benefits for water investments and policy', World Bank Technical Paper No. 338, Washington, DC, World Bank.

APPENDIX C: DETAILED WATER ACCOUNTS FOR BOTSWANA, NAMIBIA AND SOUTH AFRICA

Table C.1   Water use by supplying institution and natural source in Botswana 1993–98

A Millions of cubic metres

		1993/94	1994/95	1995/96	1996/97	1997/98	1998/99
Use by natural source							
	Groundwater	85.2	86.3	87.9	83.7	87.4	85.8
	Dams	27.6	27.9	28.3	28.5	31.3	34.6
	River	30.1	30.0	30.6	29.3	29.5	29.5
Total, all sources		142.8	144.1	146.7	141.5	148.2	149.8
Use by institution and natural source							
WUC	Dams	22.2	22.8	23.1	22.9	24.7	28.2
DWA	Groundwater	6.9	8.9	8.5	9.2	10.2	11.3
	Dams	1.3	1.0	0.8	0.8	1.0	1.1
	River	0.7	0.8	0.8	0.8	1.0	1.0
	Total DWA	8.9	10.6	10.2	10.8	12.2	13.4
DC	Groundwater	24.3	24.6	24.9	25.4	25.9	26.2
Self-providers	Groundwater	54.0	52.8	54.5	49.1	51.4	48.3
	Dams	4.0	4.1	4.4	4.8	5.6	5.2
	River	29.4	29.2	29.7	28.5	28.5	28.5
	Total	87.4	86.1	88.6	82.4	85.5	82.1

B. Percentage distribution by institutional source

	1993/94	1994/95	1995/96	1996/97	1997/98	1998/99
WUC	16	16	16	16	17	19
DWA	6	7	7	8	8	9
DC	17	17	17	18	17	17
Self-providers	61	60	60	58	58	55
Total	100	100	100	100	100	100

C. Percentage distribution by natural source

	1993/94	1994/95	1995/96	1996/97	1997/98	1998/99
Groundwater	60	60	60	59	59	57
Dams	19	19	19	20	21	23
River	21	21	21	21	20	20
Total	100	100	100	100	100	100

Source: Adapted from Lange et al. (2001).

Table C.2 Water use by detailed economic sector in Botswana, 1993 and 1998

	Cubic metres		Percentage	
	1993/94	1998/99	1993/94	1998/99
All agriculture	**71 693 610**	**67 336 815**	**50.2**	**44.9**
Traditional agriculture	49 879 471	45 728 111	34.9	30.5
Commercial agriculture	21 814 139	21 608 704	15.3	14.4
All mining	**16 207 370**	**15 546 713**	**11.4**	**10.4**
Diamond	12 038 060	9 772 720	8.4	6.5
Copper/nickel	3 825 441	5 362 622	2.7	3.6
Coal & other	343 869	411 371	0.2	0.3
Manufacturing	**2 215 297**	**3 023 146**	**1.6**	**2.0**
Food and beverages	1 488 529	1 543 176	1.0	1.0
Other manufacturing	726 768	1 479 969	0.5	1.0
Water & electricity	**1 539 260**	**1 536 684**	**1.1**	**1.0**
Construction	**309 513**	**187 522**	**0.2**	**0.1**
Services	**3 124 052**	**3 244 021**	**2.2**	**2.2**
Trade, hotels & restaurants	1 253 589	1 247 219	0.9	0.8
Transport, communications	166 066	179 670	0.1	0.1
Insurance, banking, business	472 631	567 410	0.3	0.4
Social and personal services	1 321 676	1 249 722	0.9	0.8
Government	**7 221 229**	**9 825 087**	**5.0**	**6.6**
Central	5 920 379	8 170 579	4.1	5.5
Local	1 300 851	1 654 508	0.9	1.1
Households	**40 526 175**	**49 144 792**	**28.4**	**32.8**
Urban	10 817 245	13 574 670	7.6	9.1
Peri-urban	5 446 493	9 392 100	3.8	6.3
Rural	24 262 437	26 178 022	17.0	17.5
Total	**142 836 507**	**149 844 780**	**100.0**	**100.0**

Source: Adapted from Lange et al. (2001).

Table C.3 Percentage distribution of water use, national income and employment by economic sector in Botswana, 1993 and 1998

Economic activity	1993/94			1998/99		
	Water use	National income	Employment	Water use	National income	Employment
Agriculture	**50.2**	**4.4**	**2.1**	**44.9**	**2.8**	**1.7**
Traditional	34.9	3.8	–	–	–	–
Commercial	15.3	0.4	–	–	–	–
Mining	**11.3**	**35.7**	**3.7**	**10.4**	**35.0**	**3.6**
Diamond	8.4	32.5	–	–	–	–
Copper/nickel	2.7	1.9	–	–	–	–
Coal & other	0.2	1.2	–	–	–	–
Manufacturing	**1.6**	**4.6**	**9.1**	**2.0**	**4.7**	**10.0**
Food & beverages	1.0	1.8	–	–	–	–
Other manufacturing	0.5	2.9	–	–	–	–
Water & electricity	**1.1**	**2.2**	**1.1**	**1.0**	**1.9**	**1.1**
Construction	**0.2**	**6.5**	**12.6**	**0.1**	**5.9**	**9.4**
Services	**2.2**	**26.4**	**36.2**	**2.2**	**30.3**	**32.4**
Trade, hotels & restaurants	0.9	8.3	18.4	0.8	11.8	18.0
Transport, communications	0.1	3.7	4.0	0.1	4.1	3.7
Insurance, banking, business	0.3	10.1	8.0	0.4	10.5	7.1
Social and personal services	0.9	4.3	5.8	0.8	3.9	3.6
Government	**5.1**	**15.6**	**35.2**	**6.6**	**16.0**	**41.8**
Central	4.1	13.3	–	–	–	–
Local	0.9	2.3	–	–	–	–
Households	28.4	NAP	NAP	32.8	NAP	NAP

Notes: '–': not available
        NAP: not applicable

Source: Adapted from Lange et al. (2001).

Table C.4   Use accounts for water by source and economic activity in Namibia, 1993 and 1996 (millions of cubic metres)

A. 1993

	Namwater				Rural water supply & self-providers				All	Total		
	Total	Ground	Ephemeral-Dams	Perennial River	Total	Ground	Ephemeral-Dams	Perennial River	All	Ground	Ephemeral-Dams	Perennial
Agriculture	**35.2**	**5.6**	**27.7**	**1.9**	**106.2**	**58.6**	**0.6**	**47.1**	**141.4**	**64.2**	**28.3**	**48.9**
Livestock	7.5	5.6	-	1.9	51.5	50.7	-	0.8	59.0	56.4	-	2.6
communal	7.5	5.6	-	1.9	16.7	15.9	-	0.8	24.2	21.6	-	2.6
commercial	-	-	-	-	34.8	34.8	-	-	34.8	34.8	-	-
Crops	27.7	-	27.7	-	54.7	7.9	0.6	46.3	82.4	7.9	28.3	46.3
communal	-	-	-	-	17.8	1.6	-	16.2	17.8	1.6	-	16.2
commercial	27.7	-	27.7	-	36.9	6.3	0.6	30.1	64.6	6.3	28.3	30.1
Mining	**4.4**	**3.0**	**0.5**	**0.9**	**17.3**	**17.3**	-	-	**21.7**	**20.3**	**0.5**	**0.9**
Diamond	-	-	0.5	-	13.6	13.6	-	-	13.6	13.6	0.5	-
Other mining	4.4	3.0	-	0.9	3.7	3.7	-	-	8.1	6.7	-	0.9
Manufacturing	**5.0**	**3.5**	**1.3**	**0.2**	-	-	-	-	**5.0**	**3.5**	**1.3**	**0.2**
Fish proc.	0.7	0.7	-	-	-	-	-	-	0.7	0.7	-	-
Other manuf.	4.3	2.8	1.3	0.2	-	-	-	-	4.3	2.8	1.3	0.2
Services	**5.0**	**3.4**	**1.4**	**0.2**	**0.2**	**0.2**	**0.1**	-	**5.2**	**3.6**	**1.5**	**0.2**
Utilities	0.3	0.2	0.1	0.0	-	-	-	-	0.3	0.2	0.1	0.0
Construction	0.7	0.5	0.2	0.0	-	-	-	-	0.7	0.5	0.2	0.0
Trade	0.7	0.5	0.2	0.0	-	-	-	-	0.7	0.5	0.2	0.0
Hotel/Rest.	0.9	0.6	0.3	-	0.2	0.2	0.1	-	1.1	0.8	0.4	-
Transport	0.8	0.7	0.1	0.0	-	-	-	-	0.8	0.7	0.1	0.0
Commun.	0.2	0.1	0.0	0.0	-	-	-	-	0.2	0.1	0.0	0.0
FIREB	0.6	0.4	0.2	0.0	-	-	-	-	0.6	0.4	0.2	0.0
Soc services	0.8	0.5	0.2	0.0	-	-	-	-	0.8	0.5	0.2	0.0
Government	**2.3**	**1.5**	**0.7**	**0.1**	**34.3**	**30.0**	**0.7**	**3.6**	**36.6**	**31.5**	**1.4**	**3.7**
Households	**34.7**	**22.6**	**10.4**	**1.7**	**34.3**	**30.0**	**0.7**	**3.6**	**69.0**	**52.5**	**11.2**	**5.3**
Urban	34.7	22.6	10.4	1.7	-	-	-	-	34.7	22.6	10.4	1.7
Rural												
Communal	-	-	-	-	10.0	5.7	0.7	3.6	10.0	5.7	0.7	3.6
Commercial farms	-	-	-	-	24.3	24.3	-	-	24.3	24.3	-	-
Total	**86.6**	**39.6**	**42.0**	**5.0**	**158.0**	**106.0**	**1.4**	**50.7**	**244.6**	**145.6**	**43.3**	**55.7**

B. 1996

	Namwater				Rural water supply & self-providers				Total			
	Total	Ground	Ephemeral-Dams	Perennial River	Total	Ground	Ephemeral-Dams	Perennial River	All	Ground	Ephemeral-Dams	Perennial
Agriculture	**46.6**	**1.4**	**30.0**	**15.2**	**96.4**	**47.2**	**0.6**	**48.6**	**142.9**	**48.6**	**30.6**	**63.8**
Livestock	16.6	1.4	–	15.2	41.7	39.3	–	2.3	58.2	40.7	–	17.5
communal	16.6	1.4	–	15.2	15.6	13.3	–	2.3	32.2	14.7	–	17.5
commercial	–	–	–	–	26.0	26.0	–	–	26.0	26.0	–	–
Crops	30.0	–	30.0	–	54.7	7.9	0.6	46.3	84.7	7.9	30.6	46.3
communal	–	–	–	–	17.8	1.6	–	16.2	17.8	1.6	–	16.2
commercial	30.0	–	30.0	–	36.9	6.3	0.6	30.1	66.9	6.3	30.6	30.1
Mining	**5.5**	**2.9**	**1.2**	**1.4**	**19.7**	**19.7**	**–**	**–**	**25.2**	**22.6**	**1.2**	**1.4**
Diamond	–	–	–	–	13.6	13.6	–	–	13.6	13.6	–	–
Other mining	5.5	2.9	1.2	1.4	6.1	6.1	–	–	11.6	9.0	1.2	1.4
Manufacturing	**5.3**	**3.8**	**1.5**	**–**	**–**	**–**	**–**	**–**	**5.3**	**3.8**	**1.5**	**–**
Fish proc.	0.5	0.5	–	–	–	–	–	–	0.5	0.5	–	–
Other manuf.	4.8	3.3	1.5	–	–	–	–	–	4.8	3.3	1.5	–
Services	**5.4**	**3.7**	**1.3**	**0.3**	**0.3**	**0.2**	**0.1**	**–**	**5.6**	**3.9**	**1.4**	**0.3**
Utilities	0.4	0.3	0.1	–	–	–	–	–	0.4	0.3	0.1	–
Construction	0.8	0.5	0.2	–	–	–	–	–	0.8	0.5	0.2	–
Trade	0.8	0.6	0.3	–	–	–	–	–	0.8	0.6	0.3	–
Transport	0.8	0.5	–	0.3	–	–	–	–	0.8	0.5	–	0.3
Hotel/Rest.	0.9	0.7	0.2	–	0.3	0.2	0.1	–	1.2	0.9	0.3	–
Commun.	0.2	0.1	0.1	–	–	–	–	–	0.2	0.1	0.1	–
FIREB	0.7	0.5	0.2	–	–	–	–	–	0.7	0.5	0.2	–
Soc services	0.8	0.5	0.3	–	–	–	–	–	0.8	0.5	0.3	–
Government	**2.4**	**1.7**	**0.8**	**–**	**–**	**–**	**–**	**–**	**2.4**	**1.7**	**0.8**	**–**
Households	**39.2**	**17.0**	**11.1**	**11.1**	**34.6**	**30.2**	**3.7**	**0.7**	**73.8**	**47.1**	**14.8**	**11.8**
Urban	39.2	17.0	11.1	11.1	–	–	–	–	39.2	17.0	11.1	11.1
Rural	–	–	–	–	34.6	30.2	3.7	0.7	34.6	30.2	3.7	0.7
Communal	–	–	–	–	10.3	5.9	3.7	0.7	10.3	5.9	3.7	0.7
Commercial farms	–	–	–	–	24.3	24.3	–	–	24.3	24.3	–	–
Total	**104.6**	**30.7**	**45.9**	**28.1**	**150.9**	**97.2**	**4.4**	**49.4**	**255.5**	**127.9**	**50.3**	**77.4**

Note: Under the column 'Rural water supply and self-providers', rural water supply provides water to communal agriculture and rural households in communal areas, self-providers are responsible for all other water.

Source: Adapted from Lange (1998 and 2002).

Table C.5   Distribution of water by institution and natural source in Namibia, 1993 and 1996

	1993 (%)	1996 (%)
Namwater		
Ground	16	12
Ephemeral/dams	17	18
Perennial	2	11
Total	35	41
Rural water supply		
Ground	9	11
Ephemeral/dams	*	1
Perennial	8	7
Total	18	19
Self-providers		
Ground	34	27
Ephemeral/dams	*	*
Perennial	12	13
Total	46	40
Total		
Ground	60	50
Ephemeral/dams	18	20
Perennial	23	30
Total	100	100

Note: *less than 1%.

Source: based on Table A4.

Table C.6   Economic contribution of water by sector in Namibia, 1993 and 1996 (in constant 1990 prices)

Economic activity	Water use (millions of cubic metres)		Value-added per cubic metre of water input (N\$/m^3)	
	1993	1996	1993	1996
Agriculture	**141.0**	**143.0**	**3.1**	**4.0**
Commercial	93.0	**3.4**	**3.8**	3.8
Subsistence	50.0	**2.4**	**4.4**	4.4
Fishing	–	–	–	–
Mining	**21.7**	**25.2**	**56.9**	**60.4**
Diamond mining	13.6	13.6	56.0	69.1
Other mining	8.1	11.6	58.3	50.2
Manufacturing	**5.0**	**5.3**	**173.6**	**165.2**
Fish processing	0.7	0.5	330.4	328.6
Other manufacturing	4.3	4.8	148.2	148.4
Services	**5.2**	**5.5**	**266.6**	**283.0**
Hotels & restaurants	1.1	1.2	79.5	103.1
Transportation	0.8	0.8	225.6	284.3
Other services	3.3	3.5	341.3	341.8
GDP per cubic metre of water used	**244.6**	**255.5**	**29.7**	**32.3**

Notes: GDP does not sum to total value-added because of omission of government, dummy sector, and some taxes.
The economic contribution of water in government and household use of water cannot be calculated in this way.

Source: Adapted from Lange (1998 and 2002).

Table C.7   Water supply by institutional source in South Africa, 1998 (million cubic metres)

Sector	Raw/self-extracted water	Water agency	Return flow/effluent	Loss	Total supply
Primary sources	**611 601**				**611 601**
Water suppliers					
DWAF / CMA		6766		NA	6766
Irrigation boards		4833		NA	4833
Water boards		1264		NA	1264
District councils		131		NA	131
Local authorities		426		NA	426
Evaporation				2383	2383
Sub-total		**13 420**		**NA**	**13 420**
Water use groups					
Households					
Rural			2		2
Urban			828	338	1166
Environment			830	338	1168
Evapotranspiration					
Groundwater					
IFR					
Sub-total			**1858**	**676**	**2336**

Economic activities

Irrigation Agriculture			
Subsistence			
Field crops	331	2724	3056
Horticulture crops	158	1298	1456
Livestock	221		221
Mining	76		76
Other bulk	22		22
Strategic	297	60	357
Manufacturing	56	11	67
Construction	233	48	281
Trade, hotels, restaurants	146	30	176
Transport	23	5	28
Communication	240		
Finance, real estate, business services	60	12	72
Other private services	72	15	87
Other producers	72	15	87
Sub-total	2764	NA	
Grand total	**611 601**	**13 420**	**627 785**

Notes:
Blank means zero.
NA: not available.

Source: Adapted from CSIR (2001).

Table C.8 Use of water in South Africa, 1998 (million cubic metres)

Sector (water use group)	Raw/self-extracted water	Water supply sector	Return flow/ effluent	Loss	Use
Households					
Rural	243	547			790
Urban		1249			1249
Sub-total	**243**	**1796**			**2038**
Natural environment					
Evapotranspiration & deep seepage	484 518				467 199
Groundwater	16 865				16 865
IFR	17 738				17 738
River loss	1192				1192
Sub-total	**520 313**				**520 313**
Economic activities					
Dryland uses					
Alien vegetation	11 420				11 420
Forestry	16 731				16 731
Sugar	2693				2693
Other	45 359				45 359

Irrigation Agriculture			
Subsistence	0	17	17
Field crops	155	6979	7134
Horticulture crops	74	3326	3399
Livestock	517		517
Mining	218	235	453
Other bulk	26	216	241
Strategic	441		441
Manufacturing		223	223
Construction		42	42
Trade, hotels, restaurants		176	176
Transport & communication		110	110
Transport		17	17
Communication		181	181
Finance, real estate, business services		45	45
Other private services		54	54
Other producers		45	45
Sub-total	**74 133**	**11 623**	**89 255**
Grand total	**594 688**	**13 418**	**611 607**

Note:
Blank means zero.

Source: Adapted from CSIR (2001).

201

Table C.9   *Economic contribution of water by sector in South Africa, 1998*
(Rands/cubic metre of water input)

Economic activity	Value-added per cubic metre of water (R and /m^3)
Agriculture	1.4
Field crops	0.7
Horticulture crops	0.8
Livestock	15.7
Forestry	0.6
Pine	0.4
Eucalyptus	0.7
Wattle	2.1
Fishing	298.0
Mining	80.0
Gold	77.0
Coal	262.0
Other	62.0
Manufacturing	296.0
Electricity	197.0
Water	0.8
Construction	234.0
Trade, restaurants & hotels	256.0
Transport	189.0
Communication	354.0
Finance, real estate, business services	277.0
Other private services	253.0
General government services	269.0
Other producers	82.0

Source: Adapted from CSIR (2001).

6. Managing natural capital and national wealth

Kirk Hamilton and Glenn-Marie Lange

6.1 INTRODUCTION

The preceding chapters have presented a rich set of data on the natural resource endowment of the selected African countries. This final chapter aims to place this micro information into the macro context. We wish to examine the following broad questions:

- What is the role of natural resources in development, and how can natural resource accounting assist in the analysis of this question?
- What are the links between total wealth (including natural resources), welfare and sustainability?
- What is the evidence on the evolution of national wealth in Botswana, Namibia and South Africa?
- What are the policy challenges that resource-dependent economies face?

6.2 THE ROLE OF NATURAL RESOURCES IN DEVELOPMENT

It is notable that the role of natural resource endowments in development is treated only lightly, if at all, in the traditional literature on development economics. Where they are discussed it is generally in the context of first, the agricultural sector, and second, the question of the declining terms of trade for natural resource exporting countries.

The discussion of the agriculture sector in the development economics literature focuses on two issues: the low productivity of this sector, and the inevitable decline in relative importance of the sector owing to Engel's Law. The productivity issue is key, since the process of development is dependent on the accumulation of surpluses for investment. Generally speaking, the low productivity in the agricultural sector is attributed to low levels of technology and low levels of inputs, and only occasionally is there mention of the quality of the resource itself, agricultural land.

The question of declining terms of trade is the well-known Prebisch–Singer hypothesis – the claim is that developing countries face a structural disadvantage in the form of long-run declines in the terms of trade for their major tradable goods, primary products. It is certainly true that real prices for minerals and mineral fuels have been declining gradually over the course of decades, but there is some evidence that there have been gradual increases in real prices for tropical timber, particularly hardwoods.

Natural resources play two clear roles in the process of development. First, resource exports are a source of foreign exchange, essential for the import of capital goods as economies develop. Second, natural resources represent a source of finance for development. This second role is unique. While produced assets yield profits that can be consumed or invested, natural resources yield profits over and above this level in the form of resource rents. A critical part of the development process for resource-rich nations is the process of transforming resource rents into other productive assets – this role will be discussed further in the next section.

As a potential source of development finance, the management of natural resources raises important questions:

- Are rents being captured? This is partly a question of revenues – is the government as the owner of the natural resource being compensated for the exploitation of the resource? But it is also a question of incentives. If private firms are appropriating the resource rents then they will have an incentive to exploit the resources rapidly and quite possibly wastefully, aiming to profit as much as possible before the government exercises its rights. This can lead to 'high-grading' of resources and dynamic inefficiencies.
- Is access to the resource being controlled? This is a critical issue for living resources, especially fisheries. Open access to a fishery leads to rent dissipation, and an overall decline in the value of the resource.

Competing Uses and Externalities

A key feature of forest resources is that the land on which the forests stand has an opportunity cost. Optimal deforestation implies clearing land for agriculture up to the point where the benefits under agriculture just equal the benefits under forestry for the marginal hectare. However, for this optimum to be a social optimum, all of the external benefits provided by forest cover (soil conservation, watershed regulation, carbon sequestration) have to be added to the extractive and non-extractive benefits of forests (timber, non-timber products, recreation and tourism).

Sustainability

Non-living resources are not productive (they can only yield a rate of return over time through the capital gains inherent in the Hotelling Rule) and so the question of the sustainability of the resource *per se* is not an issue. The optimal policy is to convert non-living resource assets into other productive assets. But for living resources, with a natural rate of yield or growth, sustainability of the resource is an important concern. Except for the slowest-growing of resources, the economic optimum for exploiting living resources will generally be to harvest these resources sustainably. The questions of resource rent capture and control of access to resources are highly germane to this question.

Given these characteristics of natural resources in the development process, it is important to emphasize the role that natural resource accounting can play in helping to manage resources. Many of the features of natural resource accounting in this regard have been highlighted in the preceding chapters.

First, natural resource accounting can provide physical information on harvest rates and rates of natural growth for living resources. This is key to the sustainability question. Second, natural resource accounting yields estimates of available rents, an important element of the question of rent capture. Armed with information on available rents, governments can approach the issue of levels of and instruments for rent capture on a sound basis. Finally, natural resource accounting can be used to estimate external benefits generated by resources, and potential non-extractive benefits as well. For forests in particular, this aspect of natural resource accounting is critical for governments seeking to maximize the social benefits of resource exploitation.

This section has emphasized the role that individual resources can play in economic development and the role that natural resource accounting can play in their management. But natural resources represent just one portion of the set of assets that underpins development. The next section emphasizes the process of managing the overall portfolio of assets that countries possess in order to achieve development objectives (including sustainability of development).

6.3   WEALTH, WELFARE AND SUSTAINABILITY

The question of the sustainability of economic activity in the face of declining natural resources is a concern that goes back to the early 1970s. Solow (1974), among others, derived conditions for an economy with an exhaustible resource to avoid inevitable decline as the resource depletes, and Hartwick (1977) encapsulated the key insight of this literature in the 'Hartwick Rule': invest resource rents. An economy where net investment is equal to zero (that is, where investment in produced assets is just equal to the value of depletion of natural resources) and resources are priced efficiently (the Hotelling Rule) will achieve maximal constant consumption over time, even as the resource base is depleted.

The linkage of sustainability and asset values was examined empirically by Pearce and Atkinson (1993), who found that the net rate of saving for many developing countries was actually very small or negative when account is taken of resource depletion and pollution damages. This work, and subsequent empirical work by the World Bank (1997) emphasized the commonsense notion that sustaining economic output, and levels of consumption and welfare in particular, depends on maintaining a non-declining level of total assets.

These commonsense notions have been made more precise in work by Hamilton and Clemens (1999) and Dasgupta and Mäler (2000). These papers yield the following key result for present value of total utility along a future development path W, shadow prices p_i, assets K_i, and marginal utility of consumption U_c:

$$U_c \cdot \Sigma p_i \Delta K_i = \Delta W.$$

This states that the change in the present value of utility is proportional to the change in the real value of assets (termed 'genuine saving' in Hamilton and Clemens, to distinguish it from standard measures of net saving). This expression provides a fundamental linkage between wealth, welfare and sustainability, and has three key consequences:

- A positive value of genuine saving at a point in time implies that the present value of social welfare (as measured by the utility function) is increasing.
- A development path where genuine saving is everywhere positive is a path where the present value of social welfare is always increasing.
- A negative value of genuine saving at a point in time implies that welfare at some point in the future must be less than current welfare – this is equivalent to saying that negative genuine saving implies unsustainability.

Note that this relationship between saving and the present value of social welfare will hold for any specification of the utility function. In practice, of course, there will be a linkage between the assets in question and the constituents of well-being. If people value forests for their non-timber values, for example, this will affect how shadow prices should be estimated (see Chapter 3).

This linkage between the change in the real value of assets and the change in the present value of welfare is only policy-relevant if a sufficiently broad array of assets is taken into account. This provides a fundamental justification for the importance of natural resource accounting in resource-dependent economies. Many of the resource accounting results presented in preceding chapters provide the raw materials for measuring genuine saving, in particular (1) the change in the physical quantity of assets, and (2) the change in asset value associated with a unit of extraction or harvest (these are the shadow prices in the expression above, based on resource rents and assumptions about future prices, quantities and costs).

Is a positive genuine saving rate cause for complacence? There are three reasons to think not. First, it may be that an insufficiently wide array of assets is being accounted – human health and mortality, for example, should at least be valued at the margin if not as a total stock (this has consequences for countries with high under-five mortality). Second, it may be that reforms in the economy and environmental management can yield large gains in saving, which implies large gains in the present value of social welfare. Finally, population growth may be swamping total saving effort.

The role of population growth can be explained by the following formula, where K is total wealth (including all of the assets highlighted above), ΔK is genuine saving, and P is total population:

$$\Delta \left(\frac{K}{P} \right) = \frac{K}{P} \left(\frac{\Delta K}{K} - \frac{\Delta P}{P} \right).$$

This expression says that changes in wealth per capita are proportional to the difference between the percentage change in total wealth and the percentage change in population. Hamilton (2000) estimates this relationship for roughly 100 countries in 1997 and concludes that, empirically speaking, (1) if the population growth rate is greater than 1.2 per cent, or (2) if the rate of genuine saving is less than 10 per cent of GDP, then countries are highly likely to be on a declining wealth per capita path – this implies unsustainability in an economy where population is growing.

6.4   EMPIRICAL ESTIMATES OF NATIONAL WEALTH INCLUDING NATURAL CAPITAL

An additional measure of sustainable development can be provided by total national wealth, which is a combination of produced capital and natural capital. This figure amounts to a national asset portfolio that can be analysed to assess the diversity of wealth, ownership distribution and volatility due to price fluctuations, an important feature for economies dependent on primary commodities. Diversity is important because, in general, the more diverse an economy is, the more resilient it will be to economic disturbances. Volatility is also important in planning for the future – lower volatility contributes to more stable economic development. The distribution of the ownership of assets – between public and private sector, the concentration among different groups in society, and between domestic and foreign owners – can have significant economic implications and can influence the sustainable management of resources.

Most countries with asset accounts for natural capital have typically published the accounts separately for each resource and have not attempted a measure of total natural capital (the sum of all resources), or a measure of total national wealth (the sum of manufactured and natural capital). Among the developing countries, Botswana and Namibia are doing so. Among the industrialized countries, Australia and Canada have integrated non-produced natural assets with produced assets in their consolidated balance sheets.

In some cases, policy makers may simply be unconcerned about wealth – most countries have traditionally focused much more on the income and product flow accounts of the SNA than the asset accounts. Some developing countries may not even compile capital stock accounts for manufactured capital, except informally to calculate depreciation. Many indicators of sustainability have also been based on measures of flows rather than stocks, for example, net domestic product or 'genuine savings'. In other cases, there may be a reluctance to combine conventional measures of manufactured capital with what may be viewed as experimental calculations for natural capital, especially when there is controversy over the assumptions necessary for valuation, or over the policy implications of the results, for example, fisheries in Chile (X. Aguilar, pers. comm).

In the discussion that follows, the total wealth of Botswana and Namibia are presented and compared based on work by Lange (2001a, 2001b). Wealth accounts have not yet been compiled for South Africa. In using national wealth to monitor economic sustainability, it is crucial to include all assets, or at least as many as possible (human capital is not yet included). The natural capital assets for Botswana's accounts currently include only minerals, discussed in Chapter 2; Namibia's asset accounts include minerals and fisheries, discussed in Chapters 2 and 4. There are three major omissions from the natural capital accounts for Botswana and Namibia: land, wildlife and water. The potential impact on the results is discussed before proceeding to an analysis of trends in national wealth.

While physical accounts for land are relatively easy to construct, monetary accounts have not been constructed because no market prices exist for the very large portions of the land under communal tenure. In Botswana, less than 4 per cent of land is privately held; 42 per cent is state owned and 54 per cent is held under communal tenure, of which a small share can be leased for commercial agriculture. In Namibia, 44 per cent of land is privately held; roughly 15 per cent is state owned and 41 per cent is held under communal tenure. Even private land is not taxed so there is no assessed value that can be used for constructing monetary land asset accounts. Physical accounts for wildlife and water are very incomplete; monetary accounts for these resources have not been constructed yet.

Of the omissions of natural capital, land is probably the most serious. The consolidated balance sheet for Australia indicates that natural capital – land, forests, subsoil assets – accounted for roughly 37 per cent of non-financial assets over the past decade, and that land accounted for three-quarters of the value of natural capital (ABS, 2000). On the other hand, state and traditional tenure land dominate the land accounts of Botswana and Namibia, and the value of traditional tenure land, used largely for subsistence agriculture, will not have the same value as either built-up agricultural land or urban developed land.

Another important component of a country's asset portfolio is its net foreign financial assets. It is not uncommon for resource-rich developing countries, like some of the major oil-producing countries, to invest much of the income from resource exploitation in foreign assets, especially if the economy is small and opportunities for domestic investment are limited. For such countries, net foreign financial assets form a significant share of national wealth. Indeed, for Botswana, government foreign financial assets have grown increasingly important; figures are not yet available for Namibia.

The trend of national wealth over time indicates, at an aggregate level, whether capital is maintained and whether depletion of natural capital, if it has occurred, has been compensated for by an increase in other forms of capital. In both countries the value of total capital, in constant prices, has increased over time, although at markedly different rates. Botswana's wealth increased enormously, from 14.7 billion pula in 1980 to 70.4 billion pula in 1997 (Table 6.1). Namibia's wealth increased by only 33 per cent over the same period. Whatever depletion of resources has occurred in the two countries has been compensated for by a combination of factors: an increase in produced assets and, for non-produced assets, new discoveries, an increase in economically profitable resources and an increase in the economic value of the resources due to more rapid extraction.

The period from 1990 onward is especially important for Namibia. Prior to independence in 1990, Namibia's resources were exploited by an occupying country, South Africa, with relatively little concern for Namibia's own national development. As a result, by the time Namibia had achieved independence its resources were vastly depleted – major fish stocks were less than 25 per cent of their former level and onshore diamonds were largely exhausted, forcing the industry to move to more costly offshore diamond mining. Namibia's wealth increased significantly with the establishment of its 200-mile Exclusive Economic Zone at independence in 1990, which brought its fisheries under national control for the first time, adding this asset to the national wealth. Without fisheries, Namibia's wealth would only have increased by 24 per cent between 1980 and 1998.

In addition to the volume of wealth, the composition of wealth is also an important indicator to monitor because, generally, a more diverse economy is a more resilient one. Many resource-rich developing countries have identified economic diversification as one of their development objectives. A comparison of the shares of produced and natural capital over time is one approach to monitoring this aspect of resilience and progress toward diversification.

Table 6.1   Total wealth in Botswana and Namibia, 1980–98 (in constant prices)

A.   Botswana (millions of pula in constant 1993/94 prices)

| | | Produced assets | | | |
	Govt.	Private	Minerals	Net govt. financial assets	Total
1980/81	1872	4260	8323	229	14 686
1981/82	2101	4661	8078	382	15 223
1982/83	2312	4851	12 448	428	20 039
1983/84	2491	5055	17 076	799	25 420
1984/85	2782	5516	20 431	1036	29 764
1985/86	3056	5715	20 046	2916	31 732
1986/87	3461	5983	20 799	3882	34 125
1987/88	4247	6391	20 996	4884	36 518
1988/89	4934	7494	24 053	5419	41 899
1989/90	5441	9030	24 067	6326	44 864
1990/91	6149	10 266	27 207	7206	50 828
1991/92	6797	11 179	25 921	8558	52 455
1992/93	7517	11 906	25 073	8687	53 183
1993/94	8330	12 359	23 236	9241	53 166
1994/95	8910	12 999	24 451	9837	56 197
1995/96	9678	13 497	26 267	10 001	59 443
1996/97	10 596	13 985	27 566	12 378	64 524
1997/98	11 591	14 811	30 892	13 074	70 368

Table 6.1 continued

B. Namibia (millions of Namibian $ in constant 1990 prices)

			Produced assets		
	Government	Private	Minerals	Fisheries	Total
1980	12 410	10 075	2352		24 837
1981	12 649	10 552	1778		24 978
1982	12 679	10 943	1624		25 247
1983	12 547	11 170	1534		25 251
1984	12 343	11 327	1451		25 121
1985	12 107	11 522	1923		25 552
1986	11 888	11 642	2695		26 225
1987	11 711	11 847	3036		26 594
1988	11 656	11 942	3567		27 166
1989	11 753	11 978	3883		27 614
1990	11 909	12 080	3475	1526	28 991
1991	11 860	12 127	3212	1262	28 461
1992	12 119	12 263	2878	1596	28 856
1993	12 430	12 384	2136	2155	29 104
1994	12 860	12 514	1888	2149	29 412
1995	13 279	12 628	1709	1268	28 883
1996	13 797	12 708	2397	746	29 649
1997	14 231	12 771	3061	1009	31 071
1998	15 293	13 058	3000	1709	33 060

Note: Botswana and Namibia mineral wealth calculated using 10 per cent return to fixed capital. Namibia fish wealth calculated using a 20 per cent return to fixed capital.
Blank means zero entry; fish were not counted as part of Namibia's wealth prior to 1990 because Namibia exerted little control over this resource (see Chapter 4 for further discussion).

Source: Lange (2002). Natural capital from Chapters 2 and 4. Botswana figures for produced capital from CSO (1998) and net government foreign financial assets from Bank of Botswana (2000). Namibia figures for produced capital from CBS (2000).

Natural capital is important in both countries, but especially in Botswana (Table 6.2). In Botswana, the composition of national wealth has changed, since the mid-1980s. As the share of mineral wealth declined from 57 per cent to 44 per cent between 1980 and 1997, net foreign financial assets increased from 2 per cent to 19 per cent. The share of produced capital declined slightly, from 42 per cent to 38 per cent. However, the share of private sector capital declined significantly, 29 per cent to 22 per cent, while the share of public capital grew, 13 per cent to 16 per cent. The depletion of mineral assets has been offset by investment in other assets, mainly financial assets and public sector investment. However, the economy is still dominated by mining, measured by mining's share of assets as well as GDP and exports. The declining share of private sector capital reflects slow progress in achieving government's objective of economic diversification.

The share of natural capital is much smaller in Namibia, 9 per cent in 1980 rising to 14 per cent by 1998 with the addition of fish wealth after 1990. Namibia's mineral wealth has been fairly steady at 9 per cent throughout the period, except for a temporary rise in the late 1980s. The 1980s was a period of great political uncertainty leading up to independence in 1990; investment in private sector fixed capital was very weak and the amount of private sector

Table 6.2   Distribution of wealth by type of asset in Botswana and Namibia, 1980–98

A.   Botswana

		Produced assets			
	Govt.	Private	Minerals	Net govt. financial assets	Total
1980/81	13	29	57	2	100
1981/82	14	31	53	3	100
1982/83	12	24	62	2	100
1983/84	10	20	67	3	100
1984/85	9	19	69	3	100
1985/86	10	18	63	9	100
1986/87	10	18	61	11	100
1987/88	12	18	57	13	100
1988/89	12	18	57	13	100
1989/90	12	20	54	14	100
1990/91	12	20	54	14	100
1991/92	13	21	49	16	100
1992/93	14	22	47	16	100
1993/94	16	23	44	17	100
1994/95	16	23	44	18	100
1995/96	16	23	44	17	100
1996/97	16	22	43	19	100
1997/98	16	21	44	19	100

Table 6.2 continued

B. Namibia (millions of Namibian $ in constant 1990 prices)

| | **Produced capital** | | **Natural capital** | | |
	Government	Private	Minerals	Fisheries	Total
1980	50	41	9		100
1981	51	42	7		100
1982	50	43	6		100
1983	50	44	6		100
1984	49	45	6		100
1985	47	45	8		100
1986	45	44	10		100
1987	44	45	11		100
1988	43	44	13		100
1989	43	43	14		100
1990	41	42	12	5	100
1991	42	43	11	4	100
1992	42	42	10	6	100
1993	43	43	7	7	100
1994	44	43	6	7	100
1995	46	44	6	4	100
1996	47	43	8	3	100
1997	46	41	10	3	100
1998	46	39	9	5	100

Source: Table 6.1.

capital actually declined. Since independence, private investment has returned, and private sector capital stock has increased. But the growth of all produced capital in Namibia has been quite slow over the past 20 years compared with Botswana.

Although total assets in each country have grown continuously, considerable volatility among different assets underlies this smooth growth. Considering only natural capital, the share of minerals in total wealth in Botswana first increased from 57 per cent to 69 per cent between 1980 and 1984, and then declined. The natural capital of Namibia also appears to fluctuate, a volatility that is more pronounced when its natural assets are examined individually.

The public and private sectors may have different resource management objectives, which affect the way resources are exploited. Consequently, monitoring the distribution of asset ownership between public and private sectors may be useful, not as a direct indicator of sustainability, but as an aid to resource management. The private sector is motivated largely by commercial concerns, which can favour short-term economic efficiency, but also depletion of renewable resources under certain conditions. Government may or may not utilize resources in a sustainable manner, and it may use resources to achieve other socio-economic objectives, even if this lowers the economic return from a resource.

The response to the depletion of natural capital may also differ between the private and public sector. Where depletion occurs, sustainability requires reinvestment in other forms of capital. Private ownership may result in reinvestment in private sector activities, but foreign ownership may result in reinvestment elsewhere, which does not benefit the country providing the wealth. In countries where the government owns the resource and recovers most of the resource rent, the government bears responsibility for reinvestment, often investing in public sector capital. There is disagreement over the extent to which growth in government assets is an effective substitute for other forms of capital. There is a tendency to assume that government is economically inefficient compared with the private sector, but it is also well documented that the private sector will underinvest in assets where social benefits exceed private benefits, like public infrastructure and human capital. In any case, it is useful to monitor the distribution of capital, as well as its level and composition.

In Botswana and Namibia, minerals and fisheries are owned by the state. Private sector manufactured capital has been growing faster than public sector manufactured capital in Namibia, while the opposite is true in Botswana.

So far, we have considered only trends in total wealth. However, in most countries, population is still increasing, so a constant level of wealth and income would result in a declining per capita level of wealth and income for future generations. Intergenerational equity requires that not just total wealth, but per capita national wealth is non-declining over time. Figure 6.1 shows the index of per capita wealth in constant prices from 1980 to 2000. For Botswana (1980 to 1997), the net worth figure, including net foreign financial assets, is used; for Namibia (1980 to 1998), only produced plus natural capital are available. For comparison, a similar index was constructed for Australia (1992 to 2000), which, like Botswana, includes produced assets non-produced assets, and net foreign financial assets.

Per capita wealth has grown the fastest for Botswana, averaging more than 10 per cent annually to achieve a nearly fivefold increase from 1980 to 1997. Australia's per capita wealth increased at a much slower rate, averaging less than 2 per cent annually from 1992 to 2000. However, the figures for Namibia, adjusted by population growth, show a disturbing trend: per capita wealth has

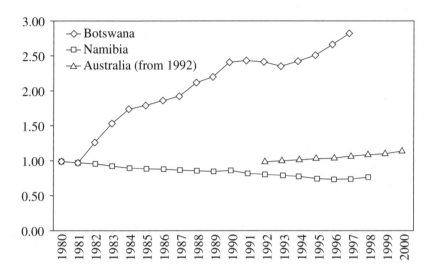

(Botswana and Namibia, 1980 =1.00
Australia, 1992 = 1.00)

Notes: Index calculated in constant prices.
National wealth is net worth for Australia and Botswana. For Namibia, only produced + natural capital are included.

Source: Table 1 and population figures from CSO (1997) and CBS (2000). Figures for Australia compiled from (Australian Bureau of Statistics, 2000).

Figure 6.1   *Index of per capita, constant-value total wealth in Botswana, Namibia and Australia*

declined by 23 per cent from 1980 to 1998. Without information about foreign financial assets, it is not certain whether the figure reported understates or overstates asset growth. However, Namibia has not had a policy of reinvesting rent from natural capital so it is highly unlikely that it has substantial foreign financial assets which might counterbalance the per capita decline in other assets.

6.5 THE POLICY CHALLENGE FOR RESOURCE-ABUNDANT ECONOMIES

The information and analysis provided in this and preceding chapters provides the evidence for substantial resource abundance in the countries of eastern and southern Africa. It is important to conclude this analysis with an exploration of the opportunities and difficulties that resource abundance poses for policy-making.

At first glance resource abundance should be a considerable advantage in the process of economic development. If two countries start out the development process with similar levels of income and produced assets per capita, but one is resource-abundant and the other not, then the greater natural endowment should favour the resource-rich country. The wealthier country should be able to grow more quickly. In fact, there is evidence to support what Auty (1993) termed the 'resource curse', formalized in the 'staple trap model' presented in Auty (2001, Chapter 1). Sachs and Warner (1995) provide cross-sectional analysis to show that the most resource-dependent economies have in fact experienced worse growth performance than their resource-poor counterparts.

This literature suggests that resource-abundant economies face many policy challenges, summarized in Sarraf and Jiwanji (2001). First, there is a risk of 'Dutch disease' for these economies as resource sectors boom. The surge in foreign exchange leads to an appreciation in the real exchange rate, changing the relative prices of tradable manufactures versus non-tradables, and hampering the competitiveness of the tradable manufacturing sector. As resource revenues are absorbed into the domestic economy, the non-tradable sector benefits the most, and there is pressure for government to protect the uncompetitive manufacturing sector.

Skills accumulation can suffer under these circumstances, as the domestic manufacturing sector languishes. This reduces both learning-by-doing and the demand for education.

Low linkage of the resource sector to the rest of the economy means that the primary way that resources benefit economies is through resource taxation. This in turn places an enormous premium on the effectiveness of the use of government revenues, including, as noted elsewhere in this book, whether these revenues are consumed or invested.

Ineffective economic management is therefore a heightened risk in these economies. In particular, it is difficult for governments to restrain expenditures once a resource boom ends, leading to risks of substantial deficits and high rates of inflation. Unproductive investment booms are also a risk during boom times, with 'white elephant' projects proliferating. And the existence of easy money in the form of resource revenues may simply reduce the urgency of reforming economies, with unfortunate consequences once the resource boom ends.

Rent-seeking is also a risk in these economies. Again, the existence of easy money makes it potentially highly profitable for individuals and institutions both within and outside government to invest time and effort in attempting to appropriate rents rather than engaging in productive economic activity.

Risks to sound policy-making abound in resource-rich countries, therefore. But resource endowments are not fate. As catalogued in Auty (2001), there are countries where prudent management of the resource sectors and resource revenues have been the springboard for economic growth. Chief among these countries are Malaysia and, of considerable relevance to this study, Botswana.

REFERENCES

Australian Bureau of Statistics (2000), Australian System of National Accounts. Consolidated Balance Sheet, ABS, Canberra, Australia.

Auty, R. (1993), *Sustaining Development in Mineral Economies: The Resource Curse Thesis*, London, Routledge.

Auty, R. (ed.) (2001), *Resource Abundance and Economic Development*, WIDER Studies in Development Economics, Oxford, Oxford University Press.

Bank of Botswana (2000), *Annual Report 2000*, Gaborone, Botswana.

CBS *see* Central Bureau of Statistics.

Central Bureau of Statistics (2000), unpublished data on population of Namibia.

Central Statistics Office (1997), *Population Projections, 1991–2021*, Gaborone, Botswana, Central Statistics Office.

Central Statistics Office (1998), 'National accounts statistics – capital stock', Stats Brief No. 98/7, June, Gaborone, Botswana, Central Statistics Office.

CSO *see* Central Statistics Office.

Dasgupta, P. and K.-G. Mäler (2000), 'Net national product, wealth, and social well-being', *Environment and Development Economics*, 5, Parts 1 and 2: 69–93.

Hamilton, K. (2000), 'Sustaining economic welfare: estimating changes in national wealth', Policy Research Working Paper No. 2498, Washington, OC, World Bank.

Hamilton, K. and M. Clemens (1999), 'Genuine saving in developing countries', *World Bank Economic Review*, 13(2): 33–56.

Hartwick, J.M. (1977), 'Intergenerational equity and the investing of rents from exhaustible resources', *American Economic Review*, 67(5): 972–4.

Lange, G. (2001a), 'The contribution of minerals to sustainable economic development in Botswana', Final report to the Botswana Natural Resource Accounting Programme. Gaborone, Botswana.

Lange, G. (2001b), 'Mineral accounts of Namibia', unpublished report to the Directorate of Environmental Affairs, Ministry of Environment and Tourism.

Lange, G. (2002), 'Natural capital, national wealth and sustainable development: contrasting examples from Botswana and Namibia, unpublished paper.

Pearce, D.W. and G. Atkinson (1993), 'Capital theory and the measurement of sustainable development: an indicator of weak sustainability', *Ecological Economics*, 8: 103–8.

Sachs, J. and A. Warner (1995), 'Natural resource abundance and economic growth', Development Discussion Paper No. 517a, Harvard Institute for International Development.

Sarraf, M. and M. Jiwanji (2001), 'Beating the resource curse: the case of Botswana', Environmental Economics Series, Paper No. 84, Washington, DC, World Bank.

Solow, R.M. (1974), 'Intergenerational equity and exhaustible resources', *Review of Economic Studies Symposium*, May: 29–46.

World Bank (1997), *Expanding the Measure of Wealth: Indicators of Sustainable Development*, ESD Studies and Monographs No. 17, Washington, DC, World Bank.

Index

agriculture
  economic contribution of water
    180–81
  and economic development 203
  water use 175–6
air pollution, mining industry 46
Alaska Permanent Fund 55
alien invasion, and fynbos yield 91–3
Arnason, R. 143
asset values
  fisheries 128–9
  forest and woodland resources 80–93
  minerals 37–8
  and sustainability 205–7
Atkinson, G. 20, 206
Auty, R.M. 2, 217

Bossi, L. 82
Botswana
  drinking water access 153–4
  economy
    and natural resources 4–6
    and water 179–81
  mineral accounts 32, 35–6
  mineral wealth 46–50
  mining industry 26–31
    environmental damage 44–5
  rainfall 154
  resource rent for minerals 37, 39
    reinvestment 50, 52–5
  socio-economic benefits of water
    168
  unaccounted-for water 167, 178–9
  water
    accounts 175–86
    supply 157–8, 177–8
    use 170–72, 175–7
  wealth 46–50, 208–15
Brundtland Commission Report 1

carbon
  density measurement, forests 83–6

sequestration valuation 76
stock accounts 85–6, 88
Christie, S.I. 85
Clemens, M. 206
coal mining, environmental impact 46
coal reserves, Botswana 35
Consolidated Diamond Mines (CDM)
  26
constant value asset accounts 16–17
copper/nickel reserves, Botswana 35
cost recovery, water 181–4
  see also resource rent recovery
costs
  extraction 15
  fish quotas 126–7
  water 161, 170
cultivated plantations (CPLNT)
  carbon stock accounts 85
  physical assets accounts 81–2

Dasgupta, P. 206
De Beers 27, 35, 38
Debswana 27
delivery costs, water 170
depletion of natural capital 18–19
depreciation
  of forest and woodland resources
    88–9
  of natural capital 18–19
developing countries, resource-rich,
  economic performance 2–3,
  215–17
diamond
  mining 26–7
  prices 38
  reserves, Botswana 35–6
direct use values, forest and woodland
  resources 75–6
diversity of wealth 207–8
drinking water access, Southern Africa
  153–4
Dutch disease 3, 216